SINEWS OF WAR

SINEWS

OF WAR

How Technology, Industry, and Transportation Won the Civil War

Benjamin W. Bacon

PRESIDIO

To my grandchildren:
Chelsea, Lauren, and Jeremy, representing that future
generation for whom the Union was saved.

Published by Presidio Press
505 B San Marin Drive, Suite 300
Novato, CA 94945-1340

Library of Congress Cataloging-in-Publication Data

Bacon, Benjamin W., 1931–
    Sinews of war : how technology, industry, and transportation won the Civil War / Benjamin W. Bacon.
        p.   cm.
    Includes bibliographical references and index.
    ISBN 0-89141-626-9
    1. United States—History—Civil War, 1861–1865—Technology.
2. United States—History—Civil War, 1861–1865—Transportation.
3. Industries—United States—History—19th century. I. Title.
E468.9.B16   1997
973.7'8—dc21   97–531
                                                                       CIP

Photographs courtesy National Archives
Printed in the United States of America

CONTENTS

Preface	vii
Introduction	xiii
I. Ben Butler Severs the Gordian Knot	1
II. We Are Coming, Father Abraham	15
III. Flag Officer Farragut Wins His Admiral's Stars	37
IV. General McClellan's Modest Proposal	50
V. General Burnside and the Wayward Pontoons	64
VI. All Roads and Rivers Lead to Vicksburg	75
VII. We Won't Starve, Thanks to the Cracker Line	91
VIII. Colonel Bailey Had a Trick or Two Up His Sleeve	113
IX. Cleaning Up After Bedford Forrest	124
X. If We Cross the James, Victory Is on the Other Side	141
XI. "Get Down, You Damn Fool, Before You Get Shot!"	156
XII. We Look Like Men of War	168
XIII. That's When I Knew We Were Beaten	186
XIV. No Such Army Since the Days of Julius Caesar	204
Epilogue: Last Steamboat North, Last Train to Springfield	227
Bibliography	239
Index	241

Bring me my bow of burnished gold
Bring me my arrows of desire
Bring me my spear—o' clouds unfold
Bring me my chariot of fire
I will not cease from mortal strife
Nor shall my sword sleep in my hand
'Til we have built Jerusalem
In this green and pleasant land.
                        —Workers' anthem

PREFACE

During the Civil War, Confederate forces looked upon many Union general officers with contempt. They frequently had good cause, as those Union soldiers who had the misfortune to serve under these generals would ruefully concede. But the Southerners viewed with increasing dread the logistical muscle that supported the Union army. As one Confederate officer reputedly observed during Sherman's march on Atlanta in the spring of 1864, "What's the point of blowing up railway tunnels in Sherman's rear? He undoubtedly carries several spare tunnels on his supply train."

Today we are accustomed to technology. We take for granted watching rockets as large as an office building blast off for the moon, and we do this from a site a thousand miles away through the medium of a television signal bounced off an Earth satellite. We can thus underestimate the unprecedented task that confronted the Union army engineers as they struggled to carry the war to the Confederacy. Even then, their exploits were largely unsung and were obscured by the more dramatic events of the battlefield. That they learned their lessons well, however, was subsequently demonstrated by such postwar marvels as the transcontinental railroad and the Brooklyn Bridge. Without their efforts the Union could not have been saved. When these engineers died, the Union they left behind was transformed from that into which they were born.

Like many latter-day Civil War buffs, I cannot remember a time when I was not fascinated with the war and its place in American history. In a literal sense I learned about it "at my father's knee." Family memories of the conflict remained strong because of the prominent, but very different, roles that two of my immediate ancestors had played.

My grandfather's grandfather was Leonard Bacon, longtime pastor of Center Church in New Haven, Connecticut, and member of the faculty of Yale University. Bacon was an early abolitionist, but unlike his contemporaries William L. Garrison and John Brown, he recognized that emancipation was more than just a moral or religious imperative. A practical question remained. How would slaves be accepted into society after emancipation? Bacon sensed that deepseated racism in the North, as well as the South, would make this a thorny question, and he argued that abolition should not be advocated without making an attempt to resolve this social dilemma. His resolution, the resettlement of American blacks in self-governing protocountries to be established in Africa, was proposed in a book of essays that he published in 1846. Bacon's modest place in American history was assured by the fact that this book was read by a young Illinois congressman, Abraham Lincoln, on whom it had a lasting influence, as Lincoln himself later acknowledged.

During the war, Bacon aided the work of the U.S. Sanitary Commission and the U.S. Christian Commission—organizations formed, respectively, to improve the treatment of the wounded and to provide Bibles and a chaplain corps to the army. Unquestionably, he also spent substantial time consoling those many bereaved parishioners who had lost sons, husbands, or fathers in combat. One of his sons was commissioned as a surgeon in a Connecticut regiment.

My grandmother's grandfather was William Buckingham, the governor of Connecticut from 1858 to 1866, and thus one of that small group of "War Governors" on whom so much of the war effort depended. He was a factory owner in Norwich, Connecticut, and had been an early convert to the newly formed Republican Party in the mid-1850s. Upon his election in 1858, he became the state's first Republican governor. His term of office also coincided with the construction of the present state capitol, in which he took a proprietary interest and whose construction site he often visited. There is a legend that his ghost haunts the building (still, presumably, running down contractors who overbilled).

After the war, Buckingham was elected to the U.S. Senate. One of our most treasured family heirlooms is an autograph book, compiled during his Washington years, that contains the signatures of President Grant, Vice President Colfax, the cabinet, and the entire Senate of his day.

Governor Buckingham had no sons, but he did have a son-in-law of military age, William Aiken, my great-grandfather. When war came, Aiken elected to join the navy. He served in 1862 as an officer aboard a gunboat in the capture of Hilton Head and Beaufort, South Carolina, for use as a naval base in support of the Union blockade. Shortly thereafter, Buckingham induced Aiken to resign his naval commission and to accept appointment as quartermaster general of the state of Connecticut, in which office he served until the end of the war. He ultimately was promoted to brigadier general. For the remainder of his life, he was known in the family as "the General."

By the time of my childhood, Abraham Lincoln, the restored Union, and the Republican Party had become virtually sacred family icons. I easily accepted this mystical bond (with at least the first two members of this trinity), but my knowledge of the war itself remained rather vapid. Thus matters remained until the early 1960s, when my first visits to Civil War battlefield sites coincided with the flood of Civil War histories that were then being published as a result of the war's centennial observances. That did it. Like many others, I became "hooked" on the war.

However, thanks to "the General," I was aware that war is not all flashing swords, battlefield smoke, and armies marching effortlessly from place to place. As Napoleon observed, "An army marches on its stomach." He might also have added that it does not march very far away from its ammo train; its replacement uniforms, overcoats, and shoes; its ambulances; or its horses and mules. Moreover, if a Civil War general wanted to move his army effectively, he would be well advised to load it on any available train or steamboat rather than to march it about. Stonewall Jackson used "foot cavalry" by necessity, not by choice.

Who, then, were the men whose job it was to move the soldiers, munitions, and supplies where they needed to go, and how did they do it? I realized that I didn't know. Moreover, as I thought about it, I began to wonder how it was possible, for example, to assemble, at a moment's notice, an armada big enough to transport 100,000 men from Washington, D.C., to Newport News, Virginia, particularly when all supplies, munitions, and so forth (including siege artillery!) for a campaign of several months' duration must also be transported. There simply had to be a story there.

Alternately, consider the situation two years later in Georgia and Tennessee. General Sherman was steadily forcing General Johnston back on Atlanta. Meanwhile, the Confederacy's brilliant cavalry leader, Nathan Bedford Forrest, was running amok in Sherman's rear, tearing up railroad lines and creating general havoc in his effort to disrupt the Union supply line. Yet Sherman continued to receive sufficient supplies to keep Johnston fully engaged. How did the Union repair the damage and replace the material fast enough to keep Sherman going? Here, too, there must have been more than met the eye.

After observing a succession of logistic marvels, one finally becomes blasé. Why continually be astounded at something that was apparently commonplace? Certainly, General Grant came to assume that his engineers could do almost anything. In the Vicksburg campaign Grant tried one unlikely route after another to get around Confederate defenses. Finally, in desperation he ordered his engineers to dig a canal that would divert the Mississippi River. They dug it, but it failed to change the river's course. The fault, however, lay in the design of the diversion, not in its execution.

Similarly, in the last summer of the war, Grant needed a pontoon bridge built over the lower James River, one of widest, swiftest rivers in the eastern United States. The engineers built the bridge in seven hours, and it was strong enough to carry the Army of the Potomac's entire wagon train, artillery, and two army corps.

Then, when the North missed its opportunity to capture Petersburg and settled down to a siege, the engineers built an entire railroad—complete with switching yards, turntables, repair sheds, and warehouses—that extended behind the full length of the fortifications. Then they connected this to a deepwater port, hospital, and jail complex to ensure that no spot on the line would fail to receive adequate supplies or be unable to evacuate its wounded. Moreover, after a Confederate bomb went off in its midst, the engineers restored the port to service almost without interruption.

This, then, is a tribute to the new technology of the nineteenth century and how it was put into service to win the war.

The central focus, chapter by chapter, is on differing logistic or technological events and how these became an integral part of the conduct of the war's various military campaigns. The book also tends to reinforce the ironic notion that many of man's more ingenious accomplishments are inspired by the need to bring about destruction from war. Finally, this book seeks to give some recognition to all those unknown skilled and unskilled support forces, in and out of uniform, whose contribution to the winning of the war was as tangible as that of the battlefield soldier.

With respect to my sources, I am particularly indebted to the works of those masters of Civil War lore Bruce Catton, Shelby Foote, and Allan Nevins. With regard to technology, I would cite those of G. B. Abdill (wartime railroads), C. Hamilton Ellis (railroad technology), and Louis Hunter (steamboat technology). Without the aid of all these authorities, this book would never have been written.

Many people helped to make this book possible starting with my wife and editor, Midge Bacon, and my typist, Michelle Smalls. Without their patient labors the book would even now not be done. Next I want to thank my attorney, Bill Eustis, my agent, Kevin McShane of the Fifi Oscard Agency, and my publisher, Presidio Press. All of them were willing to take a chance on a first time author. Without their support, the book would have remained a dream, not a reality. Finally, let me single out two individuals whose inspiration was vital, A. Wilson Greene, indefatigable tour director of the Smithsonian Institution, who taught me the necessity of examining the battlegrounds firsthand, and Janice Calkin, Director of Continuing Education in the Greenwich, Connecticut, school system, who was willing to take a chance on me as a teacher in spite of a lack of past experience.

Many others offered moral support and encouragement along the way including office colleagues, friends, students, and fellow men's club members. I thank them all. Their confidence kept me going on those occasions when the well of inspiration suffered dry spells.

INTRODUCTION

The Civil War narrative is an epic about growth, adaptation, and maturity. Politically, this translated into whether the United States truly endorsed its professed creed that all men were created equal and that they were entitled to share in democratic self-government. Economically, the war would establish whether the new technology being developed by individual entrepreneurs could, with sufficient audacity, be transformed by better organization and management to meet enormous new requirements.

The political saga of how the nation strengthened its fundamental beliefs as to the role of the national government has frequently been told elsewhere. How technology was harnessed to add to the might of Union armies, however, is often overlooked. This book was conceived to illuminate this lesser-known subject.

Many of the North's technological advances were impressive but undramatic. They involved such matters as the number of cannons, rifles, steamboats, and locomotives that were being manufactured in 1864 versus 1861, the increased efficiency of transporting these to the front lines, and the better quality of the material being produced. On occasion, the innovative use of these new capabilities had a vital and dramatic effect on the conduct of a particular battle or campaign. Such incidents, more than statistics, best illustrate the tremendous power, for good or ill, that ultimately decided the war in the North's favor.

Marching in tandem with a sophisticated application of technology were the mundane matters of assembling and training men, transporting them to the front, and providing them with an ample and continuing supply of food, clothing, shelter, and weapons. We will first dispose of these matters, before turning our attention to the technological genie in the bottle that was to come.

As the book progresses, the exploitation of both technological ingenuity and capability will come into focus. This book will describe military campaigns and discuss such diverse matters as protecting wooden warships to pass masonry forts, building railway bridges and trestles, laying pontoon bridges, creating landmines, landing the world's then largest amphibious assemblage of troops, and more. By the end of the war one can only agree with the comment of an astounded British observer as he watched the transport by water of 100,000 men to the Virginia peninsula. It was, the observer said, "the leap of a giant."

As a curtain opener, the first chapter will recall a now little remembered incident that happened less than a week after the bombardment of Fort Sumter in Charleston harbor. This chapter serves nicely as an introduction, because it displays both the bravery of green troops and their capability to use technology to overcome disadvantage. The incident starts with three Northern regiments hurriedly being sent to Washington to bolster the government against a possible onslaught from Virginia. All went well until the first of these regiments reached Baltimore, where it was confronted by a vast, angry mob. The soldiers were nonplussed. They had enlisted to fight armed rebels, not teenagers throwing rocks. Nonetheless, they behaved admirably and succeeded in reaching Washington amid truly nightmarish circumstances. Their triumph was enhanced when the two following regiments, and their commander, swiftly devised a clever means of bypassing Baltimore and thus relieved the siege of Washington within a week.

The incident ends happily with the president and chief of staff greeting the triumphant soldiers as they arrived at the Washington station. Woven through this description is the history and operation of steam locomotives and of the events that made them integral to the soldier's success. This particular incident is a personal favorite. I hope you will find it, and the rest of the book, as enjoyable to read as I have found it to tell.

CHAPTER I
Ben Butler Severs the Gordian Knot

Nobody ever accused Ben Butler of having endless patience, low self-esteem, or a shrinking violet complex. First and foremost, Ben Butler looked out for Number One. As a prewar politician he was a stalwart of the Democratic Party and rose under its aegis to become a senator in the Massachusetts state legislature. Because the Whig Party was in the majority in that state, he normally was among the highest-ranking Democratic officeholders. As the "Democracy," as the Democrats were then known, was the dominant party nationally (and typically elected the federal executive), Butler's control of the federal patronage was substantial.

There was nothing unusual in any of this. Politics, then as now, was not a game for sissies. The average politician was genuinely both a patriot and a nationalist, as he conceived the meaning of these terms, but he never took his eye off the main chance. Politics was a national pastime, and power, fortune, and public acclaim awaited those who captured the people's trust.

Two things distinguished Butler. He was better than most at self-promotion, and he was a War Democrat at a time when the Lincoln administration was seeking to rally broad support to the cause of an indissoluble union. Butler was adept at using this to his personal advantage, particularly in being selected for a variety of wartime appointments. He was memorable in another way: he was one of the oddest-looking men in public life. His enormous bald head displayed his most prominent feature—large, bulging, cocked eyes. His head sat directly upon his almost neckless body. A barrel chest and short,

1

bowed legs completed the picture. Once you saw him, you were not apt to forget him.

Even before Lincoln's initial appeal to the states for 75,000 volunteers, Butler requested Governor Andrew of Massachusetts to commission him as a brigadier general commanding a brigade of Massachusetts regiments. Governor Andrew was, no doubt, pleased to comply as a means of ridding himself of a political adversary for the duration of the war. Lincoln—wishing both to gain Butler's support and to gratify his important ally, Andrew—ratified the action. Incredibly to our modern eyes, no one seemed to question the justification of conferring such high rank and responsibility upon someone with no apparent military qualification. This was not attributable solely to political opportunism. The "minuteman" tradition was still strong, particularly in New England, and the idea that a citizen soldier could assume command of 4,000 men with nothing more than a quick perusal of the works of such strategists as Clausewitz or Jomini did not seem outlandish.

There was also the deeply held belief among a substantial segment of the Congress that military success might be directly related to the fervor of one's support of the cause. West Pointers, as a group, were not necessarily the initially favored candidates for high command. They were not deemed to be sufficiently ideologically committed. Finally, no one expected a long war. It was assumed that the mere demonstration of Northern power would intimidate the South. If that were the case, then, of course any general would do.

So on April 16, 1861, the 6th and 8th Massachusetts Regiments, having been sworn into Federal service, marched to the railway station with their regimental bands in front and the cheers, prayers, and fervent well wishes of the citizens of Boston behind them, and they embarked. With General Butler at the fore, they were off to reinforce the city of Washington against any raid that newly mobilized Confederate forces in northern Virginia might make against the Federal capital. This was by no means an unlikely possibility: after the fall of Fort Sumter on April 12, 1861, there had followed in quick succession Lincoln's call for volunteers, the secession of Virginia, and the Confederate decision to move its capital to Richmond, thus ensuring that northern Virginia would be the focus of confrontation. The lighthearted, self-confident spirit that permeated the regiments upon embarkation, however, came to an abrupt end en route, due to events that were occurring simultaneously in the city of Baltimore.

Baltimore was the most vulnerable link in the railway network that joined the New England and mid-Atlantic states to Washington, D.C. All rail traffic from the eastern seaboard had to funnel through Baltimore. Moreover, if anything were to disrupt this traffic, seaborne transport could not readily be substituted, because Confederate forces controlled the lower reaches of the Potomac River. Washington did have an alternate rail link to the North, the Baltimore and Ohio Railroad, which followed the Potomac River valley across the Appalachians to the Ohio River. Unfortunately, this line was within reach of a Confederate army in the Shenandoah Valley, which would soon interrupt service for nine months. Thus, Virginia's secession had made Washington a hostage to events in Maryland. In April 1861, Maryland was a powder keg waiting to explode.

Most Marylanders remained loyal to the Union, but as citizens of a slave state, their allegiance was tenuous. The state had not convoked a secession convention. Nonetheless, a large minority of the citizenry was disloyal, and of these, many were prepared to become active insurrectionists. It should not be surprising, therefore, that many hands were ready to apply a match to the powder keg.

The triggering event occurred on April 19, when the 6th Massachusetts Regiment was moving by rail through Baltimore. Railroads at that time were in a state of transition between private short-line companies and multistate rail networks. This led to anomalies; notably there was no connecting track between the President Street terminus of the Philadelphia, Wilmington, and Baltimore Railroad in Baltimore's northern section and the Camden Street terminus of the Baltimore and Ohio Railroad, located in the city's southwestern district. Through trains from Philadelphia to Washington were thus required to be crowbarred onto municipal trolley tracks and then hauled by horse teams through the center of the city to Camden Street, where the process was reversed. A Baltimore and Ohio engine would then be attached, and the trip to Washington resumed.

Thus, after the 6th Massachusetts reached the President Street Station on that fateful day, the men remained in their railcars as these were pulled through town. Along their route a hostile crowd formed, shouting insults and throwing occasional rocks and paving stones at the horse-drawn cars. In spite of these demonstrations, eight cars, carrying five companies, passed without serious incident. In the ninth car, several soldiers were injured as the stoning intensified. The tenth car was stopped and the trolley tracks were blocked. The occupants of the car had to run for their lives.

The regiment's last four companies were now trapped at the President Street Station with no means of joining their comrades across town, other than to march through the city. The men were thus told to load their rifles but not to fire unless ordered. A squad of Baltimore city police formed up in front, and Mayor George Brown and police chief George Kane led the procession. The group had no sooner begun their march than they were beset by the mob. The mayor and chief ordered the crowd to disband, but the unruly elements were beyond appeal and effectively controlled the streets.

There was no shortage of candidates for mob action. Baltimore, like any other major seaport, had a large contingent of occasional laborers, porters, longshoremen, and so forth, as well, of course, as the usual crowd of less gainfully employed idlers, drunks, street toughs, and assorted rowdies. In Maryland, where both affluence and slavery were constantly in evidence, such people tended to favor the South's "peculiar institution," because slavery provided an economic and social class even lower than themselves and prevented the formation of a free, black workforce of economic competitors. As a group, these Baltimore "roughs" were termed the "plug-uglies."

The passage of the 6th Massachusetts through town provided the plug-uglies with the means, motive, and opportunity to riot. It seems inescapable that their activities that day were formally organized by pro-secession members of the more respectable citizenry. Evidencing this supposition was the fact that the mob also contained a sprinkling of lawyers, merchants, and other men of substance. Presumably, these men would never have been present had they not had an ulterior motive.

By the time the last companies of the regiment were in march, it had become evident that the rioters' intent was deadly and that they meant to block passage and promote a conflict. It was, in fact, the first stroke of an intended act of secession whose ultimate purpose was not simply to add Maryland to the Confederacy but to isolate Washington and force its abandonment by the Federal government. Sensing the mob's unflinching hostility, the first reaction of the mayor and police chief was to order the police and soldiers to double-time in order to limit the length of the confrontation. This turned out to be a major mistake. The mob misread this action to be a sign of fear and redoubled its hostility.

The soldiers were not seasoned troops and had never visualized the possibility of such action by civilians. They became panic-stricken, and inevitably someone in the regiment fired into the crowd. This first shot was soon joined by many more. This infuriated the rioters, but they could not stand up to the firepower of four companies of infantry; grudgingly, they gave ground. The mob's wavering allowed the police chief to bring additional police from the Camden Street Station, where they had earlier been sent in anticipation of trouble. For the rest of the march, soldiers at the front of the line proceeded with bayonets at the ready, while the police, as a rear guard, drew their pistols and threatened to shoot any rioter who approached the column from the rear. In this fashion the final four companies finally reached the Camden Street Station, where they quickly boarded a Washington-bound train. In the process, the 6th had lost four dead and thirty-nine wounded. Civilian casualties were uncertain, but Mayor Brown reported them to be twelve dead and dozens wounded.

One poignant episode associated with the riot concerns the sad fate of some 800 Pennsylvania men who suddenly found themselves pawns of events they could neither comprehend nor control. These men, in the first flush of 1861 enthusiasm, had formed themselves into prospective military companies. For some reason, however, they had not been able to make effective contact with the Pennsylvania state authorities to gain inclusion in an organized militia. They had thus undertaken, on their own initiative, to get themselves to Washington in the hope that they might there be grafted onto some regiment in the process of formation. It was their misfortune that they had arrived at the President Street Station at the same time as the 6th Massachusetts and were thus trapped with the last four companies of the Massachusetts men.

Although roughly organized into companies, the Pennsylvania men were unarmed and not in uniform, and they maintained neither commissioned officers nor military discipline. As a military force they were absolutely useless. They elected to stay behind at the President Street Station when the 6th embarked upon its march. Neither Mayor Brown nor Chief Kane was aware of their predicament or even of their existence.

When the 6th Massachusetts successfully extricated itself and departed for Washington, the mob's mood turned even uglier. Somehow a rumor arose that some Yankee soldiers had been left behind at President Street. The mob now stormed that bastion to investigate. They discovered the hapless Pennsylvanians and severely beat most of them before the Baltimore police could intervene.

From the beginning the Pennsylvanians had not had a particular destination. Now they certainly could go no farther. Those in the worst condition were taken to a hospital; those who could manage were returned to Philadelphia. So the unit disappeared from history. We can only assume that most of its members ultimately found their way into Pennsylvania regiments. If so, one can presume that later Confederate opponents had the misfortune of discovering that they were fighting men who carried a considerable grudge.

The immediate effect of the Baltimore riot was to unnerve the police chief and the mayor, who acceded to the rioters' demands by advising the Lincoln administration that Northern troops would no longer be permitted to transit through Baltimore. As if to establish good faith in their dealings with the mob, the two politicians further authorized the blowing up of all railway bridges entering the city. This was promptly done, thus sealing off Baltimore. It should be noted that the officials were acting foolishly but not treacherously. Both were loyal, and they were trying to walk a tightrope to avoid precipitating a provocation of secession. Neither had any idea as yet of the extent to which Lincoln was prepared to go to preclude such an act.

The fat was now in the fire. How could Washington be substantially reinforced without a rail connection through Baltimore? Surprisingly, it was our friend Butler who devised the solution ("surprisingly" because many of Butler's later initiatives were not so positive). An abandoned railway spur existed between the city of Annapolis on Chesapeake Bay and the main line of the Baltimore and Ohio Railroad between Baltimore and Washington. If soldiers could be unloaded from trains at the head of Chesapeake Bay, then loaded onto steamboats for transport to Annapolis and finally reloaded onto trains for the run to Washington, the problem in Baltimore could be avoided. Butler, totally without orders, immediately undertook plans to make this happen.

There were two additional regiments now stalled on the railway north of Baltimore, the 8th Massachusetts and the 7th New York. The 8th Massachusetts had reached the Delaware-Maryland boundary; the 7th New York was stuck in Philadelphia. Butler ordered the 8th to proceed to the mouth of the Susquehanna River and there to embark upon a steamship that he had chartered. He instructed the 7th's colonel to charter the steamship *Boston* on the Philadelphia waterfront. Both vessels were to proceed down Chesapeake Bay (after the *Boston*'s passage through the Delaware-Chesapeake Canal) and to discharge their troops at Annapolis, Maryland's capital and the site of the newly formed U.S. Naval Academy.

The two regiments each mustered close to their nominal complement of 1,000 men but were otherwise totally dissimilar. The New Yorkers were a "silk stocking" regiment composed mostly of the sons of New York's prosperous merchants and professional classes. The Massachusetts men were artisans and mechanics who had been recruited in the industrial suburbs of Boston. Their skills would soon come in handy.

Upon the vessels' arrival in Annapolis on April 22, the regiments were greeted by a scene almost as ugly as the one that greeted the 6th in Baltimore. Southern sympathizers in the town had already ripped up a sizable amount of the railroad track on the spur line leading to Washington. They had also totally dismantled the one locomotive then present in the Annapolis yards. Now they were threatening to prevent the two Northern regiments from landing. Governor Thomas Hicks, though a Unionist, pleaded with Butler not to land his men for fear of provoking open conflict. Hicks mistook both the general and the temper of the Lincoln administration. Ben Butler and Abraham Lincoln were determined, decisive men who could be very obstinate when the occasion demanded.

Butler promptly gave the governor a taste of what was in store for the state of Maryland over the next several months. Butler advised Hicks that the men would at all costs be landed on the grounds of the naval academy, over which, in any event, the civil authorities had no control. Moored next to the academy was the famous War of 1812 frigate USS *Constitution (Old Ironsides),* now being used as a training ship. Butler advised Hicks that if mob action should attempt to disrupt the landing, the old warship's guns would be loaded with canister shot that would be fired into the crowd.

Hicks recoiled in horror. Canister consisted of a metal container filled with small shot, nails, and other irregular bits of metal. It effectively turned a cannon into a giant shotgun. If used on a mob, it would not just kill but obliterate. It was as frightful a weapon as then existed.

The threat was effective. No attempt was made to oppose the landing, and both regiments spent the night on the academy grounds. In the morning, however, the question of the dismantled railroad remained to be resolved. Here, the New Yorkers were of no assistance, but the 8th Massachusetts came into its own. The one available, but disassembled, locomotive was examined; it was discovered that it had been built in a Massachusetts engine works where one member of the regiment had actually worked on its construction. He said he was confident that he could reassemble it. Moreover, there were in the regiment no less than nineteen soldiers with experience as locomotive engineers as well as others familiar with most matters of railroad operation. Finally, there were innumerable metalworkers and mechanics to help. As soon as the men could get organized, the railroad would be put to rights.

How fortuitous this was becomes apparent when one considers the outcome of ordinary mechanics making amateur repairs. The steam engine was an enormous technological leap, freeing mankind for the first time from total dependence on human and animal energy. Like all technology it was complicated, and in the wrong hands it could be dangerous.

The steam railway locomotive (together with its marine counterpart, the steamboat) was the quintessential invention of the nineteenth century and resulted from the marriage of two technologies of considerable historic lineage. The first was the "tracked way." This device, which originated in antiquity, consisted simply of two parallel ruts over which a wheeled vehicle could be pulled. This arrangement provided "automatic" steering and greatly eased the task of a teamster in controlling his pulling animal. The first "track" was invented when someone ingeniously filled in muddy ruts with timbers to improve traction. By the seventeenth century the tracked way had evolved into continuous, parallel, raised wooden rails over which carts having flanged wheels could be drawn. These were used particularly for the excavation of ore from mines.

The second technology was that of the steam engine. The first such device was designed and built by an Englishman, Thomas Newcomen, who in the early eighteenth century introduced steam into a vertical cylinder sealed by a piston head to produce a vacuum within the cylinder. Atmospheric pressure drove the piston downward. This, by linkage, pulled a pump handle upward, thus pumping water from a mine shaft. Later in the century, this machine was improved by Scotland's James Watt, who added a condenser to increase the vacuum, introduced steam into the cylinder at both ends of the piston stroke, and converted vertical to rotary motion by the use of a connecting rod and flywheel. In neither instance, however, was the expansive energy of steam used by such low-pressure machines to push the piston head. Therefore, the strength of the engine was determined by and was proportional to the size of the cylinder and piston head against which atmospheric pressure was exerted. This type of engine was best suited to large, stationary machines.

The development of a practical locomotive would necessarily await the creation of a high-pressure engine in which cylinder and piston could be reduced in size and driven by the force of steam pressure rather than atmospheric vacuum. Engines of this type were created simultaneously by Richard Trevithick (in England for use in locomotives) and Oliver Evans (in America for use in milling machinery) during the first decade of the nineteenth century. Trevithick built his locomotive in 1804 and ran it experimentally (and successfully) for ten miles in Wales over a rail track normally used by horse-drawn carts to bring coal to a seaport.

Commercial usage did not occur until 1825, when improved metallurgy permitted stronger boilers and track to be built. The world's first incorporated steam-driven railroad, the Stockton and Darlington Railroad, opened in England in 1825 under the engineering direction of George and Robert Stephenson (father and son). By 1830 railway service was inaugurated between Liverpool and Manchester using the world's first standardized engine, the famous Rocket, designed and built by the Stephensons.

America's first railroad, the Baltimore and Ohio, was chartered for horse-drawn transport in 1827. In 1830 it tested its first experimental steam locomotive, the Tom Thumb. Its first commercial locomotive was purchased in June 1831, and regular steam-train service started shortly thereafter. The decades of the 1840s and 1850s produced a tremendous expansion of American railways, and by 1860 railway service was available throughout the North on a 22,000-mile grid and in the South on a 9,000-mile network.

By 1860, after thirty years' experience, a "standard American" type of locomotive had evolved. It had a 4-4-0 wheel design, that is, four small wheels forward supporting the smokestack and drive cylinders with four coupled, large driving wheels in the rear supporting the boiler and cab. Immediately forward of the cab were the firebox and boiler. An array of many hollow tubes extended from the firebox through the boiler water in the lower half of the boiler and opened into the smokestack. Flue gases from the firebox would be driven through these tubes, which maximized the heating surface between hot gases and water for the optimum production of steam (which would accumulate in the top of the boiler). Steam would be led from the boiler top to a steam chest, from which it would be introduced into the cylinders alternately through entrance valves on either side of the piston head.

When the piston stroke was partially completed, a cut-off valve would stop the injection of steam. The stroke would then be finished through the expansion of the steam already in the cylinder. After the stroke had been completed, the exhaust steam would be vented to the smokestack. This produced draft, which assisted in the exhaust of the flue gases and smoke and gave the steam engine its distinctive "huff-puff" sound.

The moving pistons drove connecting rods, which in turn would be joined to the drive wheels by attached rods termed "cranks." The drive wheels were joined together by coupling rods. Separate cylinder and piston units on either side drove the drive wheels on their respective sides of the engine.

A locomotive would of course be equipped with a headlight (usually kerosene-fired), a steam whistle, and a bell. One very essential feature was the safety valve, which vented excessive steam pressure to the air, thus preventing explosive steam buildup. Other safety features included a set of tubes that enabled the engineer to direct steam and sand onto the tracks to prevent slippage under icy conditions. Fuel (either wood or coal) would be fed continuously to the fire by the fireman. Fuel and water supplies would be carried behind the engine in a separate "tender."

Frequently, combustion would not be complete, and sparks and burning embers would enter the smokestack. The bulbous "balloon" or "diamond" stacks were designed to confine such sparks.

The steam engine was not an energy-efficient machine. It permitted excessive wasted heat and frictional drag, if measured by the standard of the later internal combustion engine. It was, however, a quantum leap over animal pulling power.

From this description, one can appreciate that a steam locomotive required precision in its assembly and operation. Particularly important was the safety valve, whose reliable operation was all that ensured that an explosion would not occur in the high-pressure boiler. Proper assembly and mounting of the moving parts were also vital if the machine were not to tear itself apart through vibration.

Laying track was much less of a skilled occupation, particularly because, in the instance at hand, a graded right-of-way from Annapolis to the Baltimore and Ohio Railroad main line already existed. A few specialists could accompany the work gangs to ensure that the track was being laid in the proper gauge and was canted at the correct angle around curves. Unskilled labor could be used to replace ties, to affix the base plates (on which the track rested) to the ties, to spike the track to the base plate, and to bolt on the "fish plates," as the horizontal connectors between track sections were called.

Thus, the purely mechanical aspect of the plan was now under control, thanks to the hungry men of the 8th Massachusetts (they had not been fed since embarking upon their steamship). Two questions remained: to what extent did Maryland secessionists remain in control of the right-of-way, and were they willing to actively contest federal occupation? The 7th New York was sent to march along the railroad right-of-way up to its junction with the Baltimore and Ohio Railroad and to contest control, as needed. They discovered no effective opposition, although some rebel sympathizers were found along the highway that paralleled the railway. The New Yorkers' main enemy was fatigue; they were forced to march all day and then all night at a snail's pace in order to permit the line to be thoroughly inspected as they passed. When they finally reached the junction, they were loaded aboard a Baltimore and Ohio special that had been sent out from Washington to pick them up. All thought of fatigue vanished when the train arrived in Washington's Union Station. There, the regiment was treated as saviors, as the city breathed a collective sigh of relief at the restoration of its connection to the North.

Shortly thereafter, the 8th Massachusetts arrived, having been delivered on the train and the track that they themselves had repaired. Within a week additional regiments would arrive. By the end of the month, rail transit through Baltimore would be restored, this time under the protection of Federal troops. Even the much-harassed Baltimore and Ohio Railroad could be circumvented now that the city of Baltimore transit was again usable. When the Baltimore and Ohio was blocked, trains with western troops or supplies could be initiated in Pittsburgh, sent east on the Pennsylvania Railroad to Harrisburg, and thence go directly to Baltimore for passage to Washington. Washington's rail crisis was over for the duration.

AFTERMATH

The end of the rail crisis begged the question as to how to dissipate the large measure of secession sentiment that persisted within Maryland. This was part of the larger question of retaining the loyalty of the remaining border slave states.

These states were vital. To concede them to the South was to court defeat, particularly because their inclusion within the Confederacy would have given the South defensible northern borders along the Ohio and Missouri Rivers. Each state, however, presented problems that needed to be confronted individually. No broad application of a formula approach to the whole region was apt to work. A major test of the pragmatism of the Lincoln administration was at hand.

One such state, Delaware, posed no problem. Only a few hundred slaves existed in the state, and there the institution was slowly dying. That fact, plus the state's geographic isolation, ensured that no further action was necessary. Virginia, on the other hand, was a major problem. Its border question was mitigated, however, by the de facto separation of western Virginia from the rest of the state. This created a buffer zone that both insulated the Ohio River and assisted in preserving Kentucky.

The latter state constituted an unresolved problem. In April 1861, it was balanced on a proverbial knife edge with a pro-Southern governor, a Union-leaning legislature, and a population that included a large disloyal minority. The governor sought a state of neutrality, a convenient legal fiction to which Lincoln acceded temporarily, as did Jefferson Davis. Such neutrality, however, was inherently unstable; both sides spent the last half of 1861 recruiting and organizing troops in and around the state. The tacit bargain collapsed during the winter of 1861–62 when the forces of Generals Thomas, Grant, and Pope drove the Confederacy out of Kentucky permanently (except for a brief incursion later in 1862 by Confederate general Bragg).

Farther west, Missouri had seemed to be a problem early in 1861 but by summer was brought under effective Union military control by perceptive military action. Thus, Virginia, Kentucky, and Missouri—through a deft blend of patience, diplomacy, and force—had been preserved for the Union. Maryland, however, constituted the gravest threat and needed the most drastic remedy.

If anyone even slightly doubted the determination of Lincoln and his administration to take whatever action was necessary to defend the Union, those doubts should have been disabused by the administration's actions in Maryland in April 1861. Lincoln here is displayed not as the empathetic president pardoning a sleeping sentinel but as the wartime commander in chief who unhesitatingly stretched the Constitution to its utmost limits. At Lincoln's specific instruction, Maryland was put under martial law, and the writ of habeas corpus was suspended throughout the state by federal executive order. Its legislature was prevented from convening, and most of its politicians and civic leaders of secessionist persuasion were arrested without specific charge or hearing and were detained as military prisoners for an unstated duration.

To enforce these edicts, Ben Butler on May 13 brought back the 6th Massachusetts to occupy Federal Hill, which dominated the city of Baltimore. The selection of that particular regiment was no accident; it was unlikely that any other regiment of the Federal army was more unsympathetic to Baltimore secessionists or more willing to enforce any regulatory order.

An enormous wail of protest arose from the citizenry. Many of the imprisoned officials sent habeas corpus writ petitions to Roger Taney, chief justice of the Supreme Court (and himself a pro-Southern Marylander). Taney approved the writ petitions, only to discover that the Lincoln administration would not enforce the writs. The imprisoned officials remained behind bars.

In time, all charges were dropped and the prisoners were released, although in several instances this did not occur until months after their original arrest. Complaints of high-handed treatment continued in the bay region for the remainder of the war, and "Maryland, My Maryland," a song of protest against the Northern "tyranny," was sung throughout the South until the war's end. Never again, however, would the state try to secede or engage in riotous action. The flames of rebellion had burned themselves out.

CHAPTER II

We Are Coming, Father Abraham

W e might be coming, but who exactly were "we"? How many men were available? What were their qualifications? Most importantly, how many had sufficient stamina to withstand the rigors of military campaigning? The Federal government had no idea, without such modern conveniences as Social Security numbers, IRS returns, and FBI fingerprints. Neither, for that matter, did the state or local governments. However, one tried-and-true method for assembling men quickly did exist: the "old boy" network. This not only had the virtue of necessity, but it also suited the temper of the times and the American preference for private, rather than public, associations.

For the North, the linchpins of the old boy system were the "War Governors" of the various states. They, after all, were the leaders of their states' dominant political parties. They also could be assumed to have the broadest acquaintance among the industrialists, merchants, editors, professional men, and the like who constituted their states' opinion leaders. The governors' loyalty was unquestioned and their patriotism solid. Thus, when President Lincoln in April and May 1861 issued appeals first for 75,000 and then 500,000 volunteers for Federal service, those numbers were immediately translated into state-by-state quotas that were assigned to the War Governors for action.

The War Governors more than fulfilled their responsibilities. Northern governors responded with alacrity and diligence, and they supported the cause faithfully during the entirety of the war. The record of Governor Buckingham of Connecticut is typical.

Three days after Fort Sumter fell, Connecticut's first regiment was organized and equipped. Another five regiments were to follow within three weeks. During the course of the war, Connecticut produced 30 infantry regiments, 1 cavalry regiment, 2 heavy artillery regiments, 3 battalions of field artillery, 250 naval officers, and 2,500 naval enlisted men

These totaled 54,900 men, of whom 20,000 would ultimately become casualties, and was 6,000 more than the Federal quota assigned to the state. Connecticut's population was then approximately 400,000. Assuming that this was divided equally between men and women and that the seventeen to thirty-five age group totaled 40 percent of the male population, this would mean that almost 70 percent of the total eligible population actually served. Civil War statistics, however, can be elusive, and the total number of enlistments may well include reenlistments. Probably about 50 percent of the total eligible population actually served. This is still extraordinary, but it was generally matched throughout the North and exceeded among the Southern states.

Governor John Andrew of Massachusetts had been the most foresighted of the War Governors. He anticipated the Sumter crisis and started recruitment in February 1861. By April, four regiments were available and brigaded under Gen. Ben Butler. Two of these were sent on their way to Washington on the day following Lincoln's appeal.

The governors' main enlistment device was to offer a colonelcy, that is, command of a regiment of 1,000 men, to any chosen acquaintance who could enlist a body of men that size. Additional patronage included the regimental second in command (lieutenant colonel) and the regimental major. The regimental officers-designate would then seek out friends who were each able to enlist companies of 100 men. After formation, the companies would elect their own captains, lieutenants, and sergeants, among whom undoubtedly would be the "friends" who formed the companies.

As the Civil War recruit was to learn the hard way, this system by no means guaranteed the military competence of one's regimental officers. However, it did ensure, in the broadest sense, that regimental and company officers had some qualification for leadership. Moreover, it provided a big intangible benefit. The recruit knew his company officers as fellow townsmen and trusted them, at least until their incompetence was made manifest on the battlefield. In any event, few obvious alternatives presented themselves. The system worked reasonably well, as attrition, dismissal, and resignation eventually weeded out the mediocre and the uninspired as well as the incompetent. In the interim, however, lives were squandered—on the battlefield and by disease caused by needlessly careless sanitary arrangements in camp.

Another approach might have been tried. The tiny, 15,000-man regular army could have been dissolved and its NCOs and junior officers could have been reassigned to command and staff functions in the volunteer state regiments. Such a course of action was instinctively rejected by the War Department, as well as by most professional officers. All indications are that these instincts were correct. Although better leadership might have spared "Billy Yank" some initial suffering, any attempt to impose regular army discipline on the volunteer soldier would have fractured the army. Even general officers were forced to learn that officers had to earn a volunteer's trust and loyalty before the volunteer would submit to military discipline.

What happened when the regulars failed to do so is illustrated by an incident that occurred during the early days of the Army of the Cumberland. General Charles Gilbert, an old-school army captain, suddenly found himself a major general heading an army corps. One midnight, he and his staff rode past a company of infantry asleep by the roadside after an all-day forced march. Gilbert was annoyed that nobody called the sleeping troops to attention as he passed and so awoke an infantry captain and demanded: "Why in hell don't you get up and salute when I pass?"

"Who in hell are you?" asked the captain.

"Major General Gilbert, by God, sir. Give me your sword. You are under arrest."

The infantry regiment's colonel, having overheard this, approached Gilbert and said that his men had been marching for a week. "I would not hold a dress parade at midnight for any damn fool living," the colonel told Gilbert.

Gilbert responded that the regiment was an armed mob, and he would take away its colors. At that point, the color sergeant declared that he would kill Gilbert if he attempted to take the colors. Another enlisted man cried out, "You damned son of a bitch, get out of here, or you're a dead man."

A second soldier thrust a bayonet into Gilbert's horse, and the animal took off in a headlong gallop. Gilbert's staff haplessly followed. The regiment called after them that they would happily shoot Gilbert if they ever saw him again. Gilbert did not last long as a major general. Martinets and volunteers (particularly westerners) did not mix!

A colonel-designate normally would recruit most of his regiment from within a particular city or county. This had the effect of raising the recruits' morale during training and instilling loyalty to their regiment. It also pitted the townsfolk of each locality against one another in a fateful, but unsuspected, game of Russian roulette, with their sons' lives at risk. Regimental casualties could run upward of 60 percent in a single action, if one were unlucky enough to be ordered to take the Sunken Road at Fredericksburg or the Bloody Angle at Spotsylvania. Forty-five minutes might be all it took to blight the future of a town for generations—if not forever.

Initial assembly of a regiment was not difficult in the spring and summer of 1861 when war was all glory and adventure. A recruitment parade could be organized within each of a county's towns, and patriotic speeches and a marching band would produce an ample number of volunteers on the spot. In fact, the problem was how to reduce the rate of enlistment, because enlistment fervor far exceeded the initial small quotas set by the national government for Federal service. Indeed, the challenge became one of trying to preserve that fervor while complying with the inflexibility of political dictation at both the Federal and state levels.

The states were, of course, free to enroll as many militia as they wished for their own benefit, regardless of the Federal quota. Their only hesitation was the cost. Who would maintain the state regiments awaiting the Federal call, and how soon would that call come? In Michigan, the state was rapidly enlisting volunteers in spite of the fact that the legislature had provided no appropriation for the purpose. Fortunately, in the early days, voluntary popular subscription could usually be counted upon to meet any short-term funding requirement.

In every state young men were clamoring to enlist during that fateful summer of 1861. To them the war was all excitement and adventure, a chance to escape the deadly boredom of farming or clerking in a small-town store. In Iowa, the state's initial quota was oversubscribed by 2,000 percent. In all the states, rejected enlistees simply refused to be turned down and would camp near enlistment centers, demanding to be enrolled. In Indiana, several nonaccepted, preformed militia companies simply joined the accepted recruits on their march to the training camp. Once there, they raised such a furor that the state had to accept them, simply to avoid disruption.

Once enlisted, the recruit would usually be instructed to report to a nearby tent city where his company would be mustered. The manner of provisions, munitions, equipment, and supplies he might expect to find there varied widely, depending upon the relative capacity and largesse of his state legislature, his sponsoring officers, and his own individual means. Some "silk stocking" regiments sported not just custom-made uniforms but such other accoutrements as field chests, camp chairs, and bunks, all of which were designed to be accommodated within a field tent of commodious size. These luxuries lasted only until it was made clear that enlisted men's baggage would not be carried in the army's baggage train (and precious little space would be devoted to the possessions of junior officers). What you wanted, you carried on your back.

The typical company recruit, however, had no such problem. He was equipped with a uniform, musket, blanket, and tent. Because these companies had not yet been received into Federal service, their uniform design could vary widely from the standard dark blue tunic and cap and light blue trousers of the regular army. Particularly popular was the Zouave uniform, copied from that of the North African troops within the French army. This consisted of baggy red pantaloons gathered at the ankle; a short, tight blue jacket; and a red fez! This was thought to symbolize both the romance and bravery of war.

Romantic it might have been. Practical it wasn't. The pants were virtually guaranteed to absorb excessive dirt and moisture and to become either caked with mud or filled with dust. Either way, their weight must have been oppressive. The tight jacket constricted all upper body movement and made awkward the nine-step procedure for loading and arming one's musket. Finally, it would be hard to conceive of a more useless piece of headgear to wear into battle than a fez. It is astounding that, in spite of everything, several regiments preserved the Zouave uniform throughout the four years of war.

Uniform color was also not standardized; blue and gray were used by both North and South. Two Union regiments under Col. William F. Barry took a devastating volley during the First Battle of Bull Run from oncoming Confederates on whom the Northerners had hesitated to fire because they were clad in blue. At Big Bethel in June 1861, the 7th New York Regiment, wearing gray, was fired upon by the 3d New York as they advanced upon the latter's line, in spite of their calling out a prearranged password, "Boston."

Generally, early recruits wanted their particular units to have some form of differentiation from the rest of the army, although most resisted the temptation of redesigning their entire uniforms. Frequently, a distinctive hat was selected for this purpose, the most famous of which were the black slouch hats of the "Iron Brigade." This brigade had earned its nickname through its unflinching determination on the battle line, and the black hats became recognized throughout the entire Army of the Potomac as a badge of honor. Thus, new regiments brigaded to the Iron Brigade would not be permitted to wear the black hat until they demonstrated their mettle in battle to the satisfaction of the brigade's veterans. A unit had to be careful, however, in its selection of headgear. The wrong choice could bring unwanted attention, as the 16th New York infantry discovered when they wore straw "boaters" into battle and thereby sustained an excessive number of head wounds.

The soldiers' desire for a special "badge" in which to take pride was recognized in 1862 by Gen. Philip Kearny, one of the North's more charismatic generals. He instructed his men to sew a diamond-shaped piece of red felt to their uniforms. This served the dual role of creating pride of association and of permitting General Kearny to identify his particular men on the battlefield.

After Kearny's death, the idea of having a distinctive badge was adopted, first by the various corps within the Army of the Potomac and eventually by the whole Union army. Thus, the 2d corps was thereafter identified by a clover leaf, the 3d (Kearny's corps) by a diamond, the 5th by a Maltese cross, and so on. Within each corps, the first division was identified by a corps badge colored red; the second, white; and the third, blue. Thus, Kearny's badge, the red diamond, continued afterward to identify his old division—the first division of the 3d corps. To this day the U.S. Army continues the use of shoulder patches to identify its various units.

The state camps to which the new recruits were sent pending muster into Federal service varied widely in the training they offered volunteers. The more fortunate regiments might have drillmasters who had served in a European army before emigrating or who were retired veterans of the Mexican War. These regiments at least received drill in marching in formation and in the manual of arms. Others had to depend on their newly elected officers and noncoms being able to interpret a manual of instructions, with which they were as unfamiliar as their troops. Some had no concept of drill whatsoever and could only imagine a soldier's role. One Massachusetts veteran remembered, "Our drill was running around the old town hall, yelling like devils and firing at an imaginary foe."

Reality, however, soon intruded on the recruit's adventure. Its first manifestation took the form of the various infectious diseases that swept the training camps even before the soldier left his home state and that would dog him throughout his service. A certain amount of illness was inevitable, as men who had rarely previously encountered a stranger were suddenly living with hundreds of them. Most such diseases could have been prevented, however, if medical science had been aware of their cause (microscopic living organisms) and manner of transmission. As it was, the only defenses against epidemics were quarantine and field sanitation, both of which were frequently improperly applied.

Virtually everything about the soldier's life ensured his susceptibility to disease. He lived in conditions of overcrowding and bad ventilation. His inability to bathe frequently or change his clothes, together with poor camp sanitation, caused flies, lice, and fleas to multiply. Food, milk, and water easily became contaminated as a result of dirty preparation areas, poor food-handling techniques, and a lack of refrigeration. The soldiers' diet consisted principally of flour, salted meat, and black coffee, which did not enhance his natural immunities and resistance, as would have been the case with a balanced diet. Finally, many fellow recruits were unknowing carriers of disease, as were the many animals with which the soldiers came in contact.

Such exposure could decimate entire regiments before they ever reached the front. Of the Union's 360,000 reported deaths, 200,000 were from disease and only 110,000 were killed in battle. Under these conditions the half-life of a regiment was about a year, even without combat. Not infrequently a projected attack or campaign was canceled or postponed because the soldiers' health couldn't sustain it. As the war progressed, however, soldiers and their commanders did learn one valuable common-sense lesson: keep the soldiers on the move if you seek to hold down illness—although they could not comprehend why this worked.

Among the infectious diseases, the most lethal were dysentery and typhoid, which together accounted for more than 50 percent of the death rate from illness. Second only to dysentery in terms of incidence was malaria, which although not usually fatal (thanks to a familiarity with quinine), disabled whole regiments. Only one infectious disease, smallpox, was under control, because vaccination had been introduced at the beginning of the century. Infectious diseases remained endemic throughout the war, and the incidence of illness did not decrease in the later stages of the conflict. The only preventative was the onset of winter. Then, however, infectious disease was replaced by rheumatism and scurvy, which, although not usually fatal, were equally disabling.

When the state regiments were called to Federal service, they were ordered to proceed to any of four assembly areas: Washington, D.C.; Cincinnati, Ohio; St. Louis, Missouri; and Cairo, Illinois. Generally, New England and middle state troops went to Washington, whereas the other three cities were the destinations of midwesterners. Although the eastern army was the largest, not a few midwesterners also were assigned to the Army of the Potomac, because Ohio and Illinois were among the more populous states.

The normal means of conveyance for the troops heading for the front were the railways. All population centers above the Ohio River were well served, although the system was fragmented. No less than four long-line railroads crossed the Appalachians: the New York Central Railroad and the Erie Railroad in New York state, the Pennsylvania Railroad in Pennsylvania, and the Baltimore and Ohio Railroad in Maryland and western Virginia, although the latter was subject to frequent Confederate disruption. A second efficient transportation system existed in the form of the steam packet boats that carried both passengers and freight on all the inland and coastal waterways of the country. The systems were interconnecting. Collectively they could handle without great strain the increasing burden of wartime traffic. Consequently, in 1861 only two bottlenecks occurred, both temporary. Troop movements to St. Louis and Cairo were delayed because of overstretched capacity on the Illinois Central Railroad, and during one week in April, Washington was denied rail and river service due to its unique vulnerability to transportation blockage.

Frequently, some combination of train and packet boat was used as the most expeditious means of transport. Thus, regiments leaving Boston might take the train to Fall River, then transfer to packet boats destined for New York, then embark on trains for Washington. Regiments leaving Albany or Hartford might take a river steamer to the coast before boarding trains for Washington. Troops converging on Cincinnati might take either river steamer or railway. The same was true for St. Louis and Cairo. Because the buildup was generally leisurely (aside from brief periods of panic in both Washington and St. Louis), the system managed to transport the troops without great strain or dislocation. This was true only because the war began in 1861—after 30,000 miles of track had been built. Had the war started a decade earlier, when only 9,000 miles existed, matters would have been very different.

Upon arrival at his destination, the recruit would often find that housing and training facilities were as haphazard as those that he had left behind. In St. Louis, operations were already under way against a Confederate-leaning state militia, and new arrivals might well find themselves immediately fed piecemeal into offensive operations. In Cincinnati and Kentucky, command was first vested in Robert Anderson, the hero of Fort Sumter, whose poor health soon rendered him unable to perform. He was relieved by William T. Sherman of latter-day fame. Sherman, however, quickly suffered a minor nervous

breakdown and had to be relieved. This instability of the high command accentuated organizational problems further down in the
ranks. In Washington before Bull Run, no one authority seemed to
be in charge. Some bizarre things occurred, among them the bil-
leting of two of the earliest arriving regiments in the Senate and
House chambers.

Getting the men in place was only half the battle. Hundreds of
thousands of new soldiers would now need a continuing supply of
food, shelter, clothing, and munitions. In the spring of 1861, this presented no problem. The arriving troops were already furnished with
necessities by their states, militia companies, ad hoc citizens' groups,
and families. Replenishment, however, was another story. That could
come only from the Federal government, and no delay could be tolerated in devising the means and methodology to accomplish it. The
task was daunting. Nothing of this magnitude had ever before been
attempted by the national government.

The job fell upon three bureaus of the War Department: Commissary, Quartermasters, and Ordnance. Leadership in these bureaus
varied. Commissary was run by Joseph Taylor, a competent administrator who performed his job in a workmanlike manner. Quartermasters was managed by an administrative genius, Montgomery
Meigs, who planned, connived, cajoled, threatened, pleaded, blus-
tered, conspired, and generally did whatever else was needed to get
the gargantuan job done. Meigs was one of the North's secret
weapons. Other than Abraham Lincoln, probably no Washington official did as much to advance the Union cause. Interestingly, he was
a Southerner, a Georgian who remained true both to the professional
army he served and to the nation.

Not so fortunate was the Ordnance bureau. Until September
1863, it was run by an insufferable bureaucrat named James Ripley
(dubbed by his peers "Ripley Van Winkle"). Ripley was hostile to
innovation, had no sense of urgency, and suffered from a penny-
pinching mania.

The easiest of the supply problems to solve concerned food. This
was the jurisdiction of Commissary, where Taylor was greeted with
simple logistics. There was no shortage of food in the North, and adequate rail and river connections existed between farm regions and

the troop assembly areas of Washington, Cincinnati, and St. Louis. All that was thus required was to purchase adequate quantities and to arrange appropriate transportation. Adequate quantities of food were thus soon available, but the quality of these supplies varied tremendously. Resolution of the quality question would come only with the painstaking development of a rigorous inspection service.

A soldier's daily ration consisted of one and a quarter pounds of meat, fresh or salted; one and a quarter pounds of bread, soft or in a stiff cracker called "hardtack"; and coffee, sugar, salt, pepper, beans, and dried peas. On occasion, onions, potatoes, rice, dried apples, vinegar, and molasses were also distributed. On the march however, only salted meat, hardtack, sugar, and coffee would be issued. The shortfall was never replaced when a new campsite was reached. Soldiers learned with resignation to accept this as simply another manifestation of the "army way."

No attempt was made to maintain a balanced diet. Even the concept was unknown. Yet the relationship between preserved foods and scurvy was realized (thanks to maritime experience). Attempts were made accordingly to combat this disease by periodically distributing fresh vegetables and fruits. Since these were usually available only in the summer, scurvy swept the camps during the winter months.

The soldiers' diet was periodically augmented by three expedients. Of primary importance were the boxes from home. These continued to be sent throughout the war and were delivered with great efficiency by the Quartermasters Corps. The boxes contained mostly preserved vegetables, fruit, jam, and baked fowl. Items such as underwear and socks were wrapped around the jars as packing materials. Not an inch of space was wasted.

A source of less nourishment was the sutlers' stores. These were shacks erected near the camps by independent merchants (sutlers). Their prices were high but probably justified, given the risks the sutlers ran and the costs they incurred. Most privates could not afford to patronize these establishments except to buy cookies (six for a quarter) or the infamous "sutlers' pies" (a quarter apiece). These pies were highly indigestible and quite indescribable. Veterans at postwar reunions had long, inconclusive discussions as to their content.

The third expedient was forage, that is, the seizure of produce and farm animals from enemy farms. Forage applied mostly in the western regions (eastern armies usually transversed a countryside that was already war ravaged). Contrary to postwar tales, soldiers rarely raided residential dwellings or took household valuables. On the other hand, stored grain, meat, or farm animals were fair game. As the war progressed and attitudes on both sides hardened, raiding soldiers became less inclined to leave behind a portion of such stores and livestock for the subsistence of the raided farm family.

The food supply was well organized while the soldiers remained in camp but became more difficult when they went on campaigns. No matter how complex the problem, however, the Quartermasters Corps (QMC) was expected to keep the provisions moving. It took a man of Meigs's genius to manage the QMC, because the corps was responsible for all shelter, clothing, fuel, horses, mules, and mess gear together with incidentals such as candles, canteens, and payroll services. It was responsible for all transportation and distribution, including that of food and arms. By war's end, the QMC ran a huge collection of railroad lines, forges, steel and iron mills, blacksmiths, warehouses, and repair shops of every kind and description.

The transition from prewar simplicity to the creation of this mammoth enterprise was not smooth. In the beginning, shortages, delays, and confusion reigned. Uniforms, tents, and blankets had not been stockpiled and thus were in short supply. Large new orders had been placed. However, factories were far too small to meet promised volume and thus consistently failed to meet delivery schedules. The quality of the goods was frequently atrocious, because the contractor had either promised better production methods than he could deliver or because he was lining his own pocket by cutting corners on specifications. The word *shoddy* is derived from the type of cloth used in early uniforms and blankets. This cloth was made from pressed cotton lint and would quickly disintegrate from moisture or even ordinary use.

There was also the matter of shoes. These were inherently uncomfortable, because factory shoe blanks did not differentiate between right and left feet. To this was added the fact that the shoes were often made of untanned leather, which caused the uppers to separate from the soles after the first rain.

If logistic problems were not enough, there was also a major policy disagreement within the high command. Early regiments were unwisely recruited for a term of only ninety days. Many of the "brass" (including general in chief Winfield Scott) accordingly felt that "good equipment" should be held back and reserved for later regiments that would be committed to longer service. Thus, a portion of what little was available in the early days was deliberately withheld.

Whenever the army embarked upon a campaign, its line of advance invariably followed rivers or railways. This was not accidental. No Civil War army could possibly subsist without the volume of materials that only boats and trains could carry. Army wagons were used only as short-haul vehicles to bring supplies from the railroad or port to the army's encampment. Even so, and in spite of draconian efforts to limit what was permitted to be loaded aboard the wagons, an army corps might require as many as 800 six-mule wagons. This would constitute a several-mile-long procession, which was both cumbersome and vulnerable. The wagon train constantly interfered with army movements and was a particular hindrance when the army was forced into retreat. Nonetheless, it had to be endured, because its role was vital.

The soldier had a clothing allowance of sixty-four dollars a year to cover a cap, blouse, dress coat, overcoat, pants, shirts, underwear, socks, and shoes plus one woolen and one rubber blanket. Invariably, this would prove inadequate, and additional items would be required to be drawn periodically from QMC stores. When the soldier did so, the cost of the replacement would be charged to his personal account. At the end of each year, all such drawings would be deducted from his pay—another illustration of the "army way."

An infantryman did not have the option of wearing each article of clothing until it became threadbare. Because on the march he would be required to carry his rifle, forty to sixty rounds of ammunition, a knapsack, three days' rations, and his canteen, blankets, and tent, in hot weather he could not resist disposing of something to lighten the load. Usually, the dress coat, overcoat, and blankets were the first items to be discarded. Almost certainly they would need future replacement.

A single concession to reality was made by the QMC. In battle, if a soldier was ordered to charge, he would immediately drop all gear

except his rifle and ammunition. Similarly, if forced into a hasty retreat, he would drop everything. In these circumstances the government did provide replacement without personal cost.

The soldier's other major personal necessity was his tent. Early in
the war these consisted of either the sibley tent, a sort of tepee, or
the "wedge" tent (like the Boy Scout variety). Other very large tents
called wall tents were used, but these were employed exclusively for
command headquarters or field hospitals. All these tents proved
cumbersome and had to be carried on the wagons.

The sleeping tents were ill ventilated, which hardly suited un-
washed and often contagiously ill men. By 1863, the smaller tents had
been mostly superseded by the "shelter half," so named because each
soldier was given half a tent with appropriate buttons and button-
holes. When evening came, he and a buddy would combine their respective halves to make a serviceable shelter for two. (When joined,
the whole tent would be referred to as a shebang, from which we get
the expression, "the whole shebang.") In winter quarters, shelter
halves would be used to form the roof of the log huts constructed by
self-selected squads of soldiers.

The QMC ultimately met every challenge. It was the primary reason why the Northern lad never suffered from famine and exposure,
as did his Southern counterpart.

The situation regarding arms and ammunition was also chaotic
in 1861. The North had approximately 250,000 small arms in storage. Of these, only 35,000 were modern rifles. The remainder were
smoothbores, of which many were unserviceable. The equipment
originally issued to the 30th Illinois infantry reflects this situation.
The regiment was furnished with 90 good rifles, 183 serviceable muskets, and 357 unserviceable muskets. No weapons at all were issued
to 120 men.

The government operated two armories, one at Harpers Ferry, Virginia, and one in Springfield, Massachusetts. The former was immediately disrupted by Confederate forces and never regained production. The Springfield facility remained in operation but initially
could produce only 1,000 rifles per month. The government did not
own a cannon foundry. The artillery was armed mostly with "brass
Napoleons," which were useful only for close-in conflict.

Obviously, the nation had to look to private manufacturers and foreign imports to meet its needs. To Ripley, however, this was not obvious. He consistently overstated his small-arms inventory and asserted that the stock of smoothbores would be sufficient and could easily (and cheaply) be made serviceable. This dictum left a vacuum in both the domestic and foreign markets that the individual Northern states and the Confederacy instantly rushed to fill. The effect was to permit prices to rise to extraordinary levels and to give the Confederates a purchasing "window."

The two best contemporary rifles were the American Springfield and the British Enfield. Both used interchangeable ammunition and were manufactured by using similar machine tools. Their designs were copied by the fifteen small manufacturers in New England and the mid-Atlantic states, whose wartime expansion became critical to the war effort. Arming of the early regiments varied considerably from state to state. Eastern regiments tended to be well equipped, thanks to their War Governors' prompt actions and the existence of local factories. Western regiments, however, were usually forced to accept whatever they could obtain.

Both the Springfield and the Enfield rifles were muzzle-loading, hammer-lock, single-shot guns whose loading entailed biting off the end of a paper cartridge, pouring and ramming the powder into the barrel, ramming down the ball, cocking the hammer, and applying a percussion cap to a nipple that led to the chamber.

The rifles were very accurate and had good range, but they were slow (three shots in two minutes was about the best obtainable action). Moreover, the soldier's right shoulder and arm were unnecessarily exposed while under fire. Sometimes a soldier would never actually fire his piece in battle because, amid the noise and confusion, he would forget to apply the percussion cap to the nipple. Successive loadings without discharge then made his rifle susceptible to breech explosions when he later remembered to fix the cap.

More efficient weapons were being developed, but Ripley stood in the way of progress. His opposition concentrated on foreign-made arms (these competed with American products), breechloaders (these might be impractical because explosive gases might escape at the breech), and rapid-fire carbines (these "wasted ammunition").

No matter how bad he was as an administrator, Ripley was first class as a departmental in-fighter. No one was able to remove him until September 1863. Finally, George Ramsay was appointed his successor. Consequently, by 1864, large quantities of Sharps and Spencer repeating carbines began to be freely issued to the army. The addition of these weapons was one of several factors that made the year 1864 decisive.

The artillery was also vastly expanded. Brass Napoleons continued to serve as the perfect weapon to fire canister and explosive shells at short range, but these were increasingly supplemented by cast-iron cannon designed for long-range and siege activities. Such weapons had two big drawbacks. They were enormously heavy and thus difficult to drag along muddy roads and across fields, and they had a propensity to explode at the breech, thus killing the gun crew. The arts of metallurgy and casting were simply not yet good enough to ensure safety. Only when steel cannons were introduced during the later war years did this problem start to be alleviated.

Two other weapons were never used but in other circumstances might have had decisive effect. These were the Gatling gun (early machine gun) and the hand grenade. A prototype Gatling gun was made in 1863, but commercial production did not start until 1866.

Thus, in a lurching and experimental fashion, the War Department learned to supply its troops, just as its equally green generals were learning how to maneuver their armies. In one respect these two processes were identical. Men died when administrators made mistakes, just as they did when generals erred. Bad food led to susceptibility to disease. Shoddy clothing and leaky tents caused deaths from pneumonia and other illnesses. Finally, there is no way to calculate the lives that might have been spared if breech-loading and rapid-firing weapons had been available earlier. In the end one can only conclude that it was all part of the price of a restored union. As Lincoln said in his Second Inaugural, God may have intended that every drop of blood drawn by the lash was to be compensated by one drawn by the sword.

Bull Run was the watershed of the war. Because of it, the need for professional control was made manifest. General George B. McClellan was appointed to create and command the eastern army, thereafter to be known as the Army of the Potomac. McClellan was brought to Washington from western Virginia, where he had been the victor in several small battles that had enabled the loyal mountaineers to make good their intended separation from the remainder of Virginia. He instantly took charge and in short order restored the pride and self-confidence that the army had lost at Bull Run. He made his men feel unbeatable, and the men loved him for it.

McClellan was appointed to command what would become the Army of the Potomac on July 27, 1861, only a week after the disaster at Bull Run. He discovered that his command consisted of a force of 53,000 men, bivouacked in various locations on both sides of the Potomac. No organization existed above the level of regiment. Among such "regiments" it was quite unusual to find one where military discipline prevailed, daily attendance was compulsory, and training was still being carried on. Most regimental organization existed only on paper. Field officers were inattentive to their men's needs, and the men idled their days away among the bars and brothels of the capital. The high command engaged in mutual recriminations over Bull Run so as to effectively preclude any remediation of these conditions.

McClellan's first steps were to create an efficient staff for the Army of the Potomac (originally consisted of twenty officers but rising to sixty-five before spring 1862), to shake up corresponding staff positions within the War Department, and to improve cooperation between these two hierarchies. This was quite novel. Napoleon had pioneered the concept of staff specialists, but the idea had fallen into general disuse since his time. First to be appointed was Col. Randolf Marcy, McClellan's father-in-law, as the Potomac army's chief of staff. This may seem like nepotism, but it was probably necessary, given the inherent conflict between McClellan's paranoiac personality and his need for implicit trust in his appointee's judgment. Moreover, Marcy was a competent administrator.

The army's most immediate need was for good order. Civilians strenuously protested the large number of drunk and disorderly soldiers, apparently under no one's control, who frequented the city's streets and parks during the day and often engaged in petty criminality at night. To deal with this, Col. Andrew Porter was appointed provost marshal general. Porter swiftly organized a military police force that employed squads of regulars to clear streets and parks, close saloons, arrest AWOL soldiers, and threaten deserters with capital punishment.

McClellan also directly confronted the problem of those regiments where discipline had completely vanished. For some, notably the 2d Maine and 4th Connecticut, this entailed the permanent imprisonment of ringleaders and the temporary stigmatization of the entire regiment. At first this seemed excessively harsh, because the soldiers' complaints of bad officers, bad food, poor sanitation, and inadequate clothing and shelter were often fully justified. McClellan's point, however, was not that these abuses should not be redressed, but that redress must come through the operation of the military chain of command, not through the volunteers' "inalienable right" to withhold service.

Nonetheless, the general much preferred to operate through incentives, not punishment. The experience of the New York 79th "Highlanders" was a case in point. The regiment was brigaded under Gen. Dan Sickles, a rather disreputable New York politician made famous by his murder of the son of Francis Scott Key (the "Star-Spangled Banner" author) for having seduced Sickles's wife. This appointment caused great discontent. Then a regular army officer was appointed as colonel to replace their former commander, who had been killed at Bull Run, instead of the regiment's being permitted to elect its own leader. This caused most of the remaining officers to resign and the men to rebel.

McClellan summarily squelched the rebellion. He had its ringleaders put in irons and accused them of "the basest cowardice" in pursuing their "frivolous and unfounded" complaints. His solution, however, was simply to take away the regiment's colors and official status, which were to be restored only at McClellan's discretion when regimental behavior so justified. When that occurred, the general staged a grand review, with great ceremony. The Highlanders became one of the Army of the Potomac's better units.

Next, McClellan focused upon the vast improvement needed in food and shelter. He appointed Brig. Gen. S. Vliet as the Potomac army's quartermaster. Vliet worked closely with the War Department's quartermaster general, Montgomery Meigs, to ensure regularity and quality of supply, while constantly fighting corruption and ineptly prepared supply contracts. The dietary health of the army improved immediately. Not so quickly remedied, however, was the inadequacy of clothing, blankets, and tents. These continued to be a problem through the winter of 1861–62, but even here progress was made.

The major problem of personal health and hygiene was put under the jurisdiction of surgeon S. Tripler, medical director of the Army of the Potomac. Because the medical department of the War Department was hopelessly outmoded, Tripler turned to the U.S. Sanitary Commission, a civilian volunteer agency, for assistance. The secretary of the commission was Frederick Law Olmsted (future architect of New York's Central Park). Olmsted assiduously toured all the camps and took charge of the enforcement of sanitary conditions. After correcting the worst of the problems, Olmsted could point with pride to a reduction in the rate of camp illness.

Rounding out the senior staff of the Army of the Potomac were Gen. Seth Williams, adjutant general (executive officer); Lt. Col. James Hardie, deputy adjutant; and Maj. John G. Barnard (designer of the Washington forts), chief of engineers.

With his staff complete, McClellan proceeded to organize the training of his men. Each newly arriving regiment (and those who had arrived earlier without effective training) was assigned to a provisional training brigade stationed on the north side of the Potomac. There it was equipped and drilled, first by squad and company, then by regiment and brigade. When it was deemed fit, it was transferred to the south side of the Potomac, where it was brigaded (four regiments to a brigade) with other "combat-ready" regiments. Then, as their training progressed, the brigades were formed into divisions (three brigades to a division). McClellan ultimately intended to form the divisions into army corps (two or more divisions to a corps). He did not do so in the winter of 1861–62, however, as he was then unsure which of his generals had the capacity to command a corps (24,000 men).

McClellan gave equal attention to the training of his artillery and cavalry. He had inherited from McDowell only 9 batteries of field artillery, totaling 30 guns. He raised this to 92 batteries of 520 guns.

These he distributed among the army at a level of 4 batteries per division, with 100 guns retained as a general artillery reserve. He also created the siege train of 500 heavy guns and mortars. Most Confederates considered the artillery to be the most effective section of the Federal army.

Unlike the Southern army, the North had no effective cavalry tradition on which to build. McClellan accordingly appointed George Stoneman to turn raw recruits into fourteen cavalry regiments within six months. All things considered, Stoneman did well. McClellan, however, having created an effective force, then largely negated the strength of his own creation by dividing the cavalry into squads and distributing these throughout the infantry. J. E. B. Stuart, commanding a unified cavalry corps in the Southern army, consistently outperformed his Northern counterparts.

McClellan's organization of the Army of the Potomac was his lasting contribution to the Union cause. It was his personal misfortune that army careers had not at his time developed specializations. Had he been enabled to fill a position as head of training command of the U.S. Army (assuming his ego would have permitted him to accept such a "subordinate" role), he would today be remembered as one of the great architects of Union victory. In McClellan's day, however, generals were modeled on Napoleon. A general was assumed to be capable of carrying out all functions of command. Thus, General McClellan could not permanently retain the one job that magnified his virtues. Instead, he was forced to eventually transform himself into a field commander of fighting men. Once that occurred, his flaws rather than his virtues came to the fore. For the time being, the Army of the Potomac responded quickly to his leadership. By fall they were drilled to perfection and ready to take on the world.

AFTERMATH

After Bull Run, the North awoke to the realization that the war would be a major endeavor that was unlikely to end in a matter of weeks or even months. Long-term planning would be required. In fact, a plan had already been devised, but prior to Bull Run it had been ignored as being both grandiose and unnecessary. After the battle, it was reexamined.

The plan had been prepared by Gen. Winfield Scott, the super-annuated hero of the Mexican War and overall commander of the Union's armies before November 1861. Scott's plan, called the "Anaconda" (after the South American constrictor snake), stipulated the following: impose a naval blockade on the entire South; invade the South via the Mississippi River and seize control of that river's entire length, thus dividing the Confederacy in two; occupy the mountainous regions of the Southern states where Union loyalty remained high; fight a holding action in Virginia in order to pin down the largest Confederate forces while the remainder of the plan was being executed; and, finally, use the positions so gained to choke the Confederacy to death.

Action pursuant to the plan was quickly implemented in the fall of 1861 and the winter and spring of 1862. The Confederacy's two major ports, Norfolk and New Orleans, were captured. The remaining Southern ports were blockaded, and the U.S. Navy occupied bases in North Carolina, South Carolina, Florida, and Alabama to permit the blockade to be maintained. General Grant captured the Southern forts on the Cumberland and Tennessee Rivers, which freed all of central and western Kentucky and Tennessee. General Thomas saved eastern Kentucky, and General Pope opened the Mississippi River to the Tennessee-Mississippi border, thus permitting Memphis to be occupied. Across the river, General Lyon prevented Missouri from joining the Confederacy, and by summer 1862 the Union was able to take control of all Southern territory north of the Arkansas River.

In Virginia, however, the plan was not implemented. This was not for want of effort by the Lincoln administration. Lincoln was a devotee of concerted action. He kept urging McClellan to coordinate the movements of the Army of the Potomac with those of the western armies, but McClellan would not listen. The general was convinced that the Army of the Potomac was outnumbered and that another defeat following Bull Run would destroy the Union. He thus would not move until he was personally persuaded of the inevitability of victory. No political or military contingency would dissuade him from this stance. (In total frustration, Lincoln at one point suggested that he might wish to borrow the army if General McClellan had no use for it.) So from October 1861 until March 1862, McClellan staged grand reviews, while the remainder of the Union's forces moved from one achievement to the next. This could not continue. By March, Lincoln told McClellan that either the army would undertake a campaign or McClellan would be relieved.

McClellan continued to reject a direct march toward Richmond. He was, however, prepared to undertake an amphibious campaign up the Virginia peninsula. Lincoln had his doubts but had to accept the sole-action recommendation that his commanding general was prepared to order. The president gave his reluctant consent, thus setting the stage for the Peninsular campaign.

CHAPTER III
Flag Officer Farragut Wins His Admiral's Stars

N ew Orleans has always been an unusual place within the American nation. It shares with only Santa Fe, New Mexico, and several small settlements in Texas and California the distinction of being a town west of the Appalachians whose existence antedates the birth of the republic. Moreover, unlike any other American city of either English or Hispanic cultural heritage, New Orleans is French with an admixture of Spanish, English, and Acadian influences that give it a unique Creole aspect.

In February 1862, however, such Chamber of Commerce "puffery" did not generally occupy the minds of those Northern strategists who were concerned with the city. Several other more tangible factors presented themselves. New Orleans was the largest and wealthiest city within the Confederacy. It was also the entrepôt where the agricultural wealth of the Prairie states, together with the cotton of the Southwest, was purchased, stored, and transshipped for export. Finally, it was a major clearing port for imports, having all necessary facilities and commercial contacts to handle the purchasing of whatever the South did not itself produce. Left untouched, the city had the capacity to be a major obstacle to the Northern war effort.

The North had no intention of allowing this to happen. New Orleans, like the remainder of the Southern coast, would first be blockaded by the Union navy. This was not as formidable an undertaking as it appeared. The Southern coast was lengthy and indented, but most of its bays were shallow and unsuited to ocean transport. As a practical matter, all seaborne traffic of the Confederacy had to choose among three Atlantic ports—Savannah, Charleston, or Wilmington, North Carolina—or three Gulf ports—Pensacola, Mobile, or New Orleans. To the north, Union control of Newport News and Fortress Monroe precluded the South's use of the Chesapeake Bay region. To the west, the Texas coast ports were too isolated to be of significant value.

The prewar U.S. Navy, unlike the army, was not an insignificant force. Its ships, although few by European standards, were modern and in good repair. Its civilian leadership—Gideon Wells and Gustavus Fox, secretary and assistant secretary, respectively—was first-rate. Under them, a handful of daring and imaginative officers filled the senior ranks. This happy combination permitted the navy to move aggressively as soon as the blockade was declared. By the end of May 1862, the navy had accomplished the following: captured Norfolk, causing the Confederate ironclad *Virginia (Merrimac)* to be scuttled and burned; breached Hatteras Gap in North Carolina's Outer Banks and captured Roanoke Island, thus closing off North Carolina's Albemarle and Pamlico Sounds to Confederate use; captured Hilton Head and Beaufort, South Carolina, thus establishing a base between Charleston and Savannah; and siezed Fort Pulaski on an island off Savannah. Accordingly, by the time the war was a year old, the Confederacy's three Atlantic ports were closely monitored and remained open only to the hazardous occupation of blockade running.

In the Gulf of Mexico things moved with equal rapidity. Throughout 1861 the Union had preserved its occupation of Fort Pickens, an island off Pensacola, Florida. In late 1861, this stronghold was reinforced and enlarged, and the area was turned into a base for the blockade of the Florida Panhandle. Ship Island, off Biloxi, Mississippi, was captured and put to a similar use for Mobile Bay and the mouth of the Mississippi River. Thus, the North by early 1862 could demonstrate that the blockade was real and enforced. This was a requirement under international law if the blockade was expected to be honored by neutral nations.

A blockade would suffice with regard to the other Southern ports, but not New Orleans. The Crescent City must be seized and permanently occupied by Union forces. This imperative derived from the city's strategic position commanding the Midwest's north-south and east-west trade routes. A major goal of the Union's strategic war plan was to deny the Confederacy the use of these routes.

The north-south route, that is, the Mississippi River, was particularly sensitive politically and economically. Most of the old northwest's produce from Ohio to Iowa was traditionally shipped down the Mississippi for transshipment at New Orleans to either the East Coast or Europe. Thus, the fortunes of this region were deemed to be tied to those of the South. It was assumed that a viable Confederacy would exert an irresistible magnetic pull on the loyalties of these states. In practical fact, this theory had been outmoded by the combination of northern railroad and Great Lakes steamer traffic that bound the old Northwest to the Northeast. That reality, however, was not apparent in 1862. The Mississippi and its tributaries also provided the means of transporting the South's cotton for transshipment, but the blockade had already reduced exports to a trickle.

Much more important was the west-to-east trade coming down the Arkansas or Red Rivers to be discharged at Memphis, Vicksburg, or Natchez for rail transshipment to the East. This was an important source of foodstuffs and leather for both the civilian population and the Confederate army. Elimination of this traffic, however, would require Union control of the entire length of the Mississippi.

That the Confederacy would vigorously resist yielding control of the river was certain. In fact, in Lincoln's phrase, "The Father of Waters [did not] again flow unvexed to the sea" until the middle of 1863. But a start had to be made somewhere, and in January 1862 the order was given to flag officer Farragut, the navy's senior professional officer, to assemble a fleet in order to sail up the Mississippi and capture New Orleans. As the British discovered in 1814, this was not an easy task.

David Glascow Farragut had joined the U.S. Navy as a midshipman in 1810 at the age of nine and served as a prize master, that is, temporary captain, of captured vessels in the War of 1812 while still at the tender age of twelve. Interestingly, he was born in Tennessee and lived in Norfolk, Virginia. There is no indication, however, upon Virginia's secession that he gave even a passing thought to joining the

Confederacy. The navy was his life, his home, and his family. His long service had been rewarded with increasing rank and responsibility. By 1861 he was looking forward to an honorable retirement. But the war intervened.

For the purpose of assembling his fleet, Farragut selected the already navy-occupied Ship Island, an island just offshore from the city of Biloxi, Mississippi. The island was nothing more than a large sandbar and was not intended to be a permanent base.

The Mississippi cuts through a delta region to enter the sea. The main defenses of the city of New Orleans were located about twenty miles upstream from the top of the delta. These defenses consisted principally of two forts, Jackson and St. Philip, which were almost opposite each other on the river. Fort Jackson, a star-shaped masonry structure, was the stronger of the two and was situated on a bend in the river. An oncoming ship thus would be required to first steam directly at the fort, then turn left directly underneath its guns and steam parallel to the fort for several hundred yards, then turn right to pass between the two forts. During the entire run, fire from both Fort Jackson and Fort St. Philip would converge on the approaching ship and would cover the entire span of the river.

Supplementing the forts' defenses would be two Confederate ironclad rams, the *Louisiana* and the *Manassas,* that were docked nearby. The *Manassas* was operational, but the *Louisiana* suffered from the usual Confederate weakness of not having a sufficiently strong and reliable engine to give it both power and maneuverability. In fact, during the battle, *Louisiana*'s engine could not be made to work at all. Thus, it served as a floating battery rather than a warship. *Louisiana* had a sister ship, the *Mississippi,* which was then under construction in New Orleans. It, therefore, played no part in the battle.

Completing the Confederate defenses were thirteen unarmored gunboats whose principal function would be to push fire rafts against the side of any approaching Union vessel. The Confederates had also planted underwater obstacles and had attempted to stretch a chain across the ship channel. The force of the current made the latter only partially successful, but overall it was a tight defense, and it was manned by courageous men who were determined to persevere. Farragut had his work cut out for him.

Further complicating Farragut's task was the fact that his command was divided. Farragut's main rival for naval preeminence was Comdr. (later Admiral) David Dixon Porter. Before Farragut's fleet action was authorized, Porter had suggested to the Navy Department that the two forts be reduced by bombardment by an assemblage of "mortar boats." It was assumed that these would render the forts uninhabitable and thus subject them to capture by an invading army. Farragut (correctly) thought this unlikely, but Porter had persuaded the Navy Department and was placed in command of a squadron of schooners. On each schooner had been constructed a wooden platform to which a large mortar was attached. Porter's squadron was then assigned to Farragut's fleet, over Farragut's protest.

Farragut's strike force consisted of 21 gunboats and steamboats supporting 6 major warships: the wooden, steam auxiliary sloops of war *Hartford* (flagship), *Brooklyn, Richmond, Pensacola, Portsmouth,* and *Oneida.* These vessels each mounted more than 25 guns and were approximately 225 feet in length, with a beam of 45 feet, and a displacement of approximately 1,000 tons. Overall, Farragut's fleet mounted more than 200 guns, not including Porter's 21 mortar schooners. Rounding out the fleet were sufficient transports to carry an army of 15,000 men. These were commanded by none other than our old friend, the ubiquitous Gen. Ben Butler. This "task force" was the largest ever assembled by the U.S. Navy up to that time.

Farragut was appointed to command the Mississippi expedition in January 1862, but it was not until late March that his fleet could be assembled. Ship Island, the captured island off the Mississippi coast, now served as the anchorage for the fleet being assembled. Barracks and tents were also erected on that island to house Butler's army. At the end of March, warships and mortar schooners embarked for the mouth of the Mississippi. The troops remained on Ship Island, awaiting results.

Within its delta the Mississippi flowed through three separate channels (called "passes") that the river itself had carved through the irregular peninsula that made up the delta region. These passes converged into a single stream at the top of the delta at a point called "Head of the Passes." Today, all such channels are continually dredged and are suitable for passage by oceangoing vessels. In the 1860s, however, the passes were partially obstructed by the naturally created sandbars. Although all of the passes could handle Porter's mortar schooners, none could accommodate the fully loaded sloops of war. Farragut, therefore, was forced to strip his major vessels down to bare essentials to enable them to cross the entrance bars at South and Southwest Passes, the major entry points. The vessels then required refitting at Head of the Passes to restore the armament and other equipment that had been off-loaded. (Virtually every warship scraped the bar and required some amount of towing to enter the river.)

During this process of off-loading and refitting, the fleet was very vulnerable. Had even a modest Confederate fleet been present, grave damage might have been done to Farragut's fleet before its attack on the forts. As it happened, a Confederate fleet was available, or at least had been available. Unfortunately for the South, they had only one fleet but two competing urgent requirements for its use. The wrong choice was made, and the vessels that might have hurt Farragut were instead sent upstream, where they were wasted in futilely trying to combat Grant's and Pope's Tennessee offensives. That fact, plus the Confederacy's inability to provide engines for its ironclads, foredoomed the forts, the Crescent City, and the South's control of the lower Mississippi.

Farragut now came into his own. In retrospect, his victory would be seen as a masterful combination of strategic appreciation, tactical mastery, and dauntless determination. It was all that, but first and foremost it was a masterpiece of meticulous planning. This not only ensured its success but also so impressed Farragut's men as to his foresight that they would have followed him into Hell, if necessary.

Farragut anticipated and sought to cope with every contingency, and everything was designed to contribute to a single strategic goal: keep the fleet moving forward at any cost until the forts were bypassed. Farragut realized, as the Confederates did not, that there was no need to battle toe-to-toe against the forts until one or the other was destroyed. The Southern commander's appreciation that masonry forts would always outlast wooden ships was not disputed by Farragut, but Farragut's goal was not to destroy or capture the forts. It was to capture the city. Once the forts were bypassed, the city's fall became inevitable. Once the city fell, the forts became isolated and therefore untenable. Thus, the Southern commander's strategy of depending on the power of the forts to resist destruction was fatally flawed. All the fleet had to do was to withstand fire for about an hour without sinking or being disabled.

To this end, Farragut ordered that the vessels' hulls be strengthened to the maximum degree. Thus, all extra anchor chain must be hung over both sides of the vessels to act as armor plating to protect their machinery. "Jacob's ladders" must be coiled, available at various locations and fastened to each ship's main deck. Next to such rope ladders there must be a supply of boards (to which felt had been glued) and long carpenter nails. When a vessel was hit by a shot, it was anticipated that damage control parties would descend such ladders and nail the boards in place to cover holes and keep the hull watertight.

All unnecessary masts and spars were to be off-loaded, and the fore- and mainmast tops (the above-deck platforms) were to be armored to protect sharpshooters stationed at such locations. Because most of the ships' cannon pointed broadside, vessels not having fore and aft guns should specially mount such armament to repel enemy vessels coming alongside at the bow or stern.

Further precautions involved "trimming all vessels by the head," that is, ballasting all ships so that their draft was deeper at the bow than at the stern. Thus, if any vessel went aground, it would do so bow first so that the river's current could not swing the ship sideways or backward to the current. Ship's boats were to be prepared for immediate launch but nonetheless secured in locations that were sheltered from cannon fire. Boat crews were to be assigned in advance, and the boats were to be provided with line and grapples to enable the boats to swiftly tow away any fire rafts that were pushed into the vessel. Tubs of water and buckets were to be placed at various locations on deck to enable fires to be immediately extinguished.

Vessels were also to have readily available anchors at both bow and stern. Should a vessel be disabled, it was to immediately drop anchor and then drift downstream by paying out anchor cable. While so doing, it was to continue to fire at the forts or opposing warships. No vessel whose propulsion machinery was still operating was permitted to disengage or retire downstream without the express order of Farragut himself. All vessels were therefore to proceed regardless of damage or casualties until they had individually passed the forts. One final precaution reveals the degree of Farragut's preparatory planning. Portions of the decks together with all fittings, equipment, et cetera, were to be painted white for improved visibility under afterdark battle conditions.

On April 14, 1862, the fleet was as ready as Farragut could make it. Its officers and men were also at a peak of physical and psychological readiness. Before Farragut could begin his foray, however, the Navy Department insisted that Commander Porter's mortar boat scheme must first be attempted. Although Farragut seethed with impatience, he nonetheless conceded that the mortar attack was worth a try. Should that effort succeed, many casualties would be spared. On April 18, therefore, the twenty-one mortar schooners were moved into a position downstream and behind a bend in the river where their hulls could not be discerned from the forts. To further camouflage them, tree branches were tied to their mast tops so that they appeared to a distant observer to be a forest, not a fleet.

After the boats were moored, Lt. F. H. Gerdes of the Coastal Survey spent four days triangulating the exact bearing and distances from the boats to the forts. Finally, all was ready. A round-the-clock mortar bombardment ensued and continued for four days. Fifty Confederates were killed and great physical damage was caused, but it soon became apparent that bombardment alone would not reduce the forts. If New Orleans were to be captured, the forts would have to be bypassed. Farragut would wait no longer. At 3:30 A.M. on April 24, 1862, his fleet started upstream.

Farragut divided his force into three squadrons. The first consisted of eight ships, including three sloops of war *(Oneida, Pensacola,* and *Portsmouth)* and two large steamers, the *Varuna* and the *Mississippi.* This squadron alone contained more than half the firepower of the entire fleet. The second squadron consisted of the three remaining auxiliary sloops led by Farragut's flagship USS *Hartford.* The third squadron, the weakest, consisted of six gunboats. The battle plan called for the first squadron to remove the river barriers and to disperse the Confederate fleet. The path would then be opened for the three-ship second squadron to steam directly upriver, first contesting and then bypassing the forts. The third squadron would follow in the second's wake. Its role was simply to add weight to the surviving fleet for subsequent upriver operations. While this was occurring, Porter's mortar boats would continue to lay a full barrage on the forts.

Farragut's first objective was the destruction of what remained of the obstruction that the Confederates had attempted to erect to block the river. Originally, this had consisted of a series of log rafts over which had been laid a chain that stretched from shore to shore. Both rafts and chain, however, had been swept away by the river's current. What remained was a lesser barrier consisting of several hulks that were sunk in the middle of the ship channel joined by a chain. Two Union gunboats were detached from the first squadron to dismantle the chain. They succeeded in part, but the channel thus opened was narrow and permitted only single vessel passage. Thus, all of Farragut's fleet was required to pass single file through the opening. Once through, as Farragut anticipated, the fleet would be fully committed to the bypass strategy. If checked, there was no feasible way for it to withdraw.

The first squadron, led by Farragut's second in command, Capt. Theodorus Bailey, in the gunboat *Cayuga,* was then sent through and was beset by three Confederate ships. The *Cayuga* was immediately aided by the *Oneida* and the *Varuna,* and a general fleet action ensued. Within minutes four Confederate ships were destroyed, and the Federals lost the USS *Varuna.* The Confederate ram *Manassas* moved to intervene but was immediately attacked by the USS *Mississippi,* a large steamboat. *Manassas* rammed *Mississippi* and succeeded in putting it out of action. *Mississippi*'s guns, however, had ignited fires aboard *Manassas.* It broke off action and, shortly thereafter, blew up.

The Confederate forts had been attempting to destroy the Federal ships, but their task was hindered by their desire not to fire into their own vessels in the general melee. Many of their gunners were also pinned down by continuing incessant fire from Porter's mortars. Finally, both forts suffered heavy damage from the steam sloop *Pensacola,* most of whose cannons were rifled and thus had greater penetrating power. While the other vessels in the first squadron had been combating Confederate ships, *Pensacola* had steamed slowly by the forts, delivering broadsides into each in turn. It paid for its audacity by suffering the largest number of casualties of any vessel in the fleet—thirty-seven men killed or wounded.

Farragut next sent the second squadron (steam sloops USS *Hartford, Brooklyn,* and *Richmond*) on a hell-for-leather drive to bypass the forts, ignoring any distractions en route. The value of his advance planning was made manifest by the experience of the flagship. *Hartford* ran aground right under the forts' guns, and a Confederate gunboat immediately pushed a fire raft against its hull. Flames flared as high as the ship's rigging. *Hartford,* however, blew up the raft, extinguished the fire, and pulled itself off the mud bank with the help of a kedge dropped off the vessel's stern. The *Hartford* was saved, and the three sloops reached the far side of the forts without further incident.

The transit of the three steam sloops effectively won the battle. Only three of the last squadron's six gunboats succeeded in their run by, but all first squadron vessels except *Varuna* (sunk) and the *Mississippi* (disabled) ultimately joined the upriver fleet. Farragut had isolated the forts, and their value to the Confederates ceased.

Second-in-command Bailey proceeded upriver to New Orleans. Accompanied only by a lieutenant, he went ashore and demanded the surrender of the city from the mayor. The situation threatened to become ugly because the two Union officers were undefended and a mob was forming. Moreover, the mayor and a militia commander were becoming obstinate over formalities (such as whether the Louisiana flag would continue to fly over city hall), although pragmatically all was already lost. In the end, common sense prevailed. The two officers were conducted out a side entrance, and the city surrendered to overwhelming Union force.

AFTERMATH

The North had won a tremendous victory, second only to the prospective capture of Richmond itself, and the war was not yet a year old. New Orleans, the largest port and largest city (population 160,000) in the Confederacy, had been captured, and all north-south transit and external trade usage of the river had been denied forever to the Confederacy (although it would retain west-east usage of some tributaries for another year). Popular attention in the North, however, was fixed on Virginia. It would be a year before the magnitude of the victory, and its potential for military and political disruption of the entire Confederacy, became apparent. Indeed throughout the war the primacy of Virginia in the public imagination blinded opinion, both North and South, to the overriding importance of the west in the prosecution of the war.

Within days of New Orleans's surrender to Bailey, General Butler's army disembarked as an army of occupation. Shortly thereafter, the two forts were abandoned and were occupied by the Union forces.

The two Confederate ironclads, *Louisiana* and *Mississippi*, were stranded by Farragut's sudden victory. *Louisiana* had played only a minor part in the battle as a floating battery, because its engines could not be made to operate. After the forts were bypassed, *Louisiana*'s crew destroyed her with explosive charges. *Mississippi* had an even less graceful demise. Uncompleted when the battle concluded, her hull was burned on its construction ways in a New Orleans shipyard before Butler's troops occupied the city. It was the sad fate of the Confederate ironclad fleet throughout the war always to be both too little and too late.

General Butler, as military governor of New Orleans, immediately made a name for himself. In fact he was given two nicknames: "Beast" Butler and "Spoons" Butler. "Beast" derived from the fact that upper-class Southern belles were verbally abusing (and, in some cases, emptying chamber pots on) Union officers as the latter walked about the city. Butler, accordingly, issued a decree that women exhibiting such behavior would be treated as "women of the street engaged in their profession." The city was shocked to its eyebrows, but the rude behavior did cease. There is no indication that Butler's threat was ever carried out. The appellation "Spoons" was based on the (apocryphal) presumption that Butler authorized the stealing of dining silverware from the aristocracy.

Butler was prepared to enforce an object lesson, where necessary. Four secessionists hauled down the national flag from its pole atop the U.S. Mint shortly after Farragut had ceremoniously raised it. Their action was praised by the press in a series of front-page articles. Butler caused their leader to be arrested and sentenced to death by court-martial. He subsequently refused all petitions for clemency and had the offender hanged in the presence of a large crowd.

Farragut realized that the full fruits of the battle of the forts would not be gained until the entire Mississippi was cleared of Confederate control. Thus, after establishing Butler in the city, he continued upriver from the Crescent City. The Confederacy's inability to muster the resources simultaneously to defend all its vital strongpoints became immediately apparent to him. The South had staked everything on its ability to ward off invasion by defending the New Orleans forts and "Island No. 10" on the Mississippi River at the Kentucky-Tennessee border, while its field army repelled Northern invasion at Pittsburgh Landing (Shiloh) on the Tennessee River. By the end of April, the South had lost all three positions, and its western defenses were exposed as an empty shell.

Farragut saw and tried to capitalize on this opportunity. He steamed up the river to Vicksburg without any significant opposition. There, on June 28, 1862, he put the city under siege. Shortly thereafter, he was joined by Capt. Charles Davis, who had brought a fleet down from Cairo, Illinois. Together the two had steamed the entire length of the southern Mississippi without significant opposition.

In spite of his accomplishment, Farragut was increasingly frustrated. He knew that Vicksburg could not be captured by naval forces alone, but his appeal for a cooperating army fell on deaf ears. This was thanks in part to typical "Virginia first" preoccupations and in part to General Halleck's (then the western commander) abiding suspicion of and hostility toward General Grant (whom Halleck suspected of being drunk during the Union reverses on the first day of Shiloh). Grant was relieved of his command, which Halleck himself assumed. Halleck had none of Grant's offensive spirit and would not commit his army to an impromptu joint operation.

Farragut remained in front of Vicksburg for sixty-seven days but, unaided, was getting nowhere. Moreover, he had been embarrassed by the sortie of the Confederate ironclad *Arkansas* through his fleet several weeks earlier. He was also experiencing a sharp rise in illness among his men. By September, he gave up and brought his fleet back to New Orleans. Vicksburg would not be captured until the summer of 1863, when, as contemplated by Farragut, a joint expedition led by Grant and Admiral Porter would accomplish it.

Farragut, in spite of his setback before Vicksburg, was promoted to the rank of rear admiral on July 16, 1862; he was the first naval officer to attain admiral's rank in the history of the U.S. Navy. In August 1864, he was promoted to vice admiral, following his equally dramatic victory at Mobile Bay. After the war he was made a full admiral. He died in 1870.

Farragut was the second of a trio of loyalist Virginians to help advance the Union cause (the first having been Gen. Winfield Scott, the father of the Anaconda plan). The third and greatest contributor was Gen. George H. Thomas. None of these men was a "hater," but all were implacable opponents of secession. Individually and collectively, their contribution was enormous. It is hard to visualize how the war might have progressed if they, like most Virginians, had joined the Confederate cause.

CHAPTER IV
General McClellan's Modest Proposal

There was no doubt about it. Lincoln was entirely correct. In the spring of 1862, the general serving as both the commander of all the Union armies and as field commander of the Army of the Potomac, Gen. George B. McClellan, had a bad case of "the slows."

It hadn't always been that way. General McClellan graduated from West Point in 1846, ranked second in his class, and was assigned to the Army Corps of Engineers, as was customary for the top-ranking graduates. Promoted twice by brevet commission during the Mexican War, he later acted as the War Department observer of the Crimean War.

McClellan resigned from the army in 1857 and accepted positions first as chief engineer of the Illinois Central Railroad and then as president of the Ohio and Mississippi Railroad. Upon the commencement of hostilities, he was soon avidly sought for major command, as guaranteed by his previous military record. In fact, he was quickly recruited by Governor Dennison of Ohio to become the major general in command of all Ohio volunteers.

McClellan had provided the Union with its first victories in the anxious early days between the Baltimore riots and the First Battle of Bull Run. He had beaten no less a personage than Robert E. Lee in two small battles, Rich Mountain and Carricks Ford, fought in the western mountains of Virginia. These victories permitted the local mountaineers, in due course, to create the new, loyal state of West

Virginia. They also enabled the important Baltimore and Ohio Railroad to remain in service. McClellan became the nation's first hero and was appointed by Lincoln to reshape the remnants of the Bull Run army into the new Army of the Potomac.

McClellan efficiently reorganized the army, drilled it to the edge of perfection, and raised its morale to a fever pitch, but there everything stopped. The army continued to drill and maneuver, but it didn't march against the enemy. Other generals were seizing the initiative. General Burnside captured Roanoke Island, sealing the North Carolina coast. General U. S. Grant captured Forts Henry and Donelson, driving the Confederates from central and western Tennessee. Finally, Admiral Farragut steamed past the Mississippi forts and captured New Orleans.

McClellan, however, always said he had "good reason" not to advance. In this he was greatly abetted by his chief of intelligence, Allen Pinkerton, the famous detective. Pinkerton was, unfortunately for all concerned, an overgrown Tom Sawyer. He loved adventure and melodrama and was a poseur of the first magnitude. This predisposition toward drama, combined with his undue reliance on the presumed accuracy of sighting reports from panicky civilians and escaped slaves, led him consistently to overestimate the size of opposing Confederate forces. McClellan, himself an exemplar of caution, being warned that he was facing an army of up to 200,000, would inevitably either avoid a fight or insist that conditions be perfect. The result was paralysis, as Lincoln and an impatient Congress were to discover.

So while Burnside, Grant, and Farragut were acting, McClellan continued to resist the overland march to Richmond that the North was demanding. Lincoln finally warned him that his downfall was imminent unless he made some move. The general initially interpreted this remark as an unwarranted intrusion by a meddlesome politician and responded by sulking. Eventually, however, it penetrated even his narcissistic personality that "the ball was in his court."

McClellan's plan, when finally described to Lincoln, was unexpected. He continued to believe that the Confederate fortifications at Centerville, thirty miles below Washington, were too strong to attack. He accordingly proposed to outflank this stronghold by transporting his force by water to the peninsula between the York and Rappahannock Rivers and, from there, by marching southwest to Richmond. Lincoln, although surprised, could see the merit of the plan. It did offer the advantage of avoiding a costly attack on fortifications without diverting the army far enough away to "uncover" Washington.

Almost immediately, things started to go awry. Ironically, McClellan was a victim of his own caution. Confederate general Joe Johnston, the victor of Bull Run, was becoming increasingly concerned about keeping his troops as far forward as Centerville. Before being forced to retreat, he unilaterally withdrew his army to Fredericksburg (on the Rappahannock, about halfway between Washington and Richmond). There, he awaited events. In the process, he completely frustrated McClellan, because this vitiated the amphibious operation. Troops landing on the Rappahannock peninsula would now find themselves once again directly facing, rather than flanking, Johnston's forces. The move also had the incidental effect of severely embarrassing McClellan: when Union forces occupied the abandoned Centerville entrenchments, they discovered that many of the "fearsome guns" that had restrained the Union advance for six months were "Quaker cannons"—tree trunks painted black and mounted on gun carriages.

McClellan had to recast his plan. He would not give up the concept of a marine flanking operation, but he was now forced to land on the next peninsula to the south—the Virginia peninsula—consisting of the land between the York and the James Rivers. This changed the picture entirely. First, it meant that the water voyage would be twice as long as that originally planned. Second, it almost guaranteed a more spirited defense. The Rappahannock peninsula had had no particular historic significance. Thus, its loss would have no great effect on Southern morale. The Virginia peninsula, however, was the "cradle of liberty," the location of the sites of Jamestown, Williamsburg, and Yorktown. It was the embodiment of the South's assertion that it was fighting a second American Revolution, as well as being the home of Virginia's Tidewater aristocracy. Even ignoring the threat to Richmond, its defense would be dogged.

A more fundamental difficulty was that a move of this length would take the Northern army "off the map" for a week or more, leaving an open field for Confederate operations in northern Virginia. Moreover, once the Army of the Potomac reasserted itself as a fighting force, it would be on one side of the Confederate army (and its supply routes) and Washington would be on the other side. All that would then restrain the Confederates from turning and marching on Washington would be that they would in turn expose Richmond to Northern occupation. Old military men were heard to speak profoundly about the chess metaphor of "swapping queens."

Any threat to Washington was totally unacceptable to Lincoln, as he had recently demonstrated in the Maryland crisis. The president therefore remained adamantly opposed to the revised plan, unless at least 50,000 troops remained in the vicinity of Washington to guard against any onslaught.

McClellan was confident that he could reassure the president. He indicated that more than 30,000 Union troops were now operating under three separate commanders in and around Virginia's Shenandoah Valley. To these he added the 20,000-member army corps, commanded by Gen. Irwin McDowell (the losing general at Bull Run). This corps would not initially accompany McClellan to the peninsula but would remain at Centerville. Only when McClellan had advanced to the outskirts of Richmond would McDowell march south. He would then link his corps to the northernmost corps of the Army of the Potomac, thus closing off any northward movement by Confederates.

It all sounded plausible on paper. Lincoln was about to be persuaded when a then little known general named "Stonewall" Jackson suddenly demolished all their preconceived notions. Jackson was the Confederate commander in the Shenandoah Valley. Robert E. Lee, then acting as senior Confederate military adviser in Richmond, ordered Jackson to go on the offensive in the valley to take pressure off Johnston on the peninsula. Superficially, that seemed ridiculous. Jackson's army totaled only 20,000, and more than twice that number of Federals opposed him. The Federals, however, were divided into three separate armies stationed in west central Virginia, at

Harper's Ferry, and to the east of the Blue Ridge Mountains—that is, west, north, and east of Jackson. In theory, this meant that Union armies had Jackson surrounded. In fact, what it meant was that Jackson could prevent any combination between the Federal armies opposing him and could beat each of them separately.

This spectacle of Jackson on the loose completely exasperated Lincoln, who was reduced to trying (unsuccessfully) to coordinate his armies by telegraph instructions from Washington. It also created a chain of circumstances that would ultimately undermine McClellan's expedition. For the moment this was not apparent, but we shall see later what grievous consequences it had.

Meanwhile, back at McClellan's headquarters in Washington, all was proceeding well. Presidential assent to the amphibious expedition had been obtained, and preparations were getting under way. On February 27, 1862, the War Department issued the order for the transport of the Army of the Potomac to the Virginia peninsula. More than 400 vessels were involved. These included everything that the War and Navy Departments could find; ocean transports, bay and river steamers, schooners, other sailing vessels, and tugs hauling barges were all utilized. Even "canal boats," no more than oversized pontoons, were utilized as cargo carriers.

All told, these were to transport 120,000 men, 14,000 animals, 44 batteries, and all necessary ambulance and baggage wagons. In the last two weeks of March alone, the Union moved 75,000 soldiers and their equipment. All of this was done with extraordinary efficiency, from the loading of men and equipment along the Potomac River docks in Alexandria, Virginia, to their discharge at Fort Monroe at the end of the peninsula. The only casualties incurred during the move were the loss of six mules when a barge sank. By April 2, the expeditionary force was ready to attack.

No movement of this scale had ever been attempted before, and foreign observers, in particular, looked upon it with astonishment. One British commentator called it "the leap of a giant." To say that matters were efficiently handled, however, should not suggest that all went smoothly. As with any other precedent-setting operation, many unanticipated difficulties were encountered. Improvisation on a large scale was required.

The easiest part of the operation was the loading. Extensive docks on the Potomac shore were already available at Alexandria, Virginia. Loading thus became mostly a logistical problem of determining that the ships, men, and material arrived in the proper combinations and in the proper sequence in order to ensure orderly embarkation and disembarkation. Similarly, the passage itself presented no great difficulty. Adequate numbers of vessels were available so that overcrowding was not a problem. The transit, moreover, was made over inland waters, so that nowhere would ships, boats, barges, men, or animals be subjected to the rough water of the open oceans. As a result, seasickness among the men and panic among the animals were held to a minimum. Finally, the late-March weather was reasonably clement, so that men with overcoats and blankets did not suffer unduly from exposure to the cold.

A major problem did arise with regard to disembarking the men and unloading the equipment. The expedition's ultimate destination was Fort Monroe, the Federal facility that extended into Chesapeake Bay at the tip of the Virginia peninsula. Although limited wharves existed at the fort itself, there were none in its immediate environs. No one had ever contemplated that anyone would wish to land an army at such a location. It appeared that an enormous bottleneck and massive delays would result.

The problem of dockage was solved ingeniously by the army engineers. They did this by using canal boats—superpontoons about sixty feet long and fourteen feet wide. Two such boats would be spaced twelve feet apart and bound together with four-inch-square cross boards. A plank deck would then be constructed across the top of the cross boards, creating a very serviceable raft. A battery of guns could be off-loaded onto such a raft, which would then be nudged ashore by a tugboat until it grounded. The tug would then push a second raft behind the first. The two rafts would then be securely joined together. Finally, the engineers would construct a pontoon bridge from the joined rafts to the shore to create a permanent dock.

A smaller version of the same thing would be created by making a raft from two standard pontoons (thirty feet by five feet). A single gun could be placed on such a raft. Because of its smaller draft, this raft could be shoved directly to the riverbank. There, it could be immediately off-loaded by a working party. In this fashion, large amounts of equipment were brought ashore rapidly while the construction of the more ponderous docks progressed.

Pontoons were also used as landing craft for soldiers, so that they might be off-loaded from the transports without tying up valuable wharves. Initial attempts to put pontoons to such use were not altogether successful, as the soldiers were expected to climb down rope ladders thrown over the side of their transports to enter bobbing boats. Because most of the soldiers were farm boys who, in all probability, had never before been in an open boat, this exercise proceeded slowly. The engineers also solved this problem by building ramps that permitted the soldiers to walk directly from the transport decks to the pontoons. Thereafter, men went ashore at the rate of up to 2,000 per hour.

Thus, in spite of confusion and some undoubtedly unnecessary delay and duplication, the army came ashore at Fort Monroe and assembled rapidly. With high hopes and great confidence that a single sustained push would end the war, the men, in late April, started their march up the peninsula. They didn't march far, however. Very quickly it was discovered that there were several other "enemies" that first had to be defeated before they could confront the Confederates.

The first of these was topography. Someone (who, to this day, is not clear) had advised General McClellan that the roads on the peninsula were composed of loam over a clay base and so would provide a firm surface, even under rainy conditions. Whoever so informed him must have been either a Confederate sympathizer or a total ignoramus trying to advance himself by demonstrating supposed expertise. The reality was that the roads turned into bottomless mud immediately after every rain and impeded every movement of men and materials.

The second "enemy" was cartography (or the lack of it). Roads did not go where the only available maps said they should go. Rivers, ponds, and hills kept emerging where the maps said that none existed. The army floundered along, never knowing quite what to expect but seemingly always able to find within its ranks those who were capable of overcoming any unexpected obstacle.

Ultimately, the army reached Yorktown, the site of the decisive battle of the Revolutionary War. There it was confronted with both an unpleasant surprise and its third "enemy." The surprise was a line of fortifications that stretched across the peninsula, taking defensive advantage of both extensive swamps and a river of whose course the army was previously unaware. The "enemy" was the seeming lack of audacity exhibited by their own commander when any obstacle was encountered. McClellan took one look at the Yorktown fortifications and called for his siege train.

A prodigious amount of work was needed to position and utilize the roughly 100 pieces of heavy ordnance that McClellan believed necessary to crack the Yorktown defenses. When one contemplates the difficulty of bringing individual cannons, each weighing several tons, up muddy roads, it defies credibility that it was ever done at all. How it occurred was alluded to by a Civil War engineer who said he no longer had any doubts as to how the pyramids were built: put enough men on a rope and you can move anything.

Little by little during the month of April, the hard labor of bringing up the siege guns and constructing the ramparts in which to house them proceeded. Finally, all was ready, and a great bombardment of the Confederate line was scheduled for May 4. Of course, the Confederates had been observing the progress of events; they were aware that the Federals were about to open up with everything they had, and they saw no reason to stay around and suffer the consequences. So, on the night of May 3, the Confederate army abandoned its line. Once again, as at Centerville earlier in the year, it appeared that McClellan had been operating mostly against his own fears rather than the real force of the enemy. However, the Army of the Potomac took comfort in the fact that Yorktown had been given up without a battle, even though it had cost the army a month's delay and an extraordinary amount of "grunt" work.

It also soon transpired that the Confederates' withdrawal was more a shifting of position rather than an actual retreat. Very quickly the Potomac men discovered that Confederate general Magruder had fortified the area around Williamsburg, Virginia's colonial capital, and was prepared to make a stand. There, the first real battle of the campaign occurred.

It was not much of a battle. Magruder (now sick and replaced by Longstreet) had only about 10,000 men to confront the entire Union army. For a while, however, two Northern divisions were stopped, and the Union rear was thrown into confusion. Eventually, numbers told, and the Confederates were forced to retire, each side having suffered about 2,000 casualties. Now, at last, McClellan's campaign appeared to be gathering momentum. By the end of May the Northern force was approaching the eastern suburbs of Richmond, after having established a convenient base of supply at West Point on the York River. Richmond's fall seemed only a matter of time, just as Yorktown's had been, regardless of how cautious McClellan's tactics were. Then fate intervened in the form of the weather, a small river that no one heretofore had noticed, and an unexpected event.

The Chickahominy River is about as insignificant a stream as anyone can imagine. Prior to the war, it is probable that most citizens of Richmond were not even aware of its existence. As with Antietam Creek and Little Round Top, however, the war, by pure chance, wrote these place names in letters of fire for posterity to read.

The Chickahominy River rose to the north of Richmond and flowed southeast until it eventually emptied into the James. Under normal conditions it was a sluggish river that a man could wade across, but it drained a swampy area and during periods of heavy rainfall, could flood badly. On May 30, a howling storm hit the area. McClellan's army, whose line of advance had been roughly perpendicular to the river's course, now found itself divided by a raging torrent; three of its army corps were north of the river, and two were to the south. Only one pontoon bridge joined the two sections of the army. That span threatened to give way at any time. The engineers did their best to strengthen the span by adding extra anchors and by driving supporting pylons, but the bridge's status remained uncertain.

Confederate general Joe Johnston, now in overall charge of the defense of Richmond, saw his opportunity. He attacked the two isolated corps with two-thirds of his entire army. The result was a confused battle called either Fair Oaks or Seven Pines (two adjoining communities).

Johnston's assault was uncoordinated. The South was generally successful in its attack in the Seven Pines area, with Union general Keyes's corps staving off disaster only by means of a desperate bayonet attack. At Fair Oaks, however, the Federals emerged victorious, thanks to Union general Sumner (a corps commander stationed on the north side of the Chickahominy) having sent his troops across the pontoon bridge in spite of its seemingly imminent collapse. One hour after their arrival, Sumner's men sharply repulsed a Southern attack.

The fighting sputtered out by the evening of June 1. The North claimed victory—it retained possession of the battlefield—but for practical purposes the battle was a draw. Nonetheless, one very significant event occurred. Toward evening on June 1, General Johnston was wounded. Although his life was not threatened, the wound was severe. It was apparent that his convalescence would be lengthy and that he was no longer in condition to lead a field army. A successor had to be appointed, and he had to be someone who could assume effective command of an army under mortal threat. Only one possibility existed. Jefferson Davis appointed his own personal military adviser, a man of great reputation (but, to date, of mediocre battlefield performance), Gen. Robert E. Lee.

AFTERMATH

What happened next is the stuff of which legends are made. On June 1, 1862, the Southern cause was in tatters. Since Bull Run, a year before, repeated disaster had befallen it. The struggling proto-nation was on the verge of losing control of everything west of the Appalachians. If it were simultaneously to lose its political capital and industrial base, its remaining life could probably be counted in months, if not weeks. Yet, less than three months later, the siege of Richmond had been lifted, the invader had been repulsed, and overwhelming defeats had been inflicted on two major eastern Union armies. Now it was the South that was on the offensive and the North (Kentucky and Maryland) that was being invaded.

How had this occurred? It was principally due to the uncanny leadership of General Lee (with a minor assist by Gen. Braxton Bragg). Lee's victories were so astounding as to make it appear that he was reading the mind of his opposite number. Moreover, thanks mostly to the inspired leadership of his three principal lieutenants, Generals Stonewall Jackson, James Longstreet, and J. E. B. Stuart, the Southern army's execution was as good as Lee's conception. A mighty host, the Army of Northern Virginia, had been created. For a year of glory it would appear invincible.

Lee, like Johnston, based his tactics before Richmond on the obstacle that a flooded Chickahominy posed to the Federal commander. Gathering Stonewall Jackson's troops from the Shenandoah Valley (and additional forces from the South Atlantic states), Lee, during the month of June, maximized the size of his army and sought out McClellan's points of vulnerability.

McClellan's force was now deployed in mirror image to its previous position. Two-thirds of the army was south of the Chickahominy, poised for a direct assault on Richmond. One-third was north of the river, defending its railway supply line to West Point. As before, the Chickahominy was swollen by heavy rains, and contact between the two segments of the army was precariously dependent upon two pontoon bridges.

Lee decided to hit McClellan north of the river where McClellan's best corps commander, Fitz-John Porter, was in charge. Lee reasoned that defeating Porter might demoralize the Army of the Potomac, unnerve McClellan psychologically, and have the added benefit of severing the Union supply line to West Point. There were, however, two problems. Porter was well positioned, and dislodging him would not be easy. Moreover, placing Lee's forces to the north of the Chickahominy meant uncovering the approach to Richmond to the south of the river. If McClellan were ever to catch on, he could walk into Richmond virtually unopposed. Lee's attack was a high-stakes gamble but had the virtue of necessity. No other option offered even the possibility of saving Richmond.

On June 26, Lee attacked Porter's corps in the town of Mechanicsville, north of Richmond. Lee's plan had called for a frontal assault while Stonewall Jackson simultaneously hit Porter's flank. Jackson, however, never came up, and the frontal assault failed. Nonetheless, Lee's unsuccessful attack acted as the catalyst that resurrected all McClellan's anxieties and buried fears. Specifically, the general became convinced that his earlier supposition of Lee's army containing approximately 150,000 men was correct. He had continued to brood that Lincoln would not release McDowell's corps to protect his northern flank. Now, he persuaded himself that sinister forces within the Lincoln administration were deliberately withholding McDowell in a treasonous effort to destroy McClellan's army and the Union cause. These fears caused a psychological shift from an offensive to a defensive mentality. From now on, Lee would be setting the pace, and McClellan would be responding.

Lincoln was as steady a leader in a crisis as the nation had ever had, but even he was becoming disconcerted by the panicky tone of McClellan's latest telegrams. At one point in exasperation he complained that sending reinforcements to McClellan was like shoveling fleas across a barnyard floor. He also reminded the general that, if the relative strength of the forces was as unfavorable as McClellan supposed, the obvious course of action was not to send McDowell to the peninsula but to bring the Army of the Potomac back to Washington. All of this, of course, further heightened McClellan's distrust and reinforced his suspicions that he remained the Union's last faithful defender.

The practical consequence was that McClellan ordered Porter to retreat to a defensive bridgehead guarding the two pontoon bridges on the north side of the Chickahominy. So the scene was set for the battle of Gaines Mill, where, for the course of a whole day, Porter successfully stood off an overwhelming attack. Porter's men fought valiantly, his position was well chosen and, once again, Stonewall Jackson's flanking attack was late. Finally, however, Lee put it all together, and Porter's line cracked. During the evening of June 27, Porter's corps retired across the pontoon bridges, thus leaving the Chickahominy's northern bank to the victorious Confederates. This consequence was not foreordained. Two-thirds of McClellan's army had remained inactive on the southern bank throughout the entire day. These men could either have reinforced Porter or marched straight ahead into Richmond against only trifling opposition. Neither move was attempted. McClellan had taken counsel of his fear, as Lee foresaw that he would. In the end, it was McClellan's own hobgoblins that defeated him. Lee had simply been their agent.

Porter's retreat produced two decisive consequences that changed the course of the campaign. First, it caused the abandonment of the army's base at West Point on the York in favor of a new base to be established on the James. Second, it set off a wave of sequential retreats by the remainder of the Army of the Potomac, as that army sought defensible positions connected to the new base. Suddenly, it was not Richmond that was threatened. It was the survival of the Army of the Potomac that was at stake.

The Union retreat from Mechanicsville to the James River has come down in history and legend as the "Seven Days." There still remains a dispute (probably forever to be unresolved) whether the retreat was brilliantly conducted by McClellan or whether he simply abandoned responsibility, leaving his lieutenants to extricate the army. Either way, the army was in major peril most of the time. Its success in avoiding disaster rested in part on the fighting ability of its component parts but also on Lee's single mistake of having divided the Confederate force into too many independent entities whose movements could not be easily coordinated. It was a mistake that Lee would not make again.

Paradoxically, Lee's sweeping triumph ended with a considerable Union victory, thanks in part to the only fundamental flaw in Lee's generalship, his lack of caution when dealing with a seemingly beaten foe. The rapid recuperative powers during the Civil War of apparently beaten, scattered, and demoralized enemies was astonishing. More than one apparently victorious general was delivered a stunning blow by this phenomenon. At the end of the Seven Days, the Northern army approaching the James was rallied by General Porter, who, on a small rise called Malvern Hill, used the Union artillery to carry out a rear-guard action. Confederate pursuit had been close, as the Southerners sought to pin the Union army against the river and destroy it totally. Because of their eagerness, the rebels fell into Porter's trap. Lee suffered thousands of casualties as Union artillery, mounted hub to hub on the hilltop, blew apart the oncoming Confederate line.

In fact, Malvern Hill was such a restorative that the more aggressive Union commanders wished to make it the basis of a counteroffensive. McClellan would have none of it. Regardless of the state of his army, he was a beaten man. All he wanted was to put down the crushing burden that he carried. He overruled his generals and ordered a retreat to Harrison's Landing, a muddy flat on the banks of the James where the army could be sheltered under the big guns of the Union navy.

The Seven Days were not quite McClellan's last hurrah, but they certainly defined his limitations as a general. McClellan was the almost perfect modern embodiment of that legendary figure of antiquity, the tragic hero destined to be destroyed by his own shortcomings. The general's extraordinary intelligence, his charisma, his empathy, and his administrative competence would carry him a long way, but when put to the test, his perfectionism, his need to find scapegoats to absolve himself from blame, and his paranoiac tendencies would undo him.

General Porter deserved better of fate and from his country than he received. The hero of Malvern Hill was promoted to major general following the peninsular campaign. Shortly thereafter, however, he was accused by General Pope of disloyalty and disobedience (for refusing to carry out an impossible order) during the Second Battle of Bull Run. Found guilty by court-martial, he was cashiered from the army and was unable to gain exoneration until 1878. Today it is obvious that Porter's only "crimes" were a detestation of General Pope (shared by many generals) and too close an identification with a fallen-from-grace General McClellan.

The irony of the campaign was that its assumed success represented the last hope that the prewar Union might be restored with its institutions and character more or less intact. McClellan's failure of nerve (and, of course, Lee's brilliant generalship) prolonged the war for three years, during which it became a social and economic revolution, the very thing that McClellan (and Lee) fervently hoped to avoid. McClellan never admitted what a more humble Lincoln was later willing to concede: "I claim not to have controlled events but confess plainly that events have controlled me."

CHAPTER V
General Burnside and the Wayward Pontoons

Northern technological prowess often saved the day for the Union, in spite of the bumbling nature of its early military leadership. What would happen, however, if military ineptitude were compounded by mismanagement of logistical support? That fateful combination did occur late in 1862 during the Fredericksburg campaign. The result, as might be imagined, was disaster. Before examining this singular occurrence, however, let us see how the Army of the Potomac went from sitting on a mud bank of the James River in June 1862 to needing pontoons on the Rappahannock River six months later.

The hopes of the North that the Southern "rebellion" could be put down within its first year were dashed by McClellan's lost campaign on the peninsula, as well as by the North's failure to exploit its simultaneous victory at Shiloh in the west. Most of the Congress, and a sizable portion of public opinion, now turned savagely against "Little Mac." Having previously hailed him as the "New Napoleon," they now exaggerated their disillusionment.

Lincoln was not averse to the concept of replacing McClellan, but there were problems. The Army of the Potomac idealized him. He was its creator and inspiration, and there was doubt about the maintenance of morale if McClellan were shelved. Also, when Lincoln queried McClellan's critics as to who should replace him, the critics replied, "*Anybody*." Replied Lincoln, "Anybody isn't good enough, I need *some*body."

For the moment the question was moot. The army had a more immediate problem, and McClellan seemed to be the only man who could solve it. When McClellan moved to Virginia, he left behind both the Shenandoah Valley armies and McDowell's corps. After his departure, these two forces were combined to form the Army of Virginia. This was put under the command of Gen. John Pope with instructions to screen Washington.

Pope rashly moved the Army of Virginia to the Rappahannock without knowing the disposition of any Southern force that might have been arrayed against him. That left Gen. Robert E. Lee with an opening that, being Lee, he promptly exploited. Notably, as soon as McClellan's siege of Richmond was lifted, Lee detached Jackson's corps (including the "foot cavalry") to circle through the Virginia Piedmont to Thoroughfare Gap. Thence Jackson was to transit the Gap back to Pope's supply base at Centerville. In the process he went totally undetected by Pope, who discovered him only upon his arriving in his (Pope's) rear, that is, directly on Pope's supply line between his army and Washington. Jackson looted all the supplies he could carry and set fire to the remainder. His soldiers observed that the tantalizing aroma of frying bacon could be discerned for miles around.

Pope's illusions were now dispelled. He was in trouble, and he knew that his only hope was a rapid retreat followed by a confrontation with Jackson's presumably smaller force. Their clash occurred immediately to the west of the old Bull Run battle site and was thus named the Second Battle of Bull Run. There, Pope attacked Jackson, who was entrenched behind the shelter of an abandoned railway embankment. Their fighting was fierce, but when Jackson was about to be overwhelmed, Longstreet's corps arrived on the scene. Attacking Pope's left flank and rear, Longstreet routed the Federals.

While the battle was raging, advance elements of the Army of the Potomac were landing at Alexandria, Virginia, approximately thirty miles from Bull Run. Some of these were being sent out piecemeal via the Orange and Alexandria Railroad to bolster the retreating Army of Virginia. In general, however, there seemed to be little urgency involved in getting the Potomac men to the front.

McClellan himself had ridden forward, accompanied only by staff officers. Darkness fell. With it came thunderstorms that further obscured visibility. Nonetheless, as McClellan's party intercepted the fleeing soldiers, they recognized him and the implications of his presence—McClellan was once more in command. The panic-stricken soldiers cheered and gathered around him. Their rally was infectious. Word spread back up the line of the retreat: "Little Mac is back."

That the general did great service that bleak night in overcoming panic is beyond doubt. Yet, its effect was to further damage what little trust remained in the relationship between Lincoln and McClellan. The president was convinced that the lethargic reaction of the Army of the Potomac in supporting Pope was deliberate. He sensed that it resulted from McClellan's detestation of Pope and his desire that Pope's reputation be shattered, regardless of the consequences to the Union cause. Moreover, although McClellan received the credit for having once again restored the Union army to fighting condition, it was, in fact, Gen. Philip Kearny and Isaac Stevens's fight at the little-remembered battle of Chantilly that stopped the Confederate drive. Both Kearny and Stevens, two of the best and bravest generals in the Union army, were killed at Chantilly. This, of course, further alienated Lincoln.

Nothing could stop General Lee's determination to carry the war to the North. The Confederacy was now at the apex of its fortunes. Lee's drive northward coincided with that of Confederate general Bragg into Kentucky. Should Lee and Bragg each manage to win victories while on Northern soil, both European and Northern public sentiment could become persuaded of the inevitability of Southern independence.

Thus, with a bitterly divided Federal civilian and military leadership confronting a triumphant Robert E. Lee, the Union entered the first of the Civil War's decisive campaigns. Lee moved the Army of Northern Virginia into the Shenandoah Valley and headed for Harper's Ferry with the intent of advancing into Maryland and Pennsylvania. McClellan paralleled his movements to the east of the Blue Ridge Mountains but remained without a clear idea as to Lee's intentions.

The two armies met on the banks of Antietam Creek in Maryland, just north of the Potomac. The conditions were particularly favorable to the Union, which brought to the field about twice as many men as did Lee. McClellan, however, provided little leadership and left the conduct of the battle largely to his subordinates. Thus, the Northern attack took the form of a series of uncoordinated thrusts. These raised the "butcher's bill" to its highest one-day level of the entire war (23,000 casualties) but never managed to deliver a knock-out blow. Nonetheless, Lee's exhausted army was forced to retreat, and the North gained a strategic victory.

Lincoln's frustration with McClellan now reached fever pitch. Lincoln had visualized Antietam as an opportunity to trap Lee's army with its back to the Potomac River and so to force Lee's surrender. The means to do this were available. The 6th corps was fresh, having arrived late and playing no part in the battle. It could have been used the following day against Lee's exhausted survivors, but McClellan, as usual, overestimated the size of Lee's army. He failed to make a decisive effort, then and in the next several days. Lee was able to extricate his army.

Lincoln's patience had come to an end. He sent orders preemptively removing McClellan and offering command to General Burnside. McClellan's military career was over permanently. General Burnside, after some hesitation, accepted the offer.

Burnside, too, had both strengths and weaknesses, and these stood in sharp contrast to those of McClellan. On the surface Burnside was everything that McClellan was not—straightforward, honest, loyal, and dependable, a man of integrity and character. What was not apparent, however, was his lack of military capability or skill. As Churchill later observed in a different context, "He was a modest man—with much to be modest about."

Burnside's first impulse was a good one—get the army out of western Virginia and move it downriver to Fredericksburg, where supplies could readily be made available either by sea or by short rail lines. His initial execution was also well done. He managed to conceal his intentions from Lee and to position his army at Falmouth, directly across the Rappahannock River from Fredericksburg, before Lee awoke to the danger. Here, however, fate—in the form of some wayward pontoons—intervened.

Pontoons, in the Civil War context, were flat-bottomed wooden rowboats that resembled New England fishing prams. They were used, then as now, to create floating bridges over unfordable rivers.

When in place, they were very efficient. However, being thirty-one feet long and of sturdy construction, they were often cumbersome to transport, particularly on land. Also, to span a river as wide as the Rappahannock required as many as seventy-five such boats. Getting such a large number of pontoons and associated equipment to Falmouth rapidly was apt to be a major undertaking. Burnside, however, foresaw no problem. His staff routinely telegraphed the War Department asking that the requisite pontoons be sent to await the army's arrival in Falmouth.

In General Burnside's defense, it must be stated that there was no shortage of pontoons in the Army of the Potomac or of engineers to transport them. Most of the army's pontoons were then at Berlin, Maryland, approximately fifty miles up the Potomac River from Washington, where they remained after having been used to bridge the Potomac following the battle of Antietam. A second pontoon bridge also spanned the Potomac at Harpers Ferry, six miles upstream from Berlin. Finally, an additional seventy-five boats were afloat in the Chesapeake and Ohio Canal (which paralleled the Potomac) and were ready for transport to Washington via the canal. All the paraphernalia needed to convert these pontoons to bridges was also packed and ready to go. In addition, engineers of the volunteer 50th New York Regiment were camped near Berlin, awaiting orders.

All that was necessary was to raft the pontoons down the canal to Washington, transfer them to the Potomac, and then tow them farther downstream to Belle Plain, Virginia. From there an overland leg would be necessary to get the boats to Falmouth. However, because 90 percent of the trip was by water (where the pontoons were reasonably manageable) and only 10 percent overland, bringing the boats to Falmouth should have been easy. Instead, it turned into a classic demonstration of "Murphy's Law," that is, what can go wrong, will.

Enter Maj. Ira Spaulding, protagonist of our story and commanding officer of the 50th New York engineers. Major Spaulding was a fine officer, a competent and innovative engineer, and a stalwart patriot. Yet for two weeks he was forced to dwell in a strange land, bound only by slapstick farce on one side and the stuff of which nightmares are made on the other.

Spaulding's odyssey began on November 6, 1862 (the chronology is very important throughout), when a foresighted functionary of the War Department observed that the army's pontoons were all in use on the Potomac. Because the army was progressively moving away from the river, it seemed to be a sensible precaution to bring the boats back to Washington, where they would be more accessible for future use. The functionary's superior agreed. It was decided that the Harpers Ferry bridge should be left in place. The Berlin bridge would be dismantled, and all spare pontoons would be placed in storage in a Washington depot.

It would have seemed equally prudent to telegraph implementing orders to Major Spaulding to start things moving as rapidly as possible. Here, however, common sense deserted the functionaries. Instead of telegraphing the orders, they sent them by mail. Thus, Major Spaulding did not receive them on November 7, as he might have, but on November 12.

November 12 also happened to be the day on which General Burnside definitely concluded to shift his army from the valley to Fredericksburg. Although he did not yet have Halleck's and Lincoln's consent to this move, he nonetheless advised Gen. Edwin Sumner, commander of one of his three "Grand Divisions" (30,000 men), to make appropriate preparations. Sumner was thus able to move immediately upon obtaining Lincoln's consent. His men were in position in Falmouth on November 17.

Back in Berlin, Major Spaulding was proceeding expeditiously to get his pontoons moving. On November 12 he made up two rafts of thirty-six and forty boats, respectively, and started them down the canal to Washington, where they arrived on the thirteenth. Meanwhile, ancillary equipment was sent overland to Washington. Spaulding's orders were to consolidate boats and equipment in Washington, where he was to load everything on a land-based pontoon train and stand by. Spaulding himself was ordered to report to his immediate superior, Brig. Gen. Daniel Woodbury at the War Department, to find out what the next pontoon mission would be.

Spaulding duly reported to Woodbury on the thirteenth. He was surprised to discover that Woodbury had no knowledge of any anticipated need for pontoons. Woodbury advised Spaulding to do nothing until the following day, when he would query General Halleck on the subject. (Halleck, the army's highest-ranking officer, was entitled general in chief; in fact, a more accurate description of his function would be chief administrative officer.) What Halleck said to Woodbury will never be known. What is known, however, are the following two paradoxical facts: Halleck knew on November 14 that Lincoln had approved Burnside's Fredericksburg plan, which would necessarily involve using pontoons to cross the Rappahannock River, and Woodbury left the meeting with Halleck having received no additional information. Woodbury ordered Spaulding to dismantle his train and to put the pontoons in storage.

Thus, as of the fourteenth, Sumner's 30,000 men were on the road to Falmouth, while their pontoons were simultaneously going into storage in Washington! Let us hope that Ira Spaulding enjoyed his dinner and a good cigar that night and that his 50th New York engineers spent a comfortable night in their base camp. For the next eleven days Spaulding's life and the lives of his men would become an unrelieved nightmare.

On the morning of the fifteenth, the War Department received a follow-up telegram from Burnside's staff inquiring as to the status of the pontoons. Because Sumner's men were not yet in place, the telegram was not urgent. It did, however, alert the department to the need. Most of its members thought the boats were still in Berlin. It took some time to finally determine that the pontoons were in Spaulding's charge and that he had been ordered to put them in the Washington depot. Spaulding's orders were then immediately countermanded and replaced with instructions to immediately bring twenty-four boats by water to Belle Plain, Virginia, on the lower Potomac for use in that location, and to pack forty boats on an overland wagon train and bring them to Falmouth. Spaulding was not told why he was taking the pontoons to either place or that haste was required.

Packing 40 boats on a wagon train was no small task. First, the engineers had to draw 200 horses, 200 harnesses, and 40 wagons. Next, 40 or more teamsters had to be located. Many would probably have to be sobered up. The horses must then be harnessed to the wagons, and sufficient food and forage had to be acquired for them. An inkling of the difficulty about to be encountered was revealed when it was discovered that the harnesses remained unassembled in their original packing cases and that most of the horses were former cavalry steeds or field officer mounts and were not used to being in a harness.

The next scene almost defies imagination. Forty hungover teamsters laboriously put the harnesses together. Then several hundred men began harnessing 200 very unwilling horses. Finally, the deed was done. By midnight on the nineteenth, the wagon train was rumbling across Washington's Chain Bridge, heading south. Two hours later, the train made camp six miles into Virginia. It had no sooner done so when a steady, drenching rain started to fall.

Meanwhile, the tug *Hero* was towing the other twenty-four boats down the river to Belle Plain. About halfway there, on the twentieth, the *Hero* went aground. This delayed matters for many hours. Eventually, the tug arrived at Belle Plain in the middle of the night, only to discover that an infuriated garrison did not appreciate being awakened to receive unordered pontoons intended for an unknown purpose. Need we mention that, of course, no one had informed Falmouth of the boats' arrival in Belle Plain.

Back on the road, Major Spaulding set out on the twentieth in the continuing rain for Falmouth. He was completely unaware that Burnside's men had now been waiting three days and that Lee was moving to seize the initiative. The road was rapidly turning into the gumbolike, bottomless mud for which Virginia was then famous. Burnside himself, two months later, was to mire his entire army in such mud near Spaulding's current location. A soldier ditty of the time is fully descriptive.

> Now I lay me down to sleep,
> In a sea of mud six fathoms deep,
> If I should sink before I wake,
> Dredge me up with an oyster rake.

Under such conditions transporting pontoons takes on the characteristics of pyramid building. The boats became impossible to pull. They literally had to be lifted by gangs of men and carried. In one day, hundreds of men spent eighteen hours moving the train a distance of only five miles. Finally, through a brown hell of mud and

water, somehow the boats were transported back to the banks of
the Potomac. Here they were finally taken in tow for delivery to
Belle Plain.

At long last, on November 24, the boats, equipment, engineers,
and destination instructions all came together at Belle Plain. On the
following day, November 25, Major Spaulding reported to General
Burnside in Falmouth that the pontoons had arrived as ordered. It
is unlikely that anyone thanked him for his heroic efforts.

AFTERMATH

By November 25, no chance remained of flanking Lee's army by
crossing the river at Fredericksburg. Lee had long since sent
Longstreet to occupy both the strategic high ground above the city
and a sunken road behind a stone wall at the foot of this high ground.
Together, these constituted an impregnable defense. Lee's other
corps, under Stonewall Jackson, also moved to occupy defensible
high ground east of the city.

General Burnside remained obsessed with the idea of occupying
the city of Fredericksburg and could not be dissuaded. Why this was
true is not evident, because Fredericksburg had no particular strategic significance. Moreover, the element of surprise on which Burnside's plan depended had now been lost.

In carrying out his plan, two opportunities had now been allowed
to pass. The pontoons could have arrived on time, enabling a bridge
to have been constructed unopposed. In this event Burnside's whole
army could have crossed on November 19. Alternately, Sumner's
Grand Division could have forded the river on the seventeenth or
eighteenth and occupied the city as a beachhead, while awaiting the
remainder of the army when the pontoons arrived. This was rejected
because of concern that heavy rains might isolate Sumner from the
rest of the army. Such an event, if it occurred, should not have been
a disaster. Lee's entire army outnumbered Sumner's by only about
two to one. Lee certainly could not have brought more than half his
force to Fredericksburg, as long as Burnside retained the capacity to
outflank him upstream.

Sumner would also have been supported by artillery mounted behind him in Falmouth and should have been able to stand off equal

numbers indefinitely. Such, however, was the legacy of McClellan's exaggerated estimates of the size of the Army of Northern Virginia (and the awesome nature of Lee's reputation) that Burnside never dared risk isolating Sumner. Sumner, himself, provided no assistance. He was a brave and resolute soldier but was also an old army man who followed orders to the letter. Finding fault with any plan formulated by a commanding officer was contrary to the instincts of a lifetime.

Burnside inexplicably waited an additional three weeks. Thus, it was not until December 12, 1862, that the 50th New York engineers found themselves attempting to lay their bridge. Now they had to do so in the face of grueling sniper fire from a Mississippi brigade posted directly across the river. Ultimately, Sumner's men had to use some of the pontoons as landing craft for a river crossing to clear away the Mississippians. Only when that was accomplished could the bridge finally be built.

On December 13, 1862, Burnside in the town attacked Lee on the heights. The result was a cataclysm, with wave after wave of Union troops dissolving under fire from the entrenched Confederates. Thus began what many veterans later called the "Valley Forge" of the Civil War. Burnside could not admit defeat. In January 1863, he tried again to take the offensive. This time, he was unable to reach even the Rappahannock. His entire army bogged down in endless mud, and all forward progress ceased, an event known to history as the "Mud March." Meanwhile, his command was coming apart. Among the men, illness and desertion rates skyrocketed. In the officers' camp, a virtual state of mutiny ensued. Two days after the end of the Mud March, Burnside was relieved of command.

Two questions remain regarding the wayward pontoons. Why did the immediacy of Burnside's need and the destination and purpose of the pontoon transfer never seem to penetrate the middle echelons of the War Department? My answer is purely speculative but, I think, correct. The orders to move the pontoons originated on November 6, 1862, as a routine anticipation of a future need. Unbeknownst to Burnside, his orders of November 13 thus became supplementary orders to these originals. Somehow the overriding nature of the supplementary orders never seemed to catch up with the original instructions. To the end, General Woodbury's office appears to have continued to believe that it was operating under the November 6 orders. Thus, neither Spaulding nor Burnside's staff were ever given the information that they might have been able to use to rectify matters. Anyone who has ever worked in a hierarchical organization where information is disseminated on a need-to-know basis will appreciate this situation.

The second question is more baffling. Why didn't General Halleck appreciate the urgency of the need for pontoons when he saw Woodbury on the fourteenth? There are only two possible answers to this question—one innocent and one sinister. Halleck was a "detail" man and thus was usually preoccupied with a multiplicity of matters. It is possible that he absentmindedly overlooked the fact that Burnside would need pontoons, even though he knew that the army planned to cross the Rappahannock. Thus, when Woodbury questioned him out of context about pontoons, he may genuinely not have connected this query with Burnside's need. This, however, seems rather far-fetched.

The sinister response is that Halleck was well aware of the need but deliberately sabotaged Burnside's plan. Halleck had never liked the Fredericksburg crossing and had recommended against it to Lincoln. He may well have thought that, by delaying the pontoons, he would force Burnside to put his army into winter quarters and thence to rethink future offensive operations. This is not inconceivable. Civil War generals had a great capacity for undercutting one another. Certainly, Halleck could never have predicted that Burnside would behave as he did and the bloody consequences that would ensue.

Burnside had thrown away more than 12,000 of the army's best men. The remainder were at least temporarily demoralized. Lincoln was terrified about the country's reaction and about its continued willingness to finance and support the war. As he had said once before, "The bottom is out of the tub." Yet, at horrible cost, the men of the Army of the Potomac had gained an important intangible. They had demonstrated to each other and to the enemy that, in the later words of Admiral Nimitz, "Uncommon valor was a common virtue." No one ever forgot it.

CHAPTER VI

All Roads and Rivers Lead to Vicksburg

I n April 1862, after Admiral Farragut bypassed the lower Mississippi forts and captured New Orleans, he was able to steam up the Mississippi without encountering any organized Confederate resistance. Had a Union army then been available for combined operations with Farragut, future bastions such as Vicksburg, Grand Gulf, and Port Hudson might have been captured with only nominal resistance. Trans-Mississippi Confederate supplies to Lee's and Bragg's armies would then have been interdicted a year before this actually occurred.

The only army that could have so acted, Grant's Army of the Tennessee, was then immobilized due to controversy over the conduct of the Battle of Shiloh. Grant had been relieved by his superior, General Halleck, who had personally assumed command. This would have been immaterial (although tough on Grant), except that Halleck's ineptitude as a field commander was monumental. To place Halleck in field command was tantamount to instantly paralyzing an army. The moment was thus lost. By the time Grant was restored to command (in November 1862), the Confederates had recognized their vulnerability and dug in; Vicksburg, Mississippi, and Port Hudson, Louisiana (just north of Baton Rouge), became bastions guarding the last stretch of river remaining within Southern control.

Within that stretch, the Red River entered the Mississippi and provided the remaining link that brought supplies and manpower from the Trans-Mississippi Confederacy to the heartland of the South.

Only by neutralizing these fortresses, and intermediary strongpoints, could the two sections of the Confederacy be severed, thus allowing Northern traffic to flow unimpeded.

The key to the Confederate line was Vicksburg, its northern anchor. For topographic reasons, Vicksburg could be attacked only from the east. Logically, to approach from the east, Grant's men must first capture and hold the line of the Mississippi Central Railroad for a distance of several hundred miles. Then they must beat General Pemberton's 40,000-man, Vicksburg-based army in a pitched battle somewhere east of the city and cause that army either to flee or to fall back within the city, where it could be besieged.

Capturing the line of the Mississippi Central was no great problem; there was no body of Confederate infantry along the river to the north of Pemberton's forces around Vicksburg. Grant's advance thus confronted only light forces, who adopted hit-and-run tactics to slow him down.

Using the railroad as a reliable continuing source of supplies, however, was a different matter. The rail lines on which Grant's Army of the Tennessee depended were vulnerable to cavalry raids and stretched back through Mississippi and Tennessee all the way to Columbus, Kentucky. To make matters worse, Nathan Bedford Forrest, the Confederacy's superb cavalry commander, was then rampaging through Tennessee. By the time Forrest was finished, Grant would be effectively disconnected from Columbus.

Grant tried to adjust. He shifted his base to Memphis on the river, thus avoiding Forrest's inland assaults, and set up his advance supply depot at Holly Springs, near Oxford in northern Mississippi. In so doing, he overlooked General Van Dorn. On December 20, 1862, Van Dorn with 3,500 cavalrymen circled behind Grant and destroyed the base at Holly Springs, together with all supplies and spare rolling stock that had been collected there.

Grant's position became untenable. There was no solution but to retreat to Memphis and postpone further offensive operations until the following spring. How such operations might be conducted, however, was anything but obvious. Clearly a resumption of the overland march down the Mississippi Central would probably again end in the same fashion. There was simply no way to prevent raids against such a long stretch of railway transiting a hostile countryside.

Nonetheless, something had to be done. General Grant's reputation and future were at stake. The North wanted Vicksburg taken and the Mississippi River reopened. If Grant couldn't do it during the spring or summer of 1863, then the country would find somebody who could. At least one volunteer to become Grant's successor, Gen. John McClernand, an Illinois politician, was already on the scene. Worse yet, Lincoln, recognizing McClernand's ability to recruit midwestern troops, was being ambiguous as to who might ultimately be selected to command the conquest of Vicksburg.

Failing an overland campaign, how was Vicksburg to be taken? The problem was as follows. Vicksburg sits on a high bluff overlooking a bend in the Mississippi River. Because of the bend, the river's ship channel is on the Vicksburg side, just beyond the foot of the bluffs. Artillery posted on the bluffs could thus fire with a plunging trajectory on vessels passing by the city. It was therefore impossible to effect a boat landing on the city's riverfront. The maneuver would, in any event, be useless, because a landing party could not then scale the steep bluffs.

It was also difficult to steam past the city. This could be done only by armored vessels moving downstream. Even then, some damage would inevitably be sustained. On the other hand, for such ships to steam upstream was tantamount to suicide. If any operation involved transporting ships and men downstream past the city, it had better succeed, because the units so committed could not be retrieved.

Upstream, the situation was no better. Just to the north of Vicksburg, the Yazoo River empties into the Mississippi from the northeast. The area between the two rivers is referred to as the delta and consisted principally of swamps. No army could march across such country, much less attack. To the east of the delta was open dry ground (this was where the railroad debouched). The problem here was that the Vicksburg bluffs extended beyond Vicksburg along the south bank of the Yazoo. Any Northern force coming downriver and turning up the mouth of the Yazoo to go east would confront plunging fire from batteries on these cliffs.

The western side of the Mississippi was not threatened by Confederates. Therefore, Grant's army could conceivably cross the river north of Vicksburg and then march downstream on the opposite bank. What this would accomplish, however, was not fully evident, because the army would then be south of the Vicksburg batteries but its transports and their protecting gunboats remained north of the city.

Thus, no matter what General Grant might try, his army would always seem to end up at the foot of a cliff on the wrong bank of a river or the wrong end of the city. The general would have to produce a prodigious plan if this conundrum were to be solved. How he did it is a fascinating tale.

Regardless of the tactical convolutions involved, Grant's ultimate strategic goal never varied: get the army safely to firm ground east of the Yazoo delta, from which an attack to the west on the city could be made.

Grant's first attempt to reach "the promised land" was based on the presumption that a water route could be established across the delta to connect the Mississippi above Vicksburg with the upper Yazoo above Yazoo City. Such a route (of sorts), called "Yazoo Pass," had existed previously. In recent years access to the pass had been closed by a levee on the Mississippi, but Grant's engineers, by digging and blasting, broke a hole in the dike. The action of the river did the rest. Soon the opening into Yazoo Pass was big enough to allow passage by Northern ironclads and sufficient transports to carry an army of 5,000 men. On March 7, 1863, an expedition was sent up the pass.

Grant's opposite number, Confederate general John Pemberton, had several failings as a military commander, but stupidity was not one of them. He had had six months to improve Vicksburg's defenses, and he too had observed the strategic potential of Yazoo Pass. Accordingly, for weeks the Confederate army had been engaged in felling trees and dumping their branches, trunks, and stumps into the waterway. Until these were removed, the waterway was unusable. This took three days (and signaled to Pemberton that an attempt to use the pass was being made).

By March 10, the expedition was steaming down the Tallahatchie River toward its confluence with the upper Yazoo. Between the two rivers was a small peninsula of swampy land. On the peninsula's only solid ground the Confederates had built a modest fort, Fort Pemberton. It had only ten guns, but it was sufficient to stop the Federals. The topography was such that the ships could approach the fort only in line, thus masking all but their forward guns, and the surrounding ground was too swampy to allow troops to be landed. For ten days the Northerners tried to find a proper approach to the fort, only to give up in futility. On March 20, the expedition was recalled.

Grant was not yet willing to give up on a water approach, particularly after his naval colleague, Admiral Porter, suggested a second possibility. To reach the firm ground east of the Yazoo, it was not necessary to cross the delta. All that was required was for the army to find its way around the fortified bluffs above Vicksburg. A small stream called "Steele's Bayou" offered this opportunity. Steele's Bayou flowed into the Yazoo just above its mouth, and its headwaters connected with several other small watercourses (every stream in the delta seemed to interconnect). If you followed these streams, you could (at least in theory) find your way back into the Yazoo River upstream, having successfully detoured around the fortifications.

What seemed sensible on a map turned into a nightmare. Porter, in his enthusiasm, sent no less than five ironclads, four mortar boats, and four tugboats up the bayou. The farther they progressed, the narrower the passage became. The streams also became more winding, so that Porter at one point remarked that his five leading ironclads, although in column formation, were pointing in five separate directions. Ominously, as the vessels struggled upstream, they heard the sound of trees being felled ahead of them. What really gave them pause, however, was when they heard the same sound behind them! Ultimately Porter became unnerved and extricated his ships before they were either captured or driven hopelessly aground.

Grant was nothing if not persistent. If a water passage could not be found on the eastern side of the Mississippi, perhaps there might be one on the west bank. At least there wouldn't be any Confederates over there. Just to the north of Vicksburg was a large bulge in the river called Lake Providence. From there a short canal might be dug to connect this backwater with a stream called "Bayou Macon," which paralleled the Mississippi for miles. This in turn led to other waterways and eventually to the Red River. Proceeding down the Red to the Mississippi, one could land the army on the eastern bank of the big river south of Vicksburg and then march northeast. This route was explored during March. It too was deemed impractical due to natural obstructions and the lack of any obvious river channel in Bayou Macon.

While all this was occurring, the men of McClernand's and Sherman's corps were attempting to dig a canal that would divert the flow of the Mississippi River (no small undertaking!) away from Vicksburg located as it was on the bank of a hairpin curve in the river. If the river could be diverted across the base of the peninsula formed by the curve, then the city would be stranded approximately two miles away from the river's new course.

Although thousands of men were available for the purpose, the job should not be compared to the digging of the Suez or Panama Canals. There was no need to dig a trench entirely across the base of the peninsula facing Vicksburg. All that would have been necessary was to break the river levee at the point where the natural flow of the river's current would follow the diversion so created. If the river could be directed into such a new bed, then the stream itself would complete the job of diversion by scouring a new channel across the peninsula to the point where the river again found its downstream riverbed. The river itself frequently made such diversions as a result of totally natural phenomena.

In the end, it all came to naught. The canal was completed, but the river stubbornly refused to follow the new course provided for it. Moreover, if the diversion had worked, the effort still would have been unavailing. While the soldiers dug, the Confederates erected new batteries below the diversion canal. Subsequent landing parties would have discovered the river's new course to be no more hospitable below the city than the old one had been within the city.

By the beginning of April, Washington was becoming ever more impatient, while Grant's army had advanced no farther than it had been at the inception of the campaign. Grant suddenly found himself confronting the same stark choice that frequently preoccupied Lee: whether to follow an aggressive policy with a substantial risk of failure or a policy of inactivity leading almost inevitably to frustration and defeat. Grant, like Lee, was to discover that nothing so focuses the mind as having all one's options removed.

Everything else had now been tried and found wanting. Only one option remained. Warships and transports must run downstream past the Vicksburg fortifications while the army marched south past the city down the west bank of the river. Men and ships would be reassembled somewhere south of the city. The men would then be transported to the river's east bank, where they would embark upon a campaign to capture the city from the east and thence to restore communications with the North.

It all seemed reasonable enough, except for two very worrisome details. Once men and ships were landed below Vicksburg, how would their future need for supplies be satisfied? Even more troublesome was the question of how the men would be extricated if a serious reverse were to occur. Still, the deed had to be done.

Grant approached the job with consummate skill. His initial effort was to overwhelm Pemberton's military intelligence, to baffle him about the Union's real intentions, and thus to slow down Confederate reactions. This entailed Grant's taking a series of simultaneous actions that suggested different battle plans that would distract Pemberton and cause him to disperse his forces to counteract divergent threats. Grant accordingly acted as follows.

First he quietly set his real battle plan in motion by sending two army corps across the Mississippi with instructions to build a military road leading south along the west bank to New Carthage, Louisiana, a town approximately fifteen miles below Vicksburg. Then Grant requested General Banks, stationed far to the south at Baton Rouge, Louisiana, to embark upon an offensive demonstration along the Red River. Meanwhile, General Sherman's corps worked on a second canal project as a diversion. Finally, after suspending canal construction, they carried out two separate feints against Greenville, Mississippi, and against the Confederate fortifications along the Yazoo bluffs.

Grant's most dramatic diversion, however, consisted of a massive cavalry offensive that not only engaged all Union cavalry in western Tennessee but was also coordinated with a raid staged by the Army of the Cumberland to the east. In brief, the eastern men crossed northern Alabama, on their way to stage a raid on Georgia's railroads, while Grant's men struck east from Corinth, Mississippi, along the Alabama-Tennessee border.

Both these raids were themselves diversions from a different diversion and were made with the intention of distracting all Confederate troopers in Tennessee and Alabama. This would give a clear field to Grant's principal diversionary striking force, a 1,700-man column led by Brig. Gen. Benjamin Grierson. Grierson was instructed to start at the northern border of Mississippi and proceed straight south through the eastern portion of that state, disrupting east-west and north-south rail connections as he went. Ultimately, he would swing west and rejoin the Union lines at Baton Rouge. Grierson's raid was spectacularly successful in raising an alarm throughout Mississippi and fully accomplished its real intention. It completely diverted Pemberton's attention between April 17 and May 2 and caused him to spread his strategic reserve force over large sections of the state of Mississippi in an unsuccessful attempt to capture Grierson's force.

Although the raids had been provocative, none so far had been irrevocable. On April 16, however, Grant crossed his Rubicon. Porter was asked to take his flotilla of twelve ironclads beyond the Vicksburg batteries. In spite of the sailors' attempts to darken ship and muffle sound, the ships were observed and attacked, but in the process only one was lost. Encouraged, on April 22 Porter also sent a fleet of transports and supply vessels past the batteries. They too passed successfully, thanks in part to the tactics of lashing coal barges against their exposed sides and of protecting their boilers with hay bales.

The die was cast. With his ships and men irretrievably south of Vicksburg, Grant must now either defeat Pemberton somewhere in central Mississippi or ignominiously retreat to Baton Rouge, where the army would await another year (and a different commander) before again trying to break the Confederate chokehold on the river.

Before discussing the specifics of Grant's subsequent campaign, which would, finally, prove successful, let us digress to examine the evolution of the Mississippi River steamboat and its use as both a warship and a transport.

As with the steam locomotive, the steamboat represented a marriage of two technologies, the high-pressure steam engine and the mill wheel. Oliver Evans in 1803 built the first practical high pressure steam engine to be constructed in the United States. This machine was used for flour milling and wire drawing. Oliver's son, during the decade 1810–20, adapted the Evans engine for use on steamboats. (The steamboats designed earlier by Robert Fulton et al. were of the condensing, atmospheric pressure–powered variety.)

The mechanics of a high-pressure engine on a steamboat are similar to those on a locomotive, the only difference being that on a steamboat the connecting rod joined to a crank on a paddle wheel rather than to a locomotive driving wheel. The steamboat also offered a variation, that of a "walking-beam" engine. This resembled Newcomen's original design whereby a vertical piston transferred motion to a horizontal beam, which in turn delivered rotary motion in the reverse direction through a crank on the paddle wheel.

Paddle wheels could be mounted either on the sides or the stern. In the latter case, however, the walking-beam engine could not be used. The paddle-wheel technology was derived from the mill wheel. The paddle wheel was effectively a mill wheel in reverse.

Steamboat navigation on the Ohio-Mississippi-Missouri system commenced in 1812. Sixty-nine vessels were in operation by 1820. By 1860, this had risen to 735 steamboats. During that forty-year period, the vessels' design changed completely. Originally the design was based on that of steam packet boats, which were then being introduced into service on the eastern coastal waterways. This design involved a strong hull, a low center of gravity, a deep-draft keel, and a sheered deck (higher fore and aft than at midship). All of these features were intended to combat the actions of wind and wave, neither of which were present on the western rivers.

On the other hand, factors that did have to be accommodated in riverboat design were shallow water (particularly in the summer dry season), snags, sandbars, and the necessity of docking the vessel along the riverbank. Consequently, light draft became the essential element of river vessel design. This meant reducing the ratio between the width and length of a vessel and increasing the ratio between its length and draft. In 1835 large steamboats had an average ratio of length to draft of 18.3. By 1860 this ratio had risen to 36.0. In 1860 a large steamer drew only six feet of water. This was down from ten feet, on average, in 1827. Smaller vessels could draw as little as four feet.

The superstructure was also extensively changed. Because the hull was so shallow, propulsion machinery and cargo rested on the main deck. Therefore, all passenger accommodation was located on the one or two higher decks. A pilothouse sat on top of those. All decks would also extend out laterally from the hull until they were flush with the outer casing of the paddle wheel, thus providing more room for cargo and passengers. The whole superstructure was constructed of light materials to avoid making the vessel top-heavy.

The river vessels that the Union forces used during the war fell into three categories: ironclads (warships), "tin-clads" (warships but of a lighter draft), and "cotton-clads" (transports). The latter consisted of ordinary prewar passenger vessels that the army obtained under charter from private owners. The term *cotton-clad* derived from the practice of either stacking cotton bales on deck to protect the vessel's machinery from rifle fire or of tying alongside for the same purpose a barge piled high with cotton or hay bales.

The first Union ironclad was the famous *Monitor* (the term *iron-clad* was used indiscriminately to designate vessels that were constructed either entirely of iron or, as in the case of the *Monitor,* those that were built of wood covered by iron armor). The *Monitor* itself was 172 feet long by 42 feet wide and drew 10.5 feet of water (the *Merrimac* drew 22 feet). It mounted two 11-inch guns and was intended as an oceangoing vessel. It also served as the model for larger vessels, such as, for example, the *New Ironsides,* a 230-foot-long vessel armed with sixteen 11-inch guns.

Vessels of this type were far too large and heavy to be used in the river campaign. The workhorses of the river fleet were known as "Pook Turtles" after their designer, Samuel Pook, and were named for river cities (such as Cairo and Cincinnati). The Pook Turtles were built in 1861 in Illinois and Missouri, weighed 500 tons, and had a draft of six feet. Their main decks were only slightly above the waterline. From there the vessels' armor sloped inward around the entire length of the vessel to the level of the next deck, giving them their turtlelike appearance. The armor casement was pierced in thirteen places (three in the bow, four on each side, two aft) by gunports for three- or four-inch guns. These were the vessels that made up the backbone of Admiral Porter's fleet at Vicksburg. They were not, however, the only type of ironclad. Some boats, such as the USS *Choctaw,* Porter's strongest vessel, were derived from the conversion of prewar steamers. The *Choctaw* drew eight feet and mounted three nine-inch guns and several smaller cannons.

Life aboard an ironclad was not easy, even when the ship was not in action. Consider, for example, the heat. Even in the open air, temperatures during a lower Mississippi River summer normally remained in the nineties with humidity in the seventies or eighties. Imagine what it must have been like belowdecks, when the sun was literally baking the air through the vessel's iron sides and main deck. The boiler-engine room must have seemed like Hell itself even without the steam heat and the incessant clatter of machinery. Such conditions were intolerable. Men could sleep only by finding a place on deck. During the day, the decks had to be constantly hosed down or they would have been impossibly hot to stand upon.

Conditions were no better when the vessel was under way. All interior spaces were inadequately ventilated and stank of a combination of flue gases, bodily wastes, and rotting food. During battle sailors were protected against direct hits. However, a point-blank hit against a turret or superstructure would knock the heads off rivets and send them flying around compartments as lethal missiles. In fact, the very protection afforded by the armor became a drawback if an enemy blast or shell penetrated: the armor kept the effect of such a penetration inside the vessel.

Finally, the ship had to be steered and the guns sighted while the vessel was engaged in combat. That meant that men and officers had to look out through slits in the armor plate. If at such a moment a shell burst close by, grievous injury could result. Consequently, a disproportionate number of wounds aboard ironclads were to the eyes, face, and head. Lieutenant Wordin, captain of the *Monitor,* was blinded in this fashion during the fight with the *Merrimac.* Fortunately, he ultimately recovered his sight after a long convalescence.

Pook Turtles and other ironclads were useful up to St. Louis on the Mississippi and on the lower reaches of tributaries such as the Ohio, Cumberland, Tennessee, Arkansas, and Red Rivers. The upper portion of the tributaries, however, required the lighter-draft vessels nicknamed "tin-clads," in which armor protection was sacrificed to gain lesser displacement.

To resume our narrative, Grant was unable to recross the Mississippi River (from west to east) at New Carthage, as he had planned, because the Confederate bastion of Grand Gulf, twenty miles downstream from Vicksburg on the eastern bank, blocked any type of ferrying operation. The army, therefore, continued its downstream march for another twenty miles until it arrived at the small village of Hard Times. There, Grant loaded his men onto transports (protected by Porter's ironclads) and crossed the river to Bruinsburg, Mississippi, where the army reassembled on April 30, 1863. At last, Grant was on dry, level ground on the east bank of the Mississippi. A march to the northeast would lead him to the state capital, Jackson. From there, a westerly attack on Vicksburg could be launched.

AFTERMATH

What followed was a brilliant campaign that was reminiscent of Stonewall Jackson's activity the year before in the Shenandoah Valley in the way that a small, cohesive army was consistently able to defeat a larger, more diffuse force arrayed against it. Grant landed 24,000 men at Bruinsburg. He was opposed by about 40,000 Confederates throughout Mississippi, but the latter were so extended guarding river strongpoints, watching Banks and Sherman, and chasing Grierson that they couldn't be concentrated. Grant easily defeated a small Confederate garrison at Port Gibson (near Grand Gulf) on May 1 and moved northeast.

Pemberton now made a very logical, but decisive, mistake. He quite naturally assumed that Grant's supply lines would extend back to his "base" at Bruinsburg (and thence up the west bank of the river). He thus spent some days attempting to find and disrupt these facilities. It was futile, because the Northerners had no base and no supply lines. Grant had observed that central Mississippi was yet unscarred by war, and he was convinced (correctly) that the countryside could supply all needed food and forage, provided that the army stayed on the move. Pemberton's efforts simply dispersed his own army, leaving the door open for Grant to penetrate the interior of the state.

After several days, Sherman's corps rejoined Grant and brought the Federal force to about 36,000. By May 11, the army had reached the town of Raymond, near Jackson. At Raymond, General McPherson's corps (12,000 men) encountered a Confederate brigade (3,000 men) under General Gregg. Gregg was pushed aside and fell back on the city of Jackson. There, Gen. Joe Johnston was trying to raise an army to assist Pemberton. (Now recovered from his Fair Oaks wound, Johnston had been made commander in chief of all Confederate armies west of the Appalachians.) Gregg informed Johnston of a troop availability in Jackson of 6,000 men. Johnston concluded that these were insufficient to stop Grant. He retired to the north and left Gregg to cover his retreat. Grant defeated Gregg, occupied the Mississippi capital, and prepared to meet Pemberton. Leaving Sherman to destroy Jackson's railroads and industrial facilities, Grant moved west.

The climactic battle came at Champion Hill, a site on the railway between Vicksburg and Jackson. Johnston had ordered Pemberton to abandon Vicksburg and to march northeast in order to join forces. Johnston's logic was that, once Grant was beaten by their combined force, he and Pemberton could reoccupy the city. Pemberton hesitated, however, because of Jefferson Davis's strong admonition to defend the city at all costs. He was also still lured by the idea of attacking Grant's supply train. Consequently, he posted Brig. Gen. W. W. Loring's division to the southeast, while his main body took a screening position in front of Vicksburg.

Grant was thus enabled to place his army between the three separate forces of Pemberton, Loring, and Johnston. He attacked and badly defeated Pemberton, who lost twenty-seven cannon and hundreds of prisoners in his retreat to the Big Black River to the east of Vicksburg. He also lost Loring, whose force became permanently separated and ultimately joined Johnston. On May 17, Pemberton (still hopefully awaiting the return of Loring) attempted to make a stand at the Big Black. His smaller army, however, was pinned down by McClernand's corps, while Grant's other corps enveloped its flanks. Pemberton's army gave way and fled in panic to its Vicksburg fortifications.

Grant had accomplished his mission: Pemberton was trapped in Vicksburg, and Sherman occupied the bluffs at the mouth of the Yazoo, thus restoring communications with the North.

The fighting wasn't quite over. It was now Grant's turn to underestimate the recovery of a beaten enemy. As his army approached the
city, he attempted to take it by storm and suffered a bloody repulse.
Grant was forced to conduct a siege that lasted from May 22 until
July 4. Pemberton chose the later date to surrender his army on the
presumption that he could gain the best possible terms (even from
"Unconditional Surrender" Grant) on the country's national day. He
was correct. Grant, in a subsequently controversial decision,
"paroled" Pemberton's army rather than sending it north for in-
ternment.

By early July, when it was too late, Johnston succeeded in raising
a 31,000-man army and tried to relieve Pemberton. By the time Johnston reached the Big Black, however, Pemberton surrendered, and
Grant sent Sherman to oppose him. Johnston retired to Jackson,
which Sherman then put under siege. Johnston retired to the east,
and Sherman once more destroyed Confederate installations in
Jackson before returning to Vicksburg.

The campaign was over. With Vicksburg gone, the other Confederate bastions could not endure. Port Hudson, the South's other anchor on the river, had withstood General Banks's attack since March
14. By early July, with food and ammunition virtually exhausted and
its hope gone, Port Hudson too surrendered to the Northern forces.
At last, in Lincoln's words, "The Father of Waters again flows unvexed
to the sea."

Grant's, Sherman's, and McPherson's military careers were now in
the ascendant. General McClernand, however, became a political ca-
sualty of the "West Point clique" (in this case headed by Grant), not
because he was incompetent but, to the contrary, because he wasn't.
He was virtually a Democratic clone of Abraham Lincoln (born in
frontier Kentucky; admitted to the bar in Springfield, Illinois; served
several terms as congressman from the Springfield district) and, although a political adversary, remained on amicable terms with the
president. As a "War Democrat" he demonstrated his patriotism during the winter of 1862–63 by enlisting vast numbers of midwestern
volunteers for the campaign against Vicksburg. Operating on the
premise that Lincoln intended to put him in command, he had sent
these enlistees to Memphis and personally commanded them in a

victory at Arkansas Post (where 5,000 Confederate prisoners were taken). Concurrently, Grant's protégé, Sherman, was suffering a costly repulse at Haynes Bluff. By spring 1863, McClernand had emerged as a rival and threat to Grant.

McClernand had sufficient seniority and clout to outrank everyone in Grant's army except Grant himself. He was thus an inconvenient presence who could not be bypassed. Grant grudgingly appointed him to the lowest possible position commensurate with his rank, that of an army corps commander. McClernand behaved as creditably during the Vicksburg campaign as either Sherman or McPherson, the other two corps commanders. This fact, however, simply increased Grant's determination to get rid of him. He succeeded by using McClernand as the scapegoat for the repulse of the attempt to take Vicksburg by storm and by condemning him for holding an unauthorized press conference. All in all, although McClernand had a very difficult personality, he deserved better. Grant's behavior was typical. Although inordinately loyal to his friends, he could be merciless when a seeming rival appeared to threaten his hard-won status in life.

General Pemberton was in due course "exchanged" and thus was again enabled to serve the Confederate cause. He was, however, looked upon by many Confederates as a traitor; they presumed that his inept performance was, in fact, deliberate treachery (arising from his Pennsylvania origins). He retained the loyalty of Jefferson Davis (ever the friend of inept generals), and the president attempted to find another suitable position for him. None being available, Pemberton resigned his general's commission and accepted rank as a colonel of artillery, in which he served until the war's end. After the war he became a farmer, first in Virginia and ultimately in his hometown in Pennsylvania.

The Vicksburg campaign marked a low point for Gen. Joe Johnston, who had been outgeneraled by Grant. Johnston was the superior officer of both Bragg and Pemberton and should have been able to effect some concentration to confront Grant, particularly in view of the idleness of Bragg's army at the time. Johnston, however, perceived the difficulties rather than the opportunities that concentration afforded. He also spent an inordinate amount of time carrying out a long-distance feud with Jefferson Davis to no purpose except to aggravate their differences and their mutual dislike. This too distracted from his generalship. Johnston remained a major Confederate asset and would continue until the end to render valuable service, but he had his limitations.

Finally, because of the later importance of the Union's two leading generals, two of the most important consequences of the campaign were the lessons learned, respectively, by Grant and Sherman. In the case of Grant, it was respect for the volunteer soldier. Prior to the war, Grant shared in the general West Point skepticism of the volunteer's worth in comparison to that of regular soldiers. His official report after Vicksburg, however, contains the following quotation: "It is a striking feature, so far as my observation goes, of the present volunteer army of the United States, that there is nothing which men are called upon to do, mechanical or professional, that accomplished adepts cannot be found for the duty required in almost every regiment." There speaks a man who watched with awe as green troops built a military road through a swampy wilderness.

With Sherman, the lesson was logistic. Until Grant showed him how, Sherman was not aware that, under certain conditions, an army can exist without supply lines. In 1864, the states of Georgia and the Carolinas would discover how well he had mastered that subject.

CHAPTER VII
We Won't Starve, Thanks to the Cracker Line

D uring the summer of 1863, the Union maintained a third major army in the field, but you never would have known it by reading the daily press. Reporters' eyes were turned to the two major theaters of war: Pennsylvania, where the Army of the Potomac was celebrating its great triumph at Gettysburg; and the Mississippi, where Grant had finally won control of the river and forced the surrender of the Confederate army at Vicksburg.

This third army operated in central Tennessee. It was designated the Army of the Cumberland and was commanded by Gen. William Rosecrans, one of Grant's West Point classmates. Rosecrans was another Civil War general who combined impressive strength under normal circumstances with equally major flaws that emerged only under battlefield conditions. In fact, the Northern war effort can be defined as a process of sorting out those West Pointers who could handle the "fog of war" from those who could not. The South was lucky enough to identify its military leaders early but was ultimately decimated by their irreplaceable loss. The North took longer in the sifting process, but when its elite finally emerged, it was devastatingly effective.

In the case of General Rosecrans, a string of early victories in western Virginia and Mississippi had brought about his appointment as commander of the Cumberland army. He assumed command in October 1862 and led the army into the Battle of Stone's River on the following New Year's Eve. On that day, Rosecrans, as veteran soldiers said of their first major battle experience, "saw the elephant."

The two armies faced each other across a north-south axis. Each commander planned an early morning attack by having a reinforced left flank strike the opposing army's right. Rosecrans made the mistake of allowing his soldiers to make breakfast. His opposite number, Braxton Bragg, did not. Bragg thus attacked first and caught Rosecrans's army by surprise. The result was several hours of desperate hand-to-hand fighting, with the right side of the Union line being bent back against its left until the two formed a V. Had the two legs of the V merged, the Union army could have been annihilated. Fortunately, Gen. George H. Thomas, in the center of the Union line, strengthened his right and fought off successive attacks. Two nights later, Bragg, for unclear reasons, retreated. The Union claimed victory.

This "victory" had nonetheless unnerved General Rosecrans. The next time, he vowed, he would be ready. Such a vow characterized Rosecrans, who was both a good organizer and an excellent planner. He was also gifted with considerable strategic insight. Given time and preparation, Rosecrans could be devastating. Before his next battle, Rosecrans decided that he would take the time he needed.

Unlimited time, however, was a luxury that the Lincoln administration could not afford. For the first time, the North was waging a coordinated offensive on two separate fronts. Lincoln had been seeking such cooperation since the beginning of the war. Now that Grant and Gen. George Meade had finally "gotten religion," it was infuriating that Rosecrans was failing to coordinate the third front. Nothing, however, that Lincoln, Secretary of War Stanton, or chief of staff Halleck could do would move Rosecrans. He would not be hurried and would not start his offensive until he was ready. So the Army of the Cumberland remained in camp from January 1 until June 24, 1863, the longest period of inactivity experienced by any major army throughout the Civil War.

Rosecrans was not entirely unjustified. He was having difficulty in obtaining supplies, because the War Department always gave priority either to the Gettysburg or the Vicksburg campaigns. Moreover, once under way, Rosecrans would be passing through some of the least accessible country in the eastern United States. Whatever he needed on his march he would have to bring with him.

As predicted, once he did move, he moved with decisive strategic effect. Maneuvering his three army corps independently of one another, he forced Bragg out of his entrenched line and then out of his base in Chattanooga. In one brief, bloodless campaign, Rosecrans chased Bragg's Army of the Tennessee completely out of middle Tennessee and across the Tennessee River into Georgia. The doorway to Atlanta stood open. For the moment, Rosecrans was the man of the hour.

Then he forgot that beaten Civil War opponents had a tendency not to stay beaten. The mistake was commonplace. Even the great Robert E. Lee was prone to it, as he had demonstrated at Malvern Hill on the peninsula. Lee might have suffered an equally heavy blow at the Battle of Chancellorsville by attacking the Army of the Potomac's fortified bridgehead on the Rappahannock had the Union commander not preempted him by retreating beforehand. Lee's initiating a charge at the center of the Union line at Gettysburg was the most glaring example of this failing. To say this mistake was commonplace among generals is not to say that it was not serious. In the first two instances cited above, Lee was reprieved by the failings of the Federal commander. In the third case he almost shattered his army. Rosecrans was also about to discover the grave consequences of such a misjudgment.

Rosecrans's elaborate maneuvers had separated his three army corps by distances of up to forty-five miles. Bragg, whose army was between these separated corps, was desperately trying to effect a concentration of his forces in order to destroy the Federal corps sequentially. Deficiencies in staff work, however, as well as squabbles with his subordinate commanders caused several such attempts to misfire and alerted the Federals to their danger. Both armies then sought to concentrate their forces. Their convergence came near the banks of Chickamauga Creek in northern Georgia. The word *Chickamauga* means "river of death." Never was a river more aptly named.

The armies skirmished for several days without bringing on a general engagement. Concurrently, however, something unusual was occurring; the Confederates were being massively reinforced. On almost every Civil War battlefield, the Federals outnumbered the Confederates by almost two to one. At Chickamauga, on the eve of the battle, the Federals also had the advantage. They numbered around 50,000; the Confederates, about 40,000. Then General Bragg received 5,000 men under General Buckner (who had been forced by General Burnside's advancing army to abandon Knoxville). These were followed by 11,500 men from central Mississippi (who had unsuccessfully sought to relieve General Pemberton at Vicksburg). Finally, there arrived some 15,000 men under General Longstreet (in an astounding feat of Confederate logistics, they were transported across Virginia, the Carolinas, and Georgia over an improbable series of virtually worn-out railroads). Thus, as the battle moved toward a general engagement, the Federals were outnumbered but did not realize it.

The two armies at that moment stood in two parallel lines of approximately equal length, facing each other with their lines running from southwest to northeast. Both armies formed continuous lines. Behind the center of the Southern line, General Longstreet stationed his 15,000 veterans as a reserve force ready to exploit opportunities. To the north, Union general Granger commanded a reserve division of about 5,000 men posted to guard the road back to Chattanooga.

Many Federals had a sense of foreboding going into this battle. It stemmed partly from the fact that Bragg's long retreat had clearly ended and partly from the general atmosphere of a place that seemed like a setting from Edgar Allen Poe—a dank woodland overshadowing a black stream. Mostly, it came from the realization that both sides were fighting with their backs to a mountain ridge. If either side broke, it faced a fair chance of annihilation in trying to extricate itself from the valley.

Both armies again had identical battle plans: strike the northern flank of the enemy, then roll up its army with a southward movement. Bragg also intended to administer a coup de grâce by sending in Longstreet's reserves to attack the Union flank once Rosecrans's army had started its southward retreat. Bragg again made the first advance, but his attack was not strong enough to displace General Thomas, the Federals' northernmost corps commander. Thomas kept asking Rosecrans for reinforcement, and toward 11:00 A.M. Rosecrans responded by ordering General Wood's division to close up on

Thomas. Unfortunately, Wood was not next to Thomas, as Rosecrans thought, but rather was separated from him by another full division. Therefore, when Wood was ordered to close up on Thomas, he ordered his men to march to the rear of the intervening division and left a large gap in the Union line.

As fate would have it, General Longstreet was growing impatient. He had waited all morning for the promised Federal retreat across his front line. That wasn't happening, and the continuing battle noise to his right seemed to indicate that the effort to roll up the Northern line was not working. He saw no reason to further hold back his men, and therefore, promptly at noon, he hit the line at the very point that Wood's division had just vacated. The effect momentarily seemed almost comical, like the cartoon character who charges against a supposedly locked door only to have it opened by a second character mere moments before the first would have hit it. Like the cartoon character, Longstreet's 15,000 men ran into a void. Within minutes, they found themselves a mile in the rear of the Union line.

Two things happened. The first was that the Union army was split in half, with its southern half immediately fleeing the field in panic, taking with it two Union corps commanders, Generals McCook and Crittenden, as well as General Rosecrans. Second, Longstreet's corps momentarily fell into a state of disarray. His men needed time to catch their breath and to restore their formations. Their commander needed time to reorient himself. Only then could an effective pursuit of the fleeing Army of the Cumberland occur. If the corps could recover swiftly, however, it stood an excellent chance of beating Rosecrans and his men to McFarland's Gap. This would cut off the Federal army's access to Chattanooga and force its surrender.

They had no sooner paused than they were engaged, sequentially, by two Union brigades. The first was an Ohio brigade under Gen. William Lytle, a published poet and a romantic. It never occurred to him to run, although it must have been obvious to him that he was vastly outnumbered. Lytle gamely rallied his men and hit the Confederate line with a counterattack. It was hopeless. Lytle and most of his men were killed, but they did retard the Confederate advance.

It was, however, the second brigade to counterattack that really slowed down Longstreet's corps. This was the most renowned brigade in the Cumberland army, the famous "Lightning Brigade" of another Ohio general, General John T. Wilder. Early in the war Wilder had been in command of a strongpoint in Kentucky that had been forced to surrender to Confederate raider John Morgan. The incident rankled ever after. Wilder, after being exchanged and restored to brigade command, vowed that he would never again be exposed to such humiliation. Accordingly, when he read of the new Spencer repeating breech-loading rifle, he immediately petitioned the War Department to equip his brigade with Spencers, only to be greeted with a stinging rebuff. The department was strenuously against such action; its Ordnance Bureau was staffed by traditionalists who didn't like this weapon because it "wasted ammunition."

Wilder would not take no for an answer. Rejected by the War Department, he personally guaranteed sufficient private financing to equip each man with a Spencer at his own cost, to be repaid in installments. In similar fashion, he arranged for each of his men to acquire a horse. Wilder had produced a rapid-firing, mounted infantry brigade. Nothing else quite like it existed in either army. It was this brigade that now hit the left side of Longstreet's advance, attacking it with the firepower of a division. They stopped the oncoming men in their tracks and briefly forced them to retreat. Ultimately, Wilder was overwhelmed by force of numbers, but the retreating Federal corps continued to gain valuable time in reaching McFarland's Gap.

Other Federal elements also rallied on Longstreet's right, further slowing him down. All in all, the opportunity of close pursuit was slipping away. Longstreet's hesitancy to pursue was also increased by his continuing awareness of the noise to his right. Clearly, some large element of the Army of the Cumberland had not left the field. Longstreet's own right flank might be exposed if he were to continue to pursue the Union retreat.

Longstreet, accordingly, sent a courier to General Bragg to explain his situation and request instructions. Unfortunately for the Southern cause, General Bragg lacked the capacity to exploit unanticipated opportunities. Having originally devised a plan to roll up Rosecrans from north to south, he continued to insist on its implementation. This immobilized Longstreet, who now could neither continue forward to chase McCook and Crittenden nor turn right to confront the resistance to his north. Longstreet's protests were futile, and his chance of catching the Federals disappeared. Time passed, and remaining in place was soon pointless. Eventually, he turned his corps to the right and marched north to join the battle in progress.

The battle that Longstreet heard was being carried on by Rosecrans's remaining corps commander, Gen. George H. Thomas. Thomas had retained control of his own corps, together with Wood's division and some other elements of Crittenden's corps, despite the general Union retreat. Although outnumbered and heavily engaged, Thomas was also the beneficiary of one small stroke of good fortune. General Granger's division had been posted to the north of the battlefield as a reserve. After hearing the intensifying fire to his south, Granger, on his own initiative, left one brigade in place to guard the road to Chattanooga and led his remaining two brigades south to help Thomas. By anticipating Thomas's need, Granger saved Thomas, who, in turn, saved the Army of the Cumberland.

Thomas had been under mounting attack all morning from Bragg's Northern corps commander, General Polk. He had held until noon by inserting piecemeal reinforcements from Rosecrans, as received, into his line. Suddenly, he lost all contact with both the commanding general and the rest of the army, and it became clear as the afternoon progressed that he was being encircled by Confederates. Thomas accordingly drew back his corps into a horseshoe-shaped formation. There for the remainder of the day he withstood (with the help of Granger's men) the combined forces of Bragg's army. At dusk, he successfully extricated his men and, fighting rearguard actions all the way, led the survivors of the battle to the safety of the Chattanooga fortifications. By so doing he had both saved his own men and enabled the panicked remainder of the Army of the Cumberland to reach safety. For this feat General Thomas was thereafter hailed as "the Rock of Chickamauga" (a nickname devised by another hero of the battle, future president James A. Garfield).

As may be imagined, the postbattle recriminations on both sides were fearsome. Among the Confederates, Bedford Forrest, the cavalry commander, questioned not just Bragg's military competence but his sanity, and he publicly refused to ever serve with him again. Longstreet kept silent, but no one was in any doubt as to how he compared Bragg with Lee. Hill, Polk, and Hardee, the remaining Confederate corps commanders, also urged Bragg's dismissal for his failure to pursue Rosecrans. Bragg, however, retained the confidence of one very important person, Jefferson Davis, president of the Confederate states. Davis had admired Bragg since their service together in the Mexican War, and such admiration remained undiminished. Bragg was retained in command, to the universal disgruntlement of his field officers and men.

Bragg had not totally thrown away the fruits of victory. He, at least, had subsequently occupied all the high ground around Chattanooga. That city was now under siege, and unless the Union could quickly do something about it, the Army of the Cumberland might soon starve to death. Before that occurred, however, its soldiers would become so debilitated as to permit the surrounding Confederates to simply walk into town and take away their guns.

The problem was this. The land around Chattanooga consists of a series of parallel mountain ranges that stretch for more than a hundred miles from southwest to northeast. East-west transportation is thus very difficult and can occur only over infrequent gaps in these parallel ranges. The biggest such gaps are those caused by the course of the Tennessee River. Chattanooga lies on the east bank of that river (which, flowing from the northeast, passes the city to the west of Missionary Ridge). The river then flows west at the foot of Lookout Mountain before turning again in a bend to the north.

The land circumscribed by this loop in the river is called "Moccasin Point"; it is relatively low-lying and is dominated by the mass of Lookout Mountain directly above it. West of Moccasin Point the river follows a meandering course to the west for approximately thirty miles past Raccoon Mountain before again turning south. Thus, overlooking Moccasin Point were Missionary Ridge to the east, Lookout Mountain to the south, and Raccoon Mountain to the west. Bragg's army was stationed on Missionary Ridge with detachments located on Lookout and Raccoon Mountains and in the valleys between them on the south side of the river. The Federals occupied the city, the north side of the river, and all the land to the west of Raccoon Mountain.

All transport into Chattanooga normally came by river or by parallel railroad along the south bank of the river from either central Tennessee to the west or from Knoxville to the northeast. A third railroad (from Atlanta) connected the city to the southeast and served as the Confederates' supply line. The Confederate army, by occupying Missionary Ridge, Lookout Mountain, and Raccoon Mountain, maintained control of all three of these routes.

The countryside to the north and northwest of the city was free of Confederates and thus provided a possible alternate route for the Federal forces, but its mountainous terrain was so difficult as to be impassable for anything except a mule. No route created there could possibly bring in the volume of supplies that the Cumberland army required on a daily basis. There was, therefore, no alternative. The Southern stranglehold would have to be broken if the Union army wanted to retain Chattanooga. Before even this minimal requirement could be accomplished, however, something would have to be done to arrest the deteriorating condition of the Army of the Cumberland. At the moment, it could do little to extricate itself from its own predicament. In part, this was due to the increasing enfeeblement of its men, as a result of their starvation rations. In at least equal part, however, it was due to a virtual paralysis in that army's high command.

It was clear that Rosecrans had suffered a severe psychological trauma at Chickamauga and was now rendered ineffectual by depression (Lincoln was quoted by his secretary, John Hay, as having observed, "Rosecrans is confused and stunned like a duck hit on the head"). He could conceive of the means of breaking the Confederate grip on the city but seemed unable to implement it. If his leadership were continued, the city would soon be starved into surrender.

Thus, by the end of September 1863, the Lincoln administration was genuinely alarmed that it was about to lose both the army and its control of eastern and central Tennessee. It reacted swiftly. First, it sent 25,000 men from the Army of the Potomac to reinforce Chattanooga. Second, it made the obvious (at least in retrospect) decision as to a new western commander. U. S. Grant (now idle after Vicksburg) was put in charge with full authority and responsibility, was given whatever resources he needed, and was held fully accountable. Grant was also given the choice as to whether Rosecrans or Thomas should command the Army of the Cumberland as his deputy. Grant was not fond of either but made the obvious choice, Thomas.

Grant immediately advised Thomas of the new command arrangements and directed Thomas to hold the town at all costs. (Characteristically, the Rock of Chickamauga responded, "We will hold this town until we starve." What Lincoln later said of Grant—"Once [he] gets possession of a place, he holds on to it as if he had inherited it"—applied even more aptly to Thomas.) Grant advised Thomas that he would join him in Chattanooga as soon as possible.

Grant had not had a good summer following Vicksburg's capture. Shortly thereafter, he had attended a grand troop review staged by General Banks just outside New Orleans. Banks had loaned Grant a spirited horse for the occasion, and on the ride back to the city, Grant had taken a fall (probably after several drinks) and broken his leg. Now, broken leg and all, he was forced to endure a painful sixty-mile horseback ride in foul weather via the tortuous northwestern detour in order to enter Chattanooga.

Grant was soaking wet and exhausted upon arrival, but nonetheless he immediately conferred with Thomas. The two swiftly agreed on a plan to break the siege. The key was the control of Lookout Valley, the lowland to the south of the river between Lookout and Raccoon Mountains. If the Confederates stationed there could be forced to fall back on Lookout Mountain (and then subsequently be expelled from that stronghold), the river-rail supply line from the west could be restored.

Grant and Thomas agreed upon a plan to accomplish this and the man to carry it out, Gen. W. F. "Baldy" Smith, one of Grant's West Point classmates and a military engineer currently on Thomas's staff. The plan entailed Smith leading a landing party of Thomas's men across the Tennessee River downstream from Chattanooga, while concurrently the 25,000-man, recently arrived Army of the Potomac contingent under Gen. Joe Hooker fought its way upstream. Hooker would start from Bridgeport, Alabama, a town on the south bank of the Tennessee River, twenty-five miles downstream. Hooker would advance while Smith built a pontoon bridge across the Tennessee to allow additional Cumberland units to cross the river. The two forces would meet at Brown's Ferry, a point south of the river and across from Moccasin Point, thereby trapping the Confederates caught in the middle and "liberating" the south bank from Bridgeport to Brown's Ferry.

At Brown's Ferry, a new pontoon bridge would be built across the Tennessee. This would be joined to a new road across Moccasin Point (far enough north to avoid accurate artillery fire from Confederate batteries atop Lookout Mountain). On the other side of the point another pontoon bridge would be erected across the Tennessee into Chattanooga. Once established, this route would be capable of bringing up supplies delivered by boat to Brown's Ferry. Chattanooga would be saved and preserved to act as a Federal base and jumping-off place.

It all went almost exactly as Grant and Thomas had planned, thanks in part to an unintended assist that arose from the hostile relationship between Bragg and Longstreet. (Nothing ever seemed to go right for Braxton Bragg, or for that matter for the Confederate cause in the west. Even Longstreet, otherwise the most stalwart and reliable of generals, seemed to fall apart during his Tennessee interlude between Chickamauga and the Spotsylvania Wilderness.) The line from Bridgeport to Brown's Ferry to Chattanooga became known as the "Cracker Line," so named after that essential staple of the soldier's diet, the hardtack cracker.

In execution the Northern plan proceeded as follows. Smith, using pontoons as landing craft, floated his men downstream under cover of night to effect an unopposed landing. This was the Federal army's most vulnerable moment. If the Southerners had then attacked the landing force, Smith's men would have been captured and Grant's plan thwarted. Instead, Longstreet, in tactical command of this segment of the battlefield, descended upon Hooker's rear guard near Bridgeport and ignored Bragg's order to attack the bridge builders at Brown's Ferry. Moreover, he attacked with only a single division in spite of Bragg's insistence that he use his whole corps. Longstreet's attack was repulsed, and the South relinquished control of Raccoon Mountain and Lookout Valley. For the moment there was a pause in the campaign, as the Union quartermaster corps put the Cracker Line into operation.

The Cracker Line when first established was wholly dependent upon shipborne supply deliveries to Brown's Ferry, because the railroad line segment between Bridgeport and Chattanooga was out of operation. This caused bottlenecks because railway cars had to be off-loaded onto vessels at Bridgeport. The vessels had to pass slowly and in single file through the "Suck," a narrow stretch of swift water in the Tennessee River just below Brown's Ferry. Such inconveniences, however, were trivial when compared to the army's previous circumstances. Moreover, now that the south bank of the river had been reoccupied below Brown's Ferry, railroad repair could proceed, and direct rail transport could be extended to the new pontoon bridge.

The railroad could not, however, be extended into Chattanooga proper until Bragg's forces were driven from the slopes of Lookout Mountain. When that occurred, Chattanooga would be converted into a forward supply base that would rival in size both Nashville and Louisville. For the time being, however, supplies had to be reloaded aboard quartermaster wagons for the trip on the Moccasin Point road into Chattanooga.

The responsibility for providing needed housing, food, clothing, and fuel together with the storage thereof and transportation of the army itself was assigned to the Quartermaster's Department under the command of Quartermaster General Montgomery Meigs. Under Meigs, each Union field army and army corps had a chief quartermaster to whom reported the staff quartermaster of each division, brigade, and regiment. Quartermaster sergeants were variously assigned at all such levels of command, and additional staff was permanently assigned to separate warehouse and loading facilities. At all times any infantry unit could be required, on request, to provide unskilled labor, except when that unit had actually been ordered into battle.

During the siege the quartermasters' top priority was to make foodstuffs available from commissary warehouses in Louisville and Nashville and to deliver these as fast as possible to Brown's Ferry for loading onto standard army wagons. These wagons were heavy and cumbersome with a pole in front to which one or more pairs of animals could be hitched. Each wagon had a toolbox under the driver's bench and a feed trough in back. A spare pole and wheel were suspended from the sides, and an iron bucket containing grease hung from the rear axle. The wagons had canvas covers that could be fastened, front and rear, for protection against rain.

Because the wagons traveled with the marching army, soldiers frequently attempted either to hitch rides or to dump such impediments as knapsacks or tent halves into empty or loaded wagons. This was strictly forbidden, and the number of wagons assigned to any marching army was kept to a minimum. Even officers were restricted in their carting allowance, with junior officers being limited to only a blanket, a small valise, and a mess kit. On the march only six wagons were assigned to a full regiment.

On long trips wagons could carry up to 600 pounds of forage for animals. A full cargo of commissary stores would include either six barrels of salted meat, four barrels of coffee, or ten barrels of sugar. Forty boxes of hardtack crackers also made up a full load.

The quartermaster in charge of a wagon train had anything but a soft life. He was responsible for ensuring that his train arrived at a particular location at the time ordered. No excuses were accepted for failure to comply in spite of the fact that sources of delay were legion. Not the least of his problems was the frequent receipt of totally contradictory orders from two different superior officers.

Baggage wagons were almost invariably pulled by mules, because cavalry and artillery needs exhausted the available supply of horses. Mules were more temperamental than horses but could better withstand hard use and neglect. As many as six mules could be hitched to a wagon; the largest pair being placed at the pole positions, a somewhat smaller team being put in the middle, and the smallest team being given the lead. Mules could be very stubborn about moving. The mule driver's only remedy was to snap his whip in the immediate proximity of the lead mule's ears, although mule drivers insisted that an extensive vocabulary of profanity was also helpful.

The worst attribute of the mule was his ability to kick with deadly accuracy. This made shoeing a mule a formidable exercise and inspired in veteran mule drivers a cautious sixth sense every time a mule was approached. Whatever the animal's shortcomings, however, its service throughout the war was invaluable and irreplaceable.

The quartermaster corps maintained large warehouses of commissary and quartermaster stores in Nashville, Louisville, and Chattanooga. There was thus plenty of storage space within the latter city to receive provisions and equipment as soon as the Cracker Line was open. The starving Army of the Cumberland soon recovered its health after the resumption of its supplies. This itself is a testimony to the innate, robust constitution of the Civil War soldier, in spite of his diet, which usually consisted mostly of salt pork, hardtack, and coffee.

AFTERMATH

Once Thomas's men were restored from their state of emaciation, Grant was ready to mount a full-scale attack on Bragg's main body on Missionary Ridge. His plan entailed using a portion of his force to make a frontal feint against Bragg, while the remainder of the army outflanked the ridge to both north and south. Before he could do this, however, he had to dislodge Bragg's vanguard from its position on Lookout Mountain. Joe Hooker's men, now mounting victorious guard over the Cracker Line, were already ideally located for this job and were given the assignment. Once this was done, Grant would bring up the Vicksburg army, now under Sherman. Then he would carry out the main attack, using Thomas to feint against the center, while Sherman and Hooker pressed flanking attacks to the north and south, respectively.

Hooker's men had something to prove. Most of them were veterans of the ill-fated 11th corps, the Potomac army's "infernal Dutchmen" (so called because it contained many German immigrants, who the rest of that army unjustly believed had been cowardly at both Chancellorsville and Gettysburg). Lookout Mountain was their chance for redemption. Joe Hooker too had a tarnished reputation. After a good record as a division and corps commander, he had come a cropper as Potomac army commander at Chancellorsville and had allowed Stonewall Jackson to whip him. He too needed redemption.

The battle of Lookout Mountain provided the perfect venue for their aspirations. Hardly more than a skirmish as major Civil War battles go, it was fought in the grandest of amphitheaters—the slopes of a mountain visible to the remainder of the Northern and Southern armies. As if this weren't enough, it was fought under the most dramatic conditions. The battle commenced in the afternoon with a Union advance up the mountain toward a division of Confederate infantry, supported by artillery. At the climactic moment a cloud obscured the vision of the armies below and kept it obstructed until nightfall. All through the night of November 24, no one below knew who had emerged victorious. At dawn on November 25, 1863, the armies looked up and saw the Stars and Stripes flying proudly over the summit. An enormous cheer went up from the assembled Union army, and a legend about "the Battle Above the Clouds" leapt into being. Hooker and his berated 11th corps men basked in the glory.

Actually, it hadn't been much of a battle. Lookout Mountain was so steep that the Confederate artillery had not been able to depress its cannon enough to combat the oncoming Federals. The Confederate cause was further ill served by having as acting division commander a below-par general named John K. Jackson (derisively nicknamed "Mudwall" to distinguish him from his renowned namesake, "Stonewall"). Jackson left his brigade commanders to their own devices, thus forcing their retirement when their ammunition ran out.

However vainglorious, the capture of Lookout Mountain completed Grant's strategic positioning. On November 25, Grant launched his attack on Missionary Ridge. His army was approximately twice the size of Bragg's; Bragg had foolishly transferred away Longstreet's corps (and Wheeler's cavalry) to the vicinity of the city of Knoxville in order to oust General Burnside, who was then in occupation. Bragg clearly believed his position to be so strong as to be unassailable, even by a much superior army. Thus, he felt safe in ridding himself of a second detested colleague, Longstreet, as he had in previously ridding himself of Forrest. This turned out to be vastly more than just a tragic mistake. It is no exaggeration to say that Bragg in so doing (with the collusion of President Davis) sounded the death knell of the Confederacy.

Grant's tactical intent was that Sherman's Army of the Tennessee would begin the attack by outflanking Missionary Ridge to the north. Thomas's Cumberland army would concurrently demonstrate in the center so as to hold Bragg's army in place until Sherman's attack succeeded. Finally, Hooker's Army of the Potomac men to the south would advance, assault, and encircle the fleeing Confederates after Bragg's army had broken. Fate, however, had a completely different plan in mind.

Sherman had crossed the Tennessee River upstream several days before (over still another pontoon bridge built by "Baldy" Smith). While Hooker was assailing Lookout Mountain, Sherman captured, against only light opposition, what he thought to be Tunnel Hill, the northernmost extension of Missionary Ridge. That victory appeared to be decisive. On the next day his flanking movement should easily dislodge Bragg.

On the following morning, however, he discovered his mistake. He had not captured Tunnel Hill. He had instead captured an isolated hill to its north. Tunnel Hill was now separated from his position by a deep ravine. Moreover, his attack had alerted the Southerners to their danger. During the night they had reinforced their works on Tunnel Hill.

As luck would have it, the commander of the Confederate division on Tunnel Hill was Gen. Pat Cleburne, an Irish immigrant with previous professional service in the British army. Cleburne was a superb soldier and was reputed to be the best division commander in either army. Moreover, his innate tactical sense had led him (in the dark) to identify precisely the right spot atop Tunnel Hill to defend, that is, the end-of-a-funnel convergence of all possible approaches. Like the Spartans at Thermopylae, Cleburne's men were positioned to hold off superior numbers indefinitely. Better men to hold this ground could not have been found in all the Confederate army. Bragg had been delivered a rare (and final) piece of good fortune.

Sherman's men repeatedly furiously attacked Cleburne, but there was simply no way that superior numbers could be brought to bear. Cleburne stopped them in their tracks, and it became clear that Sherman was permanently stalled. At the other end of the Federal line, Hooker's troops stepped off smartly enough but soon encountered a stream too large to be forded. They then discovered that they had left their pontoons behind (shades of Burnside!). They too were stalled.

Grant's tactical plan was thus rapidly becoming unraveled. He and Thomas stood on Orchard Knob, a small outcropping at the foot of Missionary Ridge, gloomily examining the Confederate works ahead and pondering what to do next. All that either could devise was to order Thomas's Cumberlanders to capture the first line of Confederate entrenchments at the foot of Missionary Ridge. Perhaps this would cause Bragg to strengthen his center and reduce resistance to either Sherman or Hooker. Thomas's men were given the order to advance.

This was what the Army of the Cumberland had been waiting for. They had a personal score to settle with Bragg and his men. Moreover, they were sick of being treated as "weak sisters" who needed rescue by the remainder of the Union army. They had had about all they could take of the "strutting peacocks" of the Army of the Tennessee or the "newly minted heroes" and "paper-collared ninnies" of the Army of the Potomac. When they advanced, it was with blood in their eyes.

Confederate entrenchments on Missionary Ridge were in three parallel lines: one at the foot of the ridge, one halfway up, and one at the summit. The line at the foot was the weakest and served mostly as a skirmish line. This thin group suddenly observed 20,000 men running directly at them (with more forming up behind). Some of the Confederates bravely got off a shot or two before being overwhelmed. Probably more immediately scrambled uphill to join the Confederates' second line of defense.

The charge was not bloodless. Confederate artillery higher on the ridge opened up on the advancing line, once it had gotten over its initial surprise, and did damage. It was immediately countered by all the Federal artillery that could be brought to bear. The din was horrendous, but its seeming effect was to increase the Federal blood lust. Even General Granger (of Chickamauga fame) seemed to catch it. Now in command of one of Thomas's corps, he abandoned his command post, commandeered the first cannon he could find, and began a very accurate fire against the Confederate line. He didn't stop until Grant personally told him to behave himself and return to his command.

Suddenly, the charge was over. The Federals held the lower ridgeline and started sending their prisoners to the rear. It soon became apparent, however, that the Federals couldn't stay where they were. Not only was the Confederate infantry firing down on them from the ridge above, but the Confederate artillery was rolling explosive shells with lighted fuses down on their heads. The Federals now milled around without clear direction. Dangerous as their current position was, it was also apparent that they could not safely return to their original line. More and more soldiers independently came to the realization that there was no place to go but up! One by one, regimental officers, junior officers, and sergeants gathered their colors and, a platoon here and a company there, started uphill.

The Confederate lines were formidable but not quite as formidable as they looked. Before the battle Bragg had concentrated mostly on his flanks. Thus, the lines in his center had been last-minute improvisations and were not necessarily sited for maximum effectiveness. Moreover, the crest of the ridge was very narrow and not of uniform height. Therefore, one must either defend it or flee. There was no room to regroup after a setback. Further complicating the crest's defense was the unevenness of its height, which hindered mutual support by lateral movement.

Nonetheless, Grant, Thomas, and Granger, back on Orchard Knob, were aghast as they suddenly observed chevrons of blue following their regimental flags up the side of Missionary Ridge. Grant demanded that Thomas give him the name of the general responsible for ordering this advance. Thomas denied responsibility. So did Granger, but the latter added, "When those fellows get started, all hell can't stop them." Grant muttered that if those men got repulsed, somebody was going to pay dearly.

They didn't get repulsed. They just kept going. Soon they reached the midlevel line, but they didn't even pause. To the horror of the Confederates posted on the crest, they just kept coming. It was totally unnerving, particularly because the Confederate defenders of the summit labored under a great disadvantage. Because of the unevenness of the ground, these defenders could see only a handful of fellow rebels to their right and left. In front of them, however, they could see what looked to be the entire Union army coming directly at their personal rifle pit.

It was too much. As the Union force approached, the crest line wavered and then gave way. First by squads and companies, then by regiments and brigades, the Confederate army fled down the reverse slope of the ridge. In the end, however, Cleburne held off Sherman, while Confederate general Alexander held Hooker. Thanks to them, what started as a Confederate rout turned into an orderly retreat. Nonetheless, the Confederacy's last bastion was gone. The heart of the Deep South now lay open to invasion.

Seven Union color-bearers had scaled the crest in the first onslaught. All were awarded the Congressional Medal of Honor. The first of these was a young officer from the 24th Wisconsin. Breveted on the field, he decided to make the army his career and thus founded a military dynasty. Arthur McArthur ultimately commanded the American army in the Philippine Insurrection. His son, Douglas, was to go on to even greater fame (but never won the Medal of Honor).

Sheridan was the first corps commander to reach the top. He immediately jumped astride a captured cannon and started yelling like a banshee. He was soon joined by Granger, who was beside himself with excitement. He too had a big grin on his face as he ran around yelling, "You were ordered to take the bottom of the hill, and you took the top. You disobeyed orders, and you know you should be court-martialed."

Grant, Thomas, Sherman, Hooker, Granger, Wood, and Sheridan had all contributed to the climactic Union victory. Even Rosecrans deserves some of the credit. Grant, Thomas, Sherman, and Sheridan now became the Union's winning team. For the others, Chattanooga had been their moment in the sun.

There is an aura of poetic justice and a dramatic sense of completion in that it was the troops of General Wood's division that were the first to reach the summit at Missionary Ridge. At last, they had expiated the mistake of their commander in blindly following the fateful order at Chickamauga. Wood, himself, would perform well in Sherman's drive on Atlanta until wounded in September 1864. He recovered sufficiently by December to participate in Thomas's victory at Nashville. He retired in 1868 because of the effects of his wounds, but he lived until 1906.

Granger, now raised to the level of corps commander, gave good service. He helped to lift the siege of Knoxville and participated in the capture of Mobile in the final days of the war. Never popular, he was nonetheless a solid soldier and an asset to his cause. He effectively wrote his own obituary in a note to Rosecrans: "The battle is neither to the swift nor to the strong, but to him that holds on to the end."

Hooker continued to live down his disastrous day at Chancellorsville and performed ably as a corps commander during the drive on Atlanta. He asked to be relieved, however, in the fall of 1864 when Sherman elected to promote Howard, Hooker's former subordinate, to become commander of the Army of the Tennessee in lieu of Hooker. Hooker served in administrative positions until he retired in 1868, following a stroke.

Following his relief as commander of the Army of the Cumberland, Rosecrans was appointed to command the Department of Missouri. Although a backwater, the Missouri "theater" was not without incident. In the fall of 1864 Confederate general Sterling Price led a 12,000-man raid north from Arkansas in a spectacular attempt to capture the state. Rosecrans's forces checked his advance at Westport (near Kansas City) and ultimately defeated him at Marais des Cygnes. Rosecrans resigned in 1867. He served briefly as minister to Mexico under President Andrew Johnson and later as a two-term congressman. He died in 1898.

Even Bragg realized after Missionary Ridge that he had lost the confidence of his army. President Davis, however, did not give up, and Bragg was appointed Davis's personal military adviser. In the last days of the war he was sent by Davis to coordinate the defense of Fort Fisher, a key strongpoint guarding the Confederacy's last port of Wilmington, North Carolina. Upon receipt of this news, the *Richmond Examiner* editorialized, "Bragg has been sent to Wilmington, Good-bye Wilmington!" They were prescient. Bragg's actions did substantially contribute to Fort Fisher's fall shortly thereafter.

Cleburne, having saved Bragg's army, was briefly considered as a possible successor to Bragg. Had the South done this (and if they had further appointed Forrest as Cleburne's cavalry commander), they would have created a formidable foe that would have made Sherman's job infinitely more difficult.

It was not to be, however, largely because of Cleburne himself. In his innocence of Southern custom and in the flush of his newly acquired Southern nationalism, Cleburne blithely suggested that the Confederacy enroll volunteer black soldiers by promising them emancipation at the conclusion of their service. That suggestion was about as welcome as a dirty joke at a Victorian lawn party. No one ever again heard Cleburne's name touted for high command. Instead Gen. J. B. Hood was selected to head the army (after an interval under Joe Johnston). Under Hood, Cleburne would be one of seven Confederate generals sacrificed at the incredibly ill-conceived battle of Franklin (Tennessee) on November 30, 1864. Neither President Davis nor anyone else apparently ever considered the idea of whether transferring Forrest back to Georgia might not be useful.

All of this leads to the fascinating speculation of what might have occurred if somehow the Confederacy had so transcended itself as both to appoint Cleburne and Forrest and to provide them with a sizable body of black recruits. (The idea is not wholly fanciful. In the last month of the war, and upon the advocacy of no less than Gen. Robert E. Lee, the Confederacy did in fact recruit several black companies. They were too late to see any service.)

The war's final outcome probably would have been unchanged. The North was simply too strong to be defeated. The final campaign in Georgia and the Carolinas, however, might have been altered beyond recognition. In the short run, the result would almost certainly have been worse for the country. Better generalship by the South would have increased casualties, North and South, before the ultimate Union victory. In the long run, however, who can say how the modern South would have developed if at least some black and white Confederates could have experienced a sense of comradeship, if the Army of Tennessee could have retained the same sense of pride in upholding "the Lost Cause" as did the Army of Northern Virginia, and if the South's civilians were spared the destruction of Sherman's march.

The South, of course, could not transcend its very being. The "ideal" is ever the enemy of the achievable, but the quest for its attainment cannot readily be cast away. The South could not achieve

optimum readiness, and with the onset of spring, all alleviation of
the war's conduct would be gone. A new era of merciless, total war
would commence. Its two chief practitioners were on hand. During
the winter, General U. S. Grant was commissioned lieutenant general and was made commander of all U.S. armies. General Sherman
assumed overall command in the west.

"Volunteer Refreshment Saloon" run by citizens of Philadelphia for 1861 recruits. One of many means by which civilians could express their patriotic fervor and their appreciation of the soldiers' sacrifice.

Recruits of the 8th New York Militia in 1861. One can read in their bearing their arrogance and conviction that they will bring an early end to the war.

General Ben Butler, U.S.A. An odd combination of patriot and rogue, able administrator and incompetent soldier, his wartime career would be eventful but erratic.

A Standard American-type locomotive, so called because its 4–4–0 wheel plan and external cylinders distinguished it from contemporary British designs. Engines of this design were the workhorses of most Civil War railroads.

Admiral David Farragut, U.S.N. A lifelong sailor and ardent nationalist, he never hesitated in choosing the Northern cause, although he was born in Tennessee and lived in Virginia.

Admiral David Dixon Porter, U.S.N. Capable and ambitious, he operated with equal ability on both rivers and oceans. In 1864 the prospective loss of the Red River gunboat fleet almost sank his career.

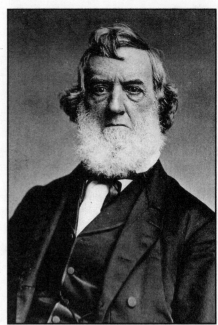

Secretary of the Navy Gideon Wells. A Connecticut editor, he ably led the Navy Department. His greater contribution, however, was to add a calm and moderating voice to the Lincoln cabinet.

The city of Fredericksburg, Virginia—1863. Focal point of the eastern conflict in 1862–63, its strategic location ensured that no less than four major battles would be fought in its immediate vicinity within an 18-month period.

Confederate dead behind the stone wall at Fredericksburg. General Burnside sent thousands of Union men unsuccessfully to storm this wall. The field in front of it was lined so tightly with prostrate bodies that people observed that one could walk across the blue uniforms as on a carpet.

The USS *St. Louis,* a "Pook Turtle." The six vessels of the class were the backbone of Porter's river fleet.

General Grant (leaning in foreground) in conference. Grant's lack of pretension and plain-spoken manner encouraged a free exchange of ideas among his staff.

General George Thomas (center in conference). Thomas was dubbed the "Rock of Chickamauga" because his actions on the day of that battle saved the Union army. Ironically, Thomas was a Virginia aristocrat who remained loyal in spite of family ostracism.

Men constructing transport steamers on the Tennessee River. Few such vessels previously existed on the upper river, since Muscle Shoals, Alabama, blocked any passage between the upper and lower rivers.

Secretary of War Edwin Stanton inherited the War Department at a low point. In spite of having a tyrannical, intimidating and arbitrary personality, he cleaned up inefficiency and corruption.

Sutlers' stores lining a street. Sutlers were merchants who exposed themselves to great personal and commercial risks to carry on a business. Their prices were usually beyond the reach of enlisted men.

A 780-foot-long railroad trestle in Tennessee. Trestles were a novelty. People were astonished as to how structures of such light construction could carry such heavy loads.

United States Military Railroad locomotive *General Haupt*. The USMRR was a section of the Quartermaster Corps and thus part of the national government. In its heyday, it operated most of the railway lines in Virginia and Tennessee.

A pontoon bridge across the James River at Richmond. This is not the famous half-mile-long bridge below Petersburg. It is nonetheless of impressive size and workmanship.

The victory parade in Washington, D.C.—May 1865 was a two-day review of both the eastern and western armies. Ironically, given the cause of the war and their dedication to that cause, black troops were not permitted to participate.

Fort Stevens in the Washington, D.C., fortifications. A typical earthen structure protecting the city, this fort is unique only in that it was visited by Lincoln during Early's raid.

General William Mahone, C.S.A. A late bloomer in the Confederate army, he distinguished himself by organizing the Confederate recovery after a Union mine exploded under vital rebel fortifications.

Depot of USMRR at City Point, Virginia. During 1864 City Point became the largest port in the United States, as Grant besieged Petersburg and then cornered Lee at Appomattox.

The McLean house in Appomattox where Lee surrendered. By an incredible coincidence, Mr. McLean had previously resided on the Bull Run battlefield. Thus, the war began and ended on Mr. McLean's property.

Union entrenchments along Sherman's route. Sherman's antagonist, General Hood, was both aggressive and unpredictable. The Union army was prudent to dig entrenchments wherever they stopped marching.

CHAPTER VIII
Colonel Bailey Had a Trick or Two Up His Sleeve

The Chattanooga campaign, coming in the wake of the Vicksburg campaign, amply demonstrated one thing to Abraham Lincoln. General U. S. Grant was the best the army had to offer, and that fact should be recognized and utilized. The general still had many detractors in spite of his successes. Most of these were fellow West Pointers who remembered him as an unreliable drunk, based on their acquaintance during the 1850s. Lincoln was well aware of this weakness, but he was also aware that this problem would not recur as long as Grant retained Brig. Gen. (and fellow townsman) John Rawlins as his chief of staff.

Lincoln thus became particularly annoyed when the same group of critics kept seizing upon one excuse after another to justify their position. The most recent was that Grant should not have accepted "parole" (that is, a written promise that a surrendered Confederate soldier would not fight again against the United States) from Pemberton's army at Vicksburg but should rather have sent all 25,000 men north to prison camp for the duration. Lincoln responded to this particular objection by telling the story about "Saunders and his old 'yaller' dog."

It seems that Saunders, a prominent townsman, had an old "yaller" dog of which he was inordinately fond. For some reason, however, the small boys of the town detested the animal and went out of the way to bedevil its existence. Finally, one Fourth of July, the boys decided to wrap the largest firecracker they could find in a piece of

meat. They would then feed it to the dog and light the fuse just as
the dog was swallowing it. Sure as fate, when Saunders arrived on the
scene a few moments later, the firecracker went off and the dog was
blown into a hundred small pieces.

Saunders watched with resignation and sadness as the pieces of
the dog settled to the ground. He finally picked up the largest piece
he could find, which consisted of the dog's back and a piece of his
tail, and observed, "I guess he ain't much use any longer—as a dog."
To this line Lincoln added dryly that Pemberton's men also weren't
much use any longer—"as an army." This rendition usually silenced
critics.

Lincoln acted upon his decision about Grant by recommending
to Congress that the rank of lieutenant general (last held by George
Washington) be restored and that Grant be promoted to it as
supreme commander of all the Union's armies. Congress readily
went along, and thus, in February 1864, Grant arrived in Washington to be invested with his new rank and to discuss strategy with the
president. Lincoln was delighted to discover that, at long last, he had
found a general who agreed that all the various Union armies should
attack simultaneously, thus denying to the Confederacy the ability to
shift troops as needed. The two, therefore, readily agreed upon a
strategic plan.

In Virginia, the Army of the Potomac would directly confront
Lee and not break off contact until Lee's army was destroyed.
Grant would make his headquarters with this army.

Also, in Virginia, two supporting offensives would be
launched. General Benjamin Butler would attack Richmond's
rail connections with the lower South; Gen. Franz Siegal would
disrupt Lee's supplies in the Shenandoah Valley.

From Chattanooga, Tennessee, Sherman (now in command
of everything outside Virginia) would attack Bragg's army (now
under Gen. Joe Johnston), with Atlanta as his goal.

Starting in Mississippi, Gen. Nathaniel Banks would lead an
expedition to capture Selma, Alabama, an important munitions
center, and, ultimately, Mobile, Alabama, the South's remaining gulf port.

All in all, it was a good plan. If it had been carried out to the letter, the war probably would have ended by the fall of 1864. Almost immediately, however, the plan started to fall apart.

The problem was that Lincoln's and Grant's strategic vision was not universally accepted. Notably, General Halleck, now officially designated as chief of staff, had a different opinion. Whereas Grant and Lincoln sought to focus on destroying the Confederacy's government and principal armies, Halleck wished to maximize the Federal occupation of territory. These objectives were not mutually exclusive. Lincoln too had territorial aspirations; he wished to accelerate the readmission of reconstructed states to the Congress. Nonetheless, each time Halleck meddled in this fashion, the army's momentum in the west was lost.

In March 1864, Halleck wanted an attack up the Red River of Louisiana to capture Shreveport. This city was the de facto capital of the Trans-Mississippi Confederacy, which consisted of southern Arkansas, northwestern Louisiana, and eastern Texas. If successful, this plan would end all Confederate governance west of the Mississippi. Halleck had an ally in General Banks, commanding officer of the Louisiana district, who would become the commander of any such expedition.

Banks was a political general and had formerly been speaker of the U.S. House of Representatives. He had major postwar political ambitions, and independent command of a successful campaign would certainly enhance his resume. Northern textile manufacturers also applied pressure. The North was starved for cotton, whereas ample supplies existed in the Red River country. Finally, capture of Shreveport would remove a buffer state between the United States and Mexico. The latter country was currently governed by an Austrian prince, installed as king by the French emperor while the United States was preoccupied with its internal problems. The Lincoln administration wanted to send a signal that this violation of the Monroe Doctrine would not be tolerated when the war ended.

All in all, the Northern leaders were able to convince themselves that a quick, useful victory could be obtained on the cheap before the campaign season began in Virginia and Georgia. As a result, Sherman was told to leave 10,000 of his Vicksburg veterans behind in

Louisiana before bringing his Army of the Tennessee back to Chattanooga for the Atlanta campaign. These men, under Gen. A. J. Smith, would be joined by 15,000 men under Gen. William Franklin, a veteran of the Peninsular and Fredericksburg campaigns, and would make up Banks's army. Attached to the army for the campaign would be a river fleet of eighteen ships, of which twelve were to be gunboats. Admiral David Dixon Porter was placed in command of this river navy.

General Banks, who was appointed overall commander of the expedition, was an able administrator and a genuinely honest politician without any taint of scandal or corruption. His generalship, however, was not of such a high order. It may perhaps best be described by the nickname that Stonewall Jackson's men gave to him during the 1862 fighting in the Shenandoah Valley: "Commissary" Banks. This described his facility for leaving his supply train exposed to capture with such regularity that the Confederates began to count on him.

Grant, in particular, was less than enthusiastic about the Red River scheme. He went along solely on the provision that the matter would be concluded swiftly and that A. J. Smith's 10,000 men would be made available to Sherman in either Georgia or Alabama in time for the spring offensives in those states. Banks would remain acutely aware of the limited time span he had been allotted.

The army and navy rendezvoused at Alexandria, Louisiana, some fifty miles from the Mississippi, and the river's head of navigation during the dry season. Below this point the river was deep and frequently filled by back surges from the Mississippi and from various Louisiana bayous. At Alexandria, however, two sets of rapids appeared during dry weather. Above such rapids one could depend only upon the river's own flow.

Porter's fleet successfully transited the rapids on their way up river, but it was noticed that the largest ironclad, *Eastport,* scraped bottom in the process. This was not a good sign. The river was engaged in its usual seasonal drop. The longer the fleet stayed upstream, the more difficult it would be to bring it back later. It was also observed that water levels during that April were lower than normal for that time of year.

Nonetheless, both army and navy proceeded in tandem upstream from Alexandria, there being a good road that paralleled the river. However, when the expedition reached Grand Ecore, a city seventy-five miles downriver from Shreveport, Banks decided to depart from the fleet and march his army over inland roads directly toward Shreveport, leaving the fleet to catch up with him later. His thinking was guided by the fact that Union general Frederick Steele was concurrently leading a force of 13,000 Federals south from Little Rock, Arkansas. These were to coordinate with Banks in a convergence upon Shreveport. Banks wished to be in position promptly to fulfill his obligations.

Confederate general E. Kirby Smith, commanding the Trans-Mississippi, recognized Banks to be the more immediate of the two threats. He thus collected all available infantry units and commissioned Gen. Richard Taylor, son of President Zachary Taylor, to lead the infantry against Banks, leaving only some 5,000 cavalry to watch Steele in lower Arkansas.

Taylor, an able and aggressive general, with 9,000 men (reinforcements of 5,000 more from Arkansas had not yet joined), immediately and unexpectedly attacked Banks's 15,000 at a place called Sabine Cross Roads. Charging like "infuriated demons," they caught Banks's three divisions sequentially, routing the first two before being stopped by the third (the hero of the day was a French aristocrat commanding a Confederate brigade, Prince Camille de Polignac; his troops could not pronounce his name, so they referred to him as "polecat").

Taylor hoped to finish off Banks the following day at Pleasant Hill, Louisiana (his Arkansas troops had now come up, bringing his total to 13,000). He again initiated the attack. This time, however, A. J. Smith and his Vicksburg veterans were on the scene. Taylor's attack was initially successful, but he was outflanked by Smith and was routed, for a clear Union victory.

Banks was now in a state of indecision as to whether or not to go on, and was particularly conscious of Grant's demand that Smith's men be promptly returned to Sherman. Meanwhile Confederate general Kirby Smith had come up for a strategy conference with Taylor. It was clear that the latter's blood was up and that he hoped to hit Banks again and again, until the Federals were destroyed. Kirby Smith, more dispassionately, realized that these tactics would simply use up his own army, leaving his district thereafter defenseless. He ordered Taylor to return to Shreveport to confront Steele, if necessary. Taylor fumed but complied.

Banks, after much soul searching, decided to retreat to Grand Ecore and rejoin Porter's fleet. Thus, both armies presented the strange spectacle of retreating from each other. When Taylor arrived back in Shreveport, however, he discovered that Steele's advance had been blunted and no longer posed a threat. Taylor then resumed his pursuit of Banks.

Banks continued the retreat to Alexandria, where he dug in so as to give Porter time to extricate his fleet. By now the worst had happened. The Red River had fallen to a point where the fleet could not pass the rapids. Porter had already lost his largest ship, the *Eastport*, to a mine near Grand Ecore, and he had lost several transports to hostile action below the rapids. Almost all his remaining ships were now above the rapids in Alexandria.

The vessels that formed Porter's fleet at Alexandria were not Pook Turtles but tin-clads—only light-draft vessels could be used under the conditions that prevailed on the upper Red River. The tin-clad was not a modified ironclad but rather a strengthened transport. Typical improvements included the structural strengthening of the hull, the lowering of boilers wholly or partially below the waterline, and the erection of oak or sheet-iron bulwarks to protect areas where sailors would otherwise be exposed to small arms fire. Unlike the ironclads, the tin-clads had no armor. They protected their crews only against rifle fire and, to some degree, against explosive shell fragments or canister. There was never any pretense that they could withstand a direct hit by a cannonball. These vessels were usually armed with six or eight small-caliber guns.

Porter was thus in a terrible quandary. If he abandoned the fleet, the Confederacy would thereby be presented with a river navy. All that the Union had accomplished in the last two years would be undone, and the two halves of the Confederacy would again be joined. If he alternately blew up his vessels rather than let them fall into enemy hands, the Union cause would be weakened, although not destroyed. Porter's reputation, however, would be devastated. All Porter's personal aspirations would be ended, and Porter was an ambitious man.

He was rescued from the horns of this dilemma by an Ohio civil engineer and lumberman, Lt. Col. Joseph Bailey, a member of Banks's staff. Bailey recalled a technique he had used in his lumbering days when timber rafts floating downstream were stacked up behind rapids. He proposed that "wing" dams be constructed from each bank of the river out into the stream at an angle of 135 degrees to the river's current. The wing dams, however, would be constructed so as to leave a gap in the middle. That gap would be closed by sinking a barge in the channel that would join the two halves of the dam and act like a cork in a bottle. The dams would be constructed at the head of the downstream rapids.

Once construction was complete, a millpond would begin to rise behind the dam. As the pond rose, the weight of the water, together with the shape of the dam (which was channeling the river's current to the center), would exert tremendous force on the sunken barge in the middle. This barge would ultimately be shoved aside by the force of the stream, upon which a huge surge of water would flow through the gap. Any ship immediately behind the dam would be carried by the surge over the rapids and escape into the deeper waters downstream.

When Bailey proposed this scheme to Banks and Porter, he received a lukewarm reception. Banks, who had no background in civil engineering, thought the idea impractical and believed that its net effect would be simply to exhaust the men without achieving any benefit. Porter, in a state of depression at the seemingly inevitable loss of his fleet, had momentarily lost the ability to make incisive command decisions. Nonetheless, neither commander could think of a better alternative and so gave their assent to Bailey. Banks arranged to have a thousand soldiers assigned to Bailey for the purpose.

The sailors thought that this was a wonderful idea. They particularly enjoyed the thought of being able to act as "sidewalk superintendents" of the soldiers' labor, while making occasional "helpful" suggestions as to how the work was being carried on. What the soldiers thought of all this was not recorded but can well be imagined.

No amount of complaining would help. They were in the army and had to accept whatever division of labor their superiors might devise.

So the soldiers sweated and the sailors hooted, but, little by little, the wing dams were being erected. Because of the differing character of the opposite sides of the river, the two wing dams were of totally different construction. The south bank of the river was wooded. Therefore, the southern wing dam was being constructed from logs. The northern wing dam originated within the confines of the city. Thus, it was being constructed from "cribs," slat-sided boxes that could be transported to the site, sunk, and then filled with brick or rubble ballast for weight.

Oddly, a coincidence occurred in the construction of the northern dam. General William T. Sherman at the beginning of the war had been the first superintendent of a newly created state military college established in Alexandria. As such, one of his first functions had been to oversee the construction of a classroom and dormitory building. This building was now demolished, and its stones were used to fill some of the cribs making up the northern wing dam. As a metaphor for what the South lost by resorting to forcible separation in 1861, this would be hard to exceed.

Finally, the wing dams were complete, the barge was sunk in the opening, and the water in the river started to rise. Now that the work was completed, its potential was obvious even to Banks and Porter. Above the dam the Union fleet started to get up steam and to make all preparations for getting under way. Several weighed anchor quickly and aligned themselves as close to the dam as they could get.

As the water rose, it was observed that the pressure on the sunken barge in the gap was enormous. It was equally clear that the barge would never stay in place long enough to allow the river level to rise to its desired height, that is, a height sufficient to permit a ship to cross the lower rapids as well as to cover the upper rapids adequately to permit boats on the upper river to get to the millpond behind the dam.

There were, however, four ships already in the pond between the rapids. Perhaps Bailey's trick would be sufficient to save at least these four vessels. All would depend on how long the barge could continue to hold back the river before letting go. In any event the four ships would be forced to ride the surge. If it were inadequate, then the four ships would be driven aground in the midst of the rapids and the four vessels would have to be destroyed. That would also seal the fate of the remaining fleet above the rapids.

There was nothing to do except to stand by and watch the river level rise, inch by inch. All eyes were on the barge, waiting for the first indication that it was giving way. The dam builders had done their job well. They had filled the barge with a great amount of ballast, and it held longer than anyone reasonably expected. Finally, it let go and was brushed cleanly out of the way. With a great whoosh the surge pushed through the dam and headed down the river. The four ships by this time had a full head of steam. They opened their throttles and headed downstream full speed ahead to catch the surge.

As the army watched, the four ships bobbed along in a great cloud of steam, smoke, and foaming water. The noise was horrendous as each vessel scraped along the bottom, but suddenly they were through. The four ships had survived with nothing worse than battered hulls to show for the experience. A great cheer went up from the assembled men on the riverbank.

Four ships made it, but what about the remaining ten? The answer now was clear to everyone. If a dam on the lower rapids had worked, then a new dam at the upper rapids should be equally successful. This time there was no shortage of volunteers, and a second dam was constructed in short order. The trick worked a second time, and with a great head of water behind it, the remaining fleet negotiated both sets of rapids to gain the lower river. The Union's control of the western rivers (not to mention Porter's reputation) had been saved.

If Porter was saved, Banks wasn't. The retreating army still had one more river to cross to escape a vengeful Taylor, who was now engaged in close pursuit. Downstream the Atchafalaya Bayou entered the Red River from the south only a few miles short of the latter's confluence with the Mississippi. Banks's army had to cross the Atchafalaya or be confronted with a battle fought with its back to two rivers meeting at a right angle, a true glory or death situation. The Atchafalaya, however, was in flood and was currently about 600 yards wide, far too great for Banks's available pontoons to span. Seemingly, the only alternative was for the navy's transports to bring units of Banks's army across the Atchafalaya in relays. In so doing, Banks's remaining army on the far shore would progressively dwindle. At some point the rear guard would become too weak to resist Taylor, who would then storm Banks's fortifications and capture the remaining troops and all the army's guns and equipment (a sort of Civil War "Dunkirk"). That really would put the icing on the cake as far as Banks's tattered military reputation was concerned, and it might well spell the end of his postwar political ambitions.

Once again, Colonel Bailey came to the rescue. This time he borrowed a trick that was approximately 2,400 years old. King Xerxes of the Persian Empire used his war galleys as pontoons to bridge the Hellespont (the word itself means "bridge to Greece") between Asia and Europe and thus permit his army to invade Greece by land. Colonel Bailey did the same. Being short of pontoons, he commandeered the navy's transports and anchored them at sufficient intervals between his available pontoons to permit the bridge to stretch to the opposite bank of the Atchafalaya. He then laid parallel transverse supports from pontoon to transport to pontoon and attached a plank roadway to the supports. The bridge so produced resembled a rollercoaster more than a highway, but it did the job. The entire army and its equipment were spared General Taylor's tender mercies.

AFTERMATH

The Red River campaign demonstrated one more time to the Lincoln administration (as if such a demonstration was necessary) that political generals, with the occasional exception of a Logan or a Blair, were at best an embarrassment and in the long run almost invariably produced disaster. On the other hand, the administration had no desire whatever to publicly humiliate Banks, who was not only a political ally but also a man known for his administrative skill and personal integrity. The solution to the dilemma was found in appointing Gen. E. R. S. Canby to the post of commander of the district of Mississippi and Louisiana and making Banks his deputy for administration in New Orleans. Banks, however, had greater things in mind.

He soon resigned from the army, returned to Massachusetts, and served six more terms in the U.S. House of Representatives.

Admiral Porter immediately put the Red River campaign behind him and went on to greater triumphs. He was appointed to command the North Atlantic Blockading Squadron in the spring of 1864. In January 1865, he assisted in the capture of Fort Fisher, closing the Confederacy's last Atlantic port. The coordination of his actions with those of General Terry, newly appointed Union coastal commander, was considered a model of army-navy cooperation. After the war, Porter became superintendent of the U.S. Naval Academy.

Confederate generals Kirby Smith and Taylor had a terrible falling out after the campaign provoked by Taylor's charge that Kirby Smith had sabotaged Taylor's chances of destroying Banks's army and capturing Porter's fleet. The breach was too great to be reconciled, and Taylor ultimately became the Confederacy's last commander of eastern Louisiana, Mississippi, and Alabama. Taylor surrendered the last Confederate army east of the Mississippi in late April 1865 and went on to become an effective advocate of Southern rights in the restored Union.

Colonel Bailey was showered with honors. He was immediately "double jumped" to the rank of brigadier general (followed by a brevet to major general in April 1865). In addition, he was officially voted the Thanks of Congress and received a presentation sword from the Navy Department, delivered to him by Admiral Porter. Unfortunately, his postwar career was short. He became the sheriff of Vernon City, Missouri, and on March 21, 1867, he was killed by two bushwhackers he had arrested.

General Smith's troops never did catch up with Sherman, although they did participate in Thomas's great victory at Nashville in December 1864 and in the capture of Mobile in April 1865.

CHAPTER IX

Cleaning Up After Bedford Forrest

From the very beginning, the Confederacy had had one great advantage over the Union—its cavalry was far superior. This was a natural consequence of the different lifestyles of the two areas. In the South, boys, particularly those from good families, were practically born in the saddle. By the time they reached adulthood, they were as natural at riding as they were at walking.

In the North, children were raised in a different environment. The typical Northern recruit was the son of a farmer, small-town artisan, or merchant. Northern youth were familiar with horses, but they used the animals for plowing and hauling, not for riding.

Not surprisingly, one of the earliest units of the Confederate Army of Northern Virginia was the cavalry corps under J. E. B. Stuart. This corps quite literally rode rings around its Northern counterpart, its most famous exploit being to ride completely around McClellan's army during the Peninsular campaign. Stuart was thus able to give to Lee an accurate appraisal of the extent and disposition of McClellan's entire force. That knowledge made possible Lee's defense of Richmond.

Such a state of affairs continued well into 1863. Much of Lee's success rested on Stuart's capacity to give him accurate intelligence, while simultaneously screening Lee's movements from the Northern commander. Not until the summer of 1863 did the Army of the Potomac reach an equal footing, and not until Stuart's death (on May 12, 1864) and the concurrent emergence of Philip Sheridan as the Federal cavalry leader did the North gain the upper hand.

In the west the Confederacy produced no less than four great cavalry leaders. Kentucky's contribution was John Hunt Morgan, whose dashing raid through Kentucky in July 1862 terrorized that state and netted Morgan many recruits. In July 1863 he crossed the Ohio River on a twenty-four-day raid through Indiana and Ohio in a failed attempt to convince Northern "Copperhead" Democrats to rebel. Morgan himself was captured, but the effect on Northern morale was devastating.

Earl Van Dorn was a failed army commander who became a successful cavalry leader. He totally destroyed the Federal base at Holly Springs, Mississippi, in late 1862 but died in the spring of 1863.

"Fightin" Joe Wheeler was the commander of the cavalry corps attached to Bragg's Army of the Tennessee and served with them until Sherman's capture of Atlanta. Then the army (now under Hood) returned to Tennessee, while Wheeler stayed in Georgia to harass Sherman on his march to the sea. Wheeler is particularly remembered for two raids into eastern Tennessee.

It was the final leader, however, who attained the pinnacle of fame and accomplishment. Nathan Bedford Forrest was in a class by himself. He probably personally caused more disruption to the Union effort than the other three combined plus an infantry division thrown in for good measure. Forrest was dubbed "The Wizard of the Saddle," and he fully lived up to the appellation. In Ken Burns's television series on the Civil War, author Shelby Foote opined that Lincoln and Forrest were probably the only two authentic geniuses that the war produced (a sentiment that had also been expressed by no less than General Sherman). That assessment seems correct. As men, the two were totally different, but they shared the same ability to rise from the humblest beginnings to become supreme champions of their respective talents.

Forrest, the son of a backwoods blacksmith, at age sixteen became a successful slave trader in order to support a large family. He enlisted in the Confederate army as a private in 1861 and by July 1862 had been promoted to brigadier general. At the war's end, he held the rank of lieutenant general, the only man in either army to accomplish such a climb. Many upper-crust Southerners, however, were reluctant to celebrate his talents. As a vulgar, illiterate slave trader, he was not invited into their homes nor was his acquaintance sought.

Forrest proved completely unbeatable by any army of remotely equal size. In desperation the North adopted a policy of pinning him down by bringing overwhelming numbers against him and doing so in remote localities so as to keep him away from critical supply routes. Then, after he had routed each such force, they would immediately bring another expedition to bear.

The pragmatism of this strategy was proved during the period between February and September 1864. During this time Forrest defeated two expeditions sent against him, forced a third to retreat, and twice raided Memphis. All told, upward of 50,000 Union troops were pinned down in western Tennessee and northern Mississippi who otherwise would have been available for service in Virginia or Georgia. During all this, Forrest's strike force never exceeded 5,000.

One thing he was not doing, however, was disrupting Sherman's vital rail supply line between Nashville and northern Georgia. This was the saving grace that made all other Northern tribulations seem trivial by comparison.

The situation in Tennessee in the spring of 1864, following the North's great victories of Lookout Mountain and Chattanooga the preceding fall, was as follows. The Northern army was now a mighty host of close to 95,000 men commanded by General Sherman and constituting a merger of four separate army groups. Its core was the Army of the Cumberland, now under Gen. George Thomas, consisting of three army corps including one corps that had been transferred from the Army of the Potomac. Next in size was the reconstituted Army of the Tennessee under Gen. James McPherson, a Sherman protégé, with two army corps. Finally, there was the Army of the Ohio under Gen. John Schofield. Schofield had spent most of the war in Missouri. In February 1864, he was assigned to command this newly formed "army," which actually was no larger than a normal army corps. These men, with General Sheridan (now a corps commander under Thomas) and Generals Grant and Meade (with the Army of the Potomac), would constitute the leadership group that one year later would win the war. Lincoln's military team finally was complete.

This Northern army stood at Tunnel Hill just across the Georgia line, west of the city of Dalton. There they were confronted by the

Army of the Tennessee, encamped across the valley at Buzzard's Roost, and now commanded by Gen. Joseph E. Johnston (Bragg having been transferred to the post of military adviser to Jefferson Davis). The army consisted of three corps under Hardee, Polk, and Hood and aggregated only slightly more than half the strength of Sherman's host. Sherman's plan was to march on Atlanta as soon as road conditions permitted, engaging Joe Johnston all the way down.

An attacking army of 95,000 requires constant replenishment of men, material, and equipment while en route. As long as the army was operating in middle Tennessee, supply lines were short, and this imposed no great problem. As Sherman's army moved southeast from Chattanooga into Georgia, however, the problem became more severe with each mile gained. Because Sherman's bases were inland, his principal source of supply was the railroad network.

At the beginning of the war, 22,000 miles of railroad lines existed in the Northern states, all of them belonging to separate private corporations. Generally they provided a continuous service throughout the New England, mid-Atlantic, and midwestern states, although some limitations existed. Specifically, the links connecting the East Coast with the Midwest were too few. Different gauge sizes on connecting lines also caused complications and delays.

The South's track network was only 9,000 miles long. Most of it consisted of short lines leading inland from the various seaports that handled the area's exports. Southern lines were more lightly constructed. Prior to the war they carried a smaller volume of traffic and employed only one-fifth of the country's total railroad employees. Moreover, because of the Southerners traditional dislike of mechanical occupations, many Northerners were employed by the Southern companies. These Northerners either went north at the outbreak of the war or were thereafter considered suspect.

In all of the South only one main "trunk" line joined its eastern and western portions. This was the Memphis and Charleston Railroad. Starting in Memphis, the line ran east along the Mississippi and Alabama northern borders to Chattanooga. There it branched in two with forks (under different names) running through Knoxville to Norfolk, and through Atlanta to Charleston, Savannah, and Pensacola. Immediately west of Chattanooga, the Memphis and

Charleston was intersected by the Nashville and Chattanooga Railroad. Sixty miles farther west, the Memphis and Charleston Railroad was joined by the Nashville, Decatur, and Stevenson Railroad. Both lines ran northward for approximately 100 miles and terminated in Nashville. Such were the interconnections of the Southern railway network that whoever controlled this rail triangle plus the Memphis and Charleston Railroad main line between Memphis and Chattanooga could block all long-line, north-south, or east-west traffic throughout the entire South. One further indication of the South's desperate plight was that, by the beginning of 1864, the Union controlled both the triangle and the main line.

Northern railroads remained in private hands throughout the war (although they were swiftly regulated after some early attempts at price gouging by several owners). Railways in Virginia and Tennessee, however, were run by a wartime agency of the Federal government, the U.S. Military Railroad System (USMRR), which operated the railroads in these states as would a trustee in bankruptcy. By 1865, the USMRR was running 16 railroads in Virginia and 19 Tennessee-Mississippi lines. In the aggregate this meant operating 2,100 miles of track, 419 engines, and 6,330 railway cars.

The USMRR also constructed "from scratch" a railway from Washington to Alexandria and a line from City Point harbor on the James River to the western end of the Petersburg fortifications. During the war the USMRR laid an estimated 650 miles of track and constructed 26 miles of bridges.

Sherman's rail supply lines were as follows. There were three railheads: Louisville, Kentucky; Columbus, Kentucky (on the Mississippi); and Memphis. All supplies originating in the old northwest could be brought down the Mississippi-Missouri River systems and landed in Columbus or Memphis. All supplies originating in Ohio River states could come down that river from Pittsburgh, Wheeling, or Cincinnati and be landed at Louisville.

From Columbus, goods would be transported by rail to Memphis. On the final leg from Memphis, the goods would travel the Memphis and Charleston Railroad to Chattanooga. From Louisville, goods would be shipped to Nashville. From Nashville, they would travel either the Nashville and Chattanooga Railroad or the Nashville, Decatur, and Stevenson Railroad to their junctions with the Memphis and Charleston Railroad and thence, via the Memphis and Charleston Railroad, to Chattanooga. Supplies stored in Chattanooga would then be sent to Sherman via the Western and Atlantic Railroad, down which he was moving toward Atlanta. From this recital one may quickly observe that the system's points of vulnerability were the Memphis and Charleston Railroad (particularly at its junctions with the two lines from Nashville) and along the Western and Atlantic Railroad extending down into Georgia.

There were serious threats to this supply line. The biggest was Johnston's army itself. If that army could get around Sherman's flank and sit on his supply line, it might be able to force Sherman to fight a battle on terrain of Johnston's choosing. This was not as fanciful as it seems. In fact, in September 1864, after the loss of Atlanta, the South would attempt to do precisely that. For the moment, however, two factors precluded it: Sherman's army was twice the size of Johnston's and thus was hard to get around; and to interpose himself between Sherman and Chattanooga meant that Johnston would be putting Sherman between himself and his own base in Atlanta, a poor idea for several reasons. Thus, Johnston's army itself was not a credible threat.

The remainder of the South between Georgia and the Mississippi River was under the jurisdiction of the Confederate Department of Alabama, Mississippi, and eastern Louisiana. There were some infantry formations in the department that posed a theoretical risk to Sherman. These troops, however, were basically garrison troops committed to a static defense of the cities of Selma and Mobile, Alabama. The department's only offensive force was Forrest and his cavalry troopers. These had been so assigned after Forrest's falling out with Bragg following Chickamauga.

There was thus no threat of Southern recapture of the rail network, but the threat of cavalry raids entailing the destruction of rails, bridges, and supplies was very real. The effectiveness of such raids had been fully demonstrated in December 1862, when Generals Forrest and Van Dorn had made a coordinated attack against the two railroads that had supported Grant's Overland Campaign against Vicksburg. The upshot of those raids was the destruction of the supply base at Holly Springs, Mississippi, with a consequent loss of 1,500 prisoners and $1.5 million worth of supplies, to say nothing of stopping Grant's campaign in its tracks. A year and a half later, Nashville and its rail connections presented an even more tempting target. Sherman probably shuddered when he thought of what a Holly Springs type of raid might do to them.

In the end, therefore, the question boiled down to a contest between a Union garrison of upward of 40,000 troops stationed at various strongpoints between Memphis, Nashville, and Chattanooga plus its railway repair gang versus Forrest and Wheeler, either singly or in combination. Each cavalry commander headed forces whose maximum strength was about 5,000. Fortunately for the North, Morgan and Van Dorn were now both out of the picture: Morgan died shortly after he escaped from a Federal prison, and Van Dorn fell at the hands of an irate husband after one love affair too many.

When left alone, the USMRR was very efficient. The Tennessee rail systems' ability to meet the army's needs was demonstrated initially at the end of September 1863. As the Army of the Cumberland reeled back from the defeat at Chickamauga into besieged Chattanooga, Lincoln turned first to the Army of the Potomac and ordered it to dispatch two full army corps to Tennessee's support. Secretary of War Stanton boasted that they would arrive in five days. He was wrong, but in only eleven and a half days, 25,000 men and 60 cannons, together with their horses, were delivered from Washington to Chattanooga via West Virginia, Ohio, Indiana, Louisville, and Nashville by 30 trains totaling 600 cars. It was the biggest rail movement of the war.

The system's biggest challenge would come in the spring of 1864, after Sherman's Georgia campaign began. From this time until November, when Sherman severed his communications with the North to begin his famous march to the sea, a total of 16 trains a day, each with 10 railcars, had to reach the army over the 473 miles of single-track railroad that stretched between Louisville and Atlanta. Even without Bedford Forrest, it took exquisite coordination to ensure that this schedule was maintained.

All the Kentucky and Tennessee railroads were under the direct administration of Brig. Gen. Dan McCallum, director of the USMRR and former superintendent of the Erie Railroad's Susquehanna Division, whose office was in Washington. McCallum's military title, as well as those of his subordinates, was provided as a courtesy. All were essentially civilian employees whose rulings were supreme regarding railroad operations. The sole military authority recognized by the USMRR was that of Gen. Montgomery Meigs, quartermaster general, who served as McCallum's superior officer and to whom he and his department reported.

McCallum's direct deputy was Col. Adna Anderson, chief superintendent and engineer, also based in Washington and having overall responsibility for construction and reconstruction. Chief of operations in Tennessee was Maj. W. W. Wright, general superintendent in Nashville. Wright would become famous after the war as the man who rebuilt the Chattanooga-Atlanta line as well as the line that connected New Bern to Goldsboro, North Carolina, and thus enabled Sherman to reestablish contact with the North after his Carolinas campaign.

Reporting to Wright were Capt. W. J. Stephens, Chattanooga superintendent, and Capt. A. F. Goodhue, Memphis superintendent. Major E. C. Smeed supervised bridge reconstruction. His masterpiece was the Chattahoochee River bridge near Atlanta, which was 780 feet long and 90 feet high and was built in four and a half days using timber cut in the immediate vicinity. Wright and Smeed were also responsible for the rapid rebuilding of the Bridgeport segment of the Nashville and Chattanooga Railroad. Lieutenants G. Spear and G. Nagle served as the bridge-building foremen. The USMRR directed a 300-man construction division, which was divided into 10-man labor teams; the division maintained ample repair facilities, machine ships, roundhouses, and equipment warehouses. The USMRR even ran its own rolling mill in Nashville for the production of rails.

One of the first acts performed by the Union army after it reached the Alabama-Tennessee border was the repair of the Nashville, Decatur, and Stevenson Railroad. This job was done under the leadership of Gen. Grenville Dodge, a line officer who was also a civil engineer and prewar railway man. Dodge's work parties of soldiers and laborers repaired 100 miles of track and 182 bridges in only 40 days. In general, the speed at which the USMRR repaired lines and

restored service on disrupted lines seems phenomenal, until one re-
members that it had virtually unlimited materials, equipment, and
labor immediately available. This is not intended to disparage the
work of such experts as Anderson, Wright, and Smeed, whose organizational and engineering efforts were monumental. It is simply
to suggest that their activities should not be compared to those of
private companies where limits are imposed by cost and profit considerations.

The most challenging task of the construction division was bridge
and trestle building. Before the war, railway bridges had been built
mostly of masonry in the form of either stone or brick arches or of
iron spans resting on a series of masonry piers. During the war, stone
or brick materials were not at hand, and the time that would have
been expended in using them would have been excessive. In any
event, military needs were transient and thus did not require the permanence of a stone structure. On occasion, however, military engineers were delighted that their prewar predecessors had built so
solidly. When an opposing army blew up a railway bridge, the iron
span would normally drop to the ground and the stone foundation
piers would be left standing. The stone piers would then be available
to serve as foundations for a new trestle. This greatly simplified and
accelerated construction.

Wartime engineers used wood as their main building material—
trees were always available. The preferred bridge design was that of
the "military truss." This was an open rectangle whose "top" consisted
of two long longitudinal members and two shorter transverse members. This would be connected to a similarly constructed "bottom"
by both vertical and diagonal support timbers that were intercepted
on either side by a semicircular wooden truss—an arch that distributed the load throughout the structure.

The advantage of a military truss was that it could be made of interchangeable timbers that could be precut and stored until needed.
It could also be assembled by unskilled labor under the direction of
a knowledgeable foreman.

When a deep ravine between two hills had to be bridged, a trestle was normally used. A trestle was merely a wooden replica of the
ancient Roman multistoried arched aqueduct. The principle of the

arch was used to distribute the load so that heavy tonnages could be supported on structures that appeared to Lincoln to be made out of "beanpoles and cornstalks."

This is not to say that wartime construction was not dangerous. Much of it was built hurriedly by unskilled labor and without adequate safety checks. Thus, the occupational hazards of railway engineers and their crews included not only being shot by the enemy, exposure to the elements, short rations, and exhaustion but also derailments and blown bridges.

Let us now add Forrest and Wheeler to the equation. Wheeler raided Tennessee twice during this period: on October 1–9, 1863, in the Chickamauga aftermath; and from August 10 to September 10, 1864, as a means to relieve the pressure that Sherman was putting on Atlanta immediately prior to its capture.

After Chickamauga, mutual recriminations between Bragg and his lieutenants largely determined Confederate strategy. Both Forrest and Longstreet adamantly refused to serve any longer under Bragg's command (Forrest publicly, Longstreet privately). President Jefferson Davis thus had to choose either to reassign Bragg or to detach Longstreet and Forrest. Sadly for the Confederacy, Davis, almost alone in all the South, retained his respect for Bragg. This derived from Davis's brigade having been saved from destruction during the Mexican War by Bragg's artillery. Davis refused even to consider relieving Bragg.

Forrest and Longstreet had to go. Not only would the Army of the Tennessee lose the services of its two best corps commanders, but the army itself would lose about one-quarter of its strength. Given that the Army of the Cumberland undoubtedly would be massively reinforced, this was madness. Nonetheless, that is what happened. Forrest was detached and sent to Mississippi; Longstreet was also detached and sent to Knoxville (farther up the Tennessee River, northeast of Chattanooga) to contest General Burnside's occupation of that city.

Burnside was in Knoxville to satisfy Lincoln's two-year-old objective of liberating eastern Tennessee, where pro-Union sentiment was strong. Burnside was the obvious choice (however dubious Burnside's military credentials were, his political clout was first-rate); he was then the commander of the Department of Ohio and thus strategically placed to lead an expedition from the Ohio River to eastern Tennessee. Happily, even Burnside could do little harm, since the fortifications of Knoxville provided him with a Fredericksburg-in-reverse situation against Longstreet. The latter general was far too smart to duplicate Burnside's previous mistakes in their present confrontation. He therefore subjected Knoxville to a siege.

This dispersion of forces would ultimately be the Confederacy's undoing. In the short run, however, it proved to its advantage. Longstreet's presence severed Rosecrans's river and rail connections with Knoxville. Bragg's occupation of Missionary Ridge and Lookout Mountain cut his supply line downriver. Rosecrans was left with a supply line that started twenty miles downstream, then went north through the Sequatchie Valley, over Walden's Ridge, and finally into Chattanooga. This was a very arduous trip and entailed using mules carrying saddle packs.

Wheeler, in his 1863 raid, sought to disrupt even this last-resort supply line. After brushing back several Union infantry and cavalry detachments, Wheeler's men crossed Walden's Ridge and fell on Union supply wagons in the Sequatchie Valley. For a week they operated largely at will, capturing or destroying more than a thousand wagons, hundreds of animals, miles of railroad, five bridges, and millions of dollars in supplies.

The Federals were now in a tight fix indeed, or at least so it seemed as long as Rosecrans and Burnside remained in charge. Once Grant and Thomas took over, matters were remedied swiftly. The Cracker Line restored the situation, and Wheeler's 1863 raid had no permanent effect (except to add to the U.S. Treasury's woes).

Wheeler's 1864 raid was a desperate measure to break Sherman's encirclement of Atlanta. It was not as successful as the 1863 effort. Initially he did succeed in destroying miles of track in northern Georgia belonging to the Western and Atlantic Railroad. Large formations of Union infantry finally drove him away from the railroad into central Tennessee, where he destroyed a few miles of track south of Nashville. Union detachments, however, were now closing in, and Wheeler was forced to flee to Alabama. Union repair crews managed to restore service swiftly in Tennessee and Georgia, and Sherman experienced no major supply problem. Wheeler's cavalry never again returned to Tennessee.

Forrest was the commander who really gave Union generals and railway authorities sleepless nights, and 1864 was his year of triumph. The problem was that while he was humiliating the Yankees (and in the process destroying the careers of several Union generals), he wasn't inflicting lasting damage on the Northern cause because he was fighting in the wrong place against the wrong army. This was the ultimate price of Davis's having left Bragg in charge surrounding Chattanooga. Forrest was thereby consigned to Mississippi, and after the reduction of Vicksburg, the North no longer had any vital interest in that state.

Nonetheless, Forrest's 1864 accomplishments were startling. In February, he routed a superior cavalry force under William Sooy Smith at Oklona and in the process disrupted Sherman's campaign against the Southern rail junction at Meridian, Mississippi. In April, Forrest raided the Memphis area, capturing Fort Pillow on the Mississippi and probably massacring black troops (only 58 of 262 engaged were taken prisoner).

In June, Forrest fought the battle for which he is most remembered, Brice's Cross Roads. To keep Forrest away from the vital railroads, Sherman ordered Brig. Gen. Samuel Sturgis to lead an army of 8,100 infantry and cavalry into Mississippi to find Forrest. It was well that he did, because Forrest was already on his way to cross the Tennessee River for a raid on the railways when the district commander called him back to deal with the threat that Sturgis represented.

Forrest had approximately 3,000 troopers to fight Sturgis's 4,800 infantry and 3,300 cavalry (under General Grierson of Grierson's Raid fame). Forrest, however, had an uncanny eye for topography and an extraordinary ability to foresee how his foe would react to circumstances. Sturgis's forces were advancing down a muddy road with Grierson's cavalry far in front. Forrest predicted that he could defeat Grierson first. Sturgis's infantry would then attempt to double-time their advance in order to save Grierson. They would arrive hot and exhausted and would be vulnerable to a frontal attack. It all happened just the way Forrest foresaw. Ultimately, the Federals were routed and lost their artillery and wagons. It was a brilliant victory, but the Tennessee railroads were left untouched.

In July another Union army, this time consisting of 14,200 infantry and cavalry under Gen. A. J. Smith (of Red River fame), was sent against Forrest. Forrest massed 6,000 troops and was joined by his department commander, Gen. Stephen Lee, with 2,000 more. With Lee in command, the two armies met near Tupelo, Mississippi. Forrest proposed making hit-and-run attacks against Smith while he was still on the march. Lee, however, opted for a frontal assault. In two hours Lee had lost 1,300 men to Smith's 700. Smith, however, was short on rations and so retreated instead of counterattacking. To date, this was the best that any Union general had ever done against Forrest. It had the added benefit of forcing him to reorganize, thus further postponing his attack on the railroads.

In August, Forrest again raided Memphis. This time he hoped to kidnap the district's Federal military commander. He didn't succeed, but he did terrorize Union "collaborators" while giving hope to Southern sympathizers.

In September a major change in strategy occurred. The command of the Confederate Department of Alabama, Mississippi, and eastern Louisiana was transferred from Gen. Stephen Lee to Gen. Richard Taylor (of Red River fame). Taylor shared with Forrest the distinction of being the South's only successful general in the west and had the respect of the Confederate War Department. Taylor was also coincidentally the brother-in-law of President Jefferson Davis and thus had a political advantage that his predecessors lacked. Finally, Taylor had the vision to realize that the South's ultimate future rested on the outcome of Sherman's campaign in Georgia. He believed that Forrest's first priority therefore ought to be to stymie Sherman, regardless of whether this resulted in the unavoidable circumstance of Mississippi's being left undefended, and he was able to act on that belief.

At long last, the South had a commander who would use Forrest's talents properly. Unfortunately, this epiphany didn't occur until three days after Atlanta fell. Nonetheless, Forrest went promptly to work. On September 22, he started his raid at Athens, Alabama, a station on the Nashville, Decatur, and Stevenson Railroad. He overcame the Federal garrison, capturing 1,300 prisoners, two cannons, and huge amounts of equipment including two locomotives and associated cars. He destroyed the rolling stock and then started moving northward along the railway toward Nashville, destroying track as he went for another twenty miles. Forrest was forced to turn aside at Pulaski, where the Federals concentrated against him. He made a brief feint to the east, where he caused minor damage to the Nashville and Chattanooga Railroad. Turning north, he struck the Nashville, Decatur, and Stevenson Railroads again thirty-five miles north of Pulaski at Spring Hill on October 1. Then he turned south and for another ten miles destroyed track, bridges, and culverts. Finally he recrossed the Tennessee River on October 3 to complete his mission.

The Tennessee crossing was made on hand-poled ferry barges. Forrest, busy working on an oar, observed a young lieutenant not doing any work. When Forrest inquired why, the lieutenant said that as an officer he didn't feel obliged to do manual work. Forrest personally knocked the young officer into the river and then fished him out with the comment, "Now, damn you, get hold of an oar and go to work! If I knock you out of the boat again, I'll let you drown." Forrest, given to a hot temper and personal violence under the best of circumstances, did not gladly suffer members of the planter aristocracy.

The raid had been an enormous success. Forrest had captured 2,350 Federals; killed or wounded 1,000 more; destroyed many bridges, trestles, and blockhouses; and had taken 7 cannons, 800 horses, 2,000 rifles, and 50 wagons loaded with other spoils. It was the high-water mark of his military career. It was also its effective end. From here on, his only role would be to stave off disaster (temporarily) within the South's deteriorating western armies.

AFTERMATH

In spite of Wheeler's and Forrest's best efforts, Sherman, on September 2, 1864, occupied Atlanta, after having severed all four of the city's railroads, thus making it untenable as a base for the Confederate army. Shortly before this occurred, Gen. John Bell Hood, formerly a division commander under Longstreet in Virginia, replaced

Gen. Joe Johnston as commander of the Army of the Tennessee. In response to President Jefferson Davis's desire to have the army go over to the offensive, Hood immediately launched three successive frontal attacks. These not only failed to drive Sherman away but inflicted more casualties on the Confederates, who could ill spare them, than on the Federals.

Upon Sherman's seizure of the city, Hood attempted to cut off his supplies by destroying the Western and Atlantic Railroad behind him. Sherman, however, remembered how easy it had been for Grant's army to live without supplies during the Vicksburg campaign, as long as it stayed on the move. He decided to sever his ties with Chattanooga, burn Atlanta, and march directly for the seacoast, living off the land. He planned to "make Georgia howl" as his 60,000 men drove a wedge through the middle of the Confederacy. To guard against Hood (now in his rear), Sherman sent Thomas to Nashville with 20,000 men to be combined with the 40,000 to 50,000 men now in Kentucky and Tennessee as a reconstituted Army of the Cumberland. Sherman was confident that Thomas could handle any stratagem that Hood and Forrest could devise against him.

Hood now retired to Decatur, Alabama, where he refitted his army and acquired Forrest as his cavalry commander. Together they marched on Nashville, using the same route that Forrest had followed the month before. A portion of Thomas's army (under General Schofield) fell back before him, buying time for Thomas to assemble his forces in Nashville. After almost trapping Schofield at Spring Hill, Hood in frustration threw his army at the Federals in an ill-conceived, massive frontal attack (the battle of Franklin). This caused Hood's own army to suffer massive casualties (including seven generals).

The survivors staggered on to Nashville, where Thomas hit them simultaneously from the flanks and the rear in a classic double envelopment. Hood's army was pulverized and could not re-form short of the Tennessee River, more than 100 miles away. Even then, it could not make a stand, and it finally retreated to Mississippi. As an army they were finished, although some of their veterans did ultimately join other units in Alabama and North Carolina. For all practical purposes, the war west of the Appalachians had ended.

Wheeler spent the balance of the war harassing Sherman. His troopers were the only force opposing the march to the sea. In 1865, they combined with the Savannah and Charleston garrisons and a few Tennessee veterans to compose Johnston's final army (which surrendered about two weeks after R. E. Lee's surrender). After the war, Wheeler became a successful cotton planter in Alabama and served in the U.S. House of Representatives. He was appointed by President McKinley as a major general of volunteers in the Spanish-American War and commanded a cavalry division at the battle of San Juan Hill.

Forrest defended the city of Selma, Alabama, during the last months of the war. He was finally defeated by General Wilson, Thomas's cavalry commander, who had pursued him after Nashville, when Forrest had acted as the rear guard covering Hood's retreat. After the war, Forrest pursued farming and business interests. He also became the first national leader of the Ku Klux Klan.

Hood was relieved of command at his own request in January 1865. After the war he failed in business and died, impoverished, of yellow fever in 1879.

Thomas was almost fired by Grant just prior to the battle of Nashville in spite of his unbroken record of success. Grant was experiencing a case of nerves and feared that Hood would outflank Thomas and march to the Ohio River before Thomas could catch him. It was also true that Grant simply didn't like Thomas. The "chemistry" between the Ohio tanner's son and the Virginia aristocrat just didn't work. Grant actually cut orders for General Schofield to relieve Thomas; the orders, of course, were superseded when Thomas again became a national hero as "the Sledge of Nashville." Nonetheless, as 1865 progressed, Grant kept diverting troops away from Thomas so that by war's end, Thomas's command was rather hollow.

In the war's aftermath, the commanding general of the army was raised to four-star rank and his immediate deputy was elevated to lieutenant general. No other officer held rank higher than major general. At first the two top jobs were held by Grant and Sherman. When Grant became president, Sherman became general and Sheridan became deputy. Thomas (and Meade) protested, claiming seniority over Sheridan. Yet Sheridan prevailed. Thomas swallowed his disappointment and in 1869 requested command of the Department of the Pacific. This was granted. He died of a stroke in his San Francisco office in March 1870.

Schofield ended the war as an army commander under Sherman in North Carolina. After the war he remained a professional army officer, serving as superintendent of West Point; upon Sheridan's death in 1888, Schofield became commanding general.

The South's record in the war in the west was a bad mixture of ineptitude and lost opportunities. It was the South's misfortune that inspired leadership was largely confined to its cavalry generals. The cumulative total of damage done by these in terms of strongpoints surrendered, prisoners taken, and supplies destroyed was sufficient to infuriate the North and to materially add to its cost, but it did no strategic damage. In the end, in spite of the Confederate cavalry's incredible daring against formidable odds, its only tactical accomplishment was to delay Grant's capture of Vicksburg from the fall of 1862 until the summer of 1863.

The North's situation was, of course, the mirror image of this. While it was constantly being humiliated by its behind-the-line garrisons and supply depots falling into enemy hands, its armies compiled an almost unbroken record of success. From beginning to end, the North lost only one campaign, the meaningless Red River escapade, and only one important battle, Chickamauga. Even there, Bragg and Longstreet were outgeneraled by Thomas, and the fruits of victory were lost within sixty days.

Of the South's various western commanders, A. S. Johnston, P. G. Beauregard, B. Bragg, J. C. Pemberton, J. E. Johnston, R. Taylor, and J. B. Hood, only Taylor performed laudably. A. S. Johnston, Beauregard, and J. E. Johnston were lackluster, and the remainder were calamities. For the North, the war in the west provided the generals (and admirals) who won the war and dominated the peace: Generals Grant, Sherman, Thomas, Schofield, and Sheridan and Admirals Farragut, Foote, and Porter.

If We Cross the James, Victory Is on the Other Side

The Army of the Potomac traveled a long way, both literally and figuratively, in the sixteen months between Burnside's Mud March in January 1863 and the beginning of its last campaign in May 1864.

The Mud March and the squalid living conditions that followed were the army's nadir. It was apparent that Burnside had to go. He had lost the confidence not only of the country but of his own corps commanders, field officers, and enlisted men. Who his replacement would be, however, was not obvious. Lincoln finally settled on "Fighting Joe" Hooker, the army's most aggressive corps commander, who was duly appointed on January 26, 1863.

Hooker was everything that Burnside was not. On the one hand, he was a courageous and competent general who had served valiantly in the Peninsular Campaign and at Antietam. On the other, he was vain, deceitful, and manipulative, with a proclivity for stabbing his fellow officers in the back. Of the pack seeking Burnside's scalp, Hooker had been in the lead. Temperamentally, he was an odd mixture of genuine patriot and self-promoting opportunist with a bad habit of boasting of his exploits to the press. On one notable occasion he was quoted as saying that the country needed a dictator if it were to successfully prosecute the war, leaving little doubt as to who he thought the dictator should be. Lincoln's letter of notification of his appointment masterfully alluded to this comment. After stating that it was in spite of, not because of, his shortcomings that the appointment was being made, Lincoln concluded to the effect that only victorious generals could expect to become dictators. If Hooker produced victory, then, Lincoln said, he would take his chances on the dictatorship.

Conditions in the army immediately improved upon Hooker's taking command. By spring, the army's morale had recovered, and Hooker embarked upon another "On to Richmond" campaign. As at Fredericksburg, at first all went well. Hooker stole a march around Lee and firmly anticipated that Lee, threatened on his left flank, would retreat. Instead, at the battle of Chancellorsville (west of Fredericksburg), Lee divided his already outnumbered army in two. With one half he pinned down Hooker's far larger army, while he sent the other half, under Stonewall Jackson, on a concealed march to attack the far side of Hooker's army. Had Hooker caught on while Jackson was on the move, Lee would have been destroyed.

The South was in luck. Jackson arrived in position without incident and successfully carried out his attack, routing a full army corps in the process. Hooker was unnerved and a day later abandoned the field and canceled his offensive. Lee's victory was brilliant, and the South's triumph would have been complete except for one thing: Stonewall Jackson was wounded by his own men while trying to continue his advance after dark. Complications set in, and within a week Jackson was dead. Lee grieved that he had lost his "right arm." His generalship would never again be so deft.

Lee then turned north for a raid into Pennsylvania with two objects in mind: to relieve the pressure on Vicksburg, half a continent away, and to encourage British and French diplomatic recognition by gaining a major victory on Northern soil. A chastened Hooker moved to pursue him, but the heart seemed to have left him. Another command change clearly was needed, and Gen. George Meade of Pennsylvania was duly designated.

Three days later, the two armies met, by happenstance, at the farm town of Gettysburg to fight the largest battle ever fought in the Western Hemisphere. There were upward of 50,000 casualties.

The "battle" really consisted of three one-day battles fought on three successive days. The first day was a clear Southern victory, as overwhelmed Federals fell back in disorder through the town to re-form on a fishhook-shaped ridge of hills southeast of the village. The second day was a draw with beleaguered Federals fighting off persistent Southern attacks on both ends of its line. The third day was a decisive Northern victory, with Lee hurling 15,000 men at the center of the Union line, from which only half returned. To Lincoln's great chagrin, Meade hesitated to follow up by cornering Lee with his back to the Potomac (then at flood stage). Lee slipped away, and the war continued. Meade pursued Lee into Virginia, but for the remainder of 1863 the two armies marched and countermarched inconclusively.

By the spring of 1864 the Confederacy had effectively been reduced to the coastal states between Virginia to the north and Alabama to the south. The two ends of this "rump" state were each guarded by an army—Lee to the north, Johnston to the south. The "rump" had been weakened to the point where it could no longer win the war. All it could hope was to inflict such pain that the North would become war weary, abandon Lincoln, and accept secession. Because the South's only war aim was political separation, this would suffice. Only General Lee could inflict pain of this magnitude. The North's major war aim thus became the destruction or surrender of Lee's army.

To accomplish that aim, Grant pitched his headquarters tent with the Army of the Potomac and embarked upon a fight to the finish with Lee. After crossing the Rapidan River in central Virginia, Grant (and Meade, still commander of the Army of the Potomac) fought a succession of bloody battles against Lee (known as the "Overland Campaign"). Contact between the armies was never broken off during more than forty days. By the middle of June, Grant and Meade had suffered casualties equal to 50 percent of the force that they had brought across the Rapidan River forty-five days before. Lee's casualties were fewer, but he too had been bled white. Unlike Grant, his casualties could not be replaced.

The worst of these battles had been the last, Cold Harbor. In what Grant called his "worst day of the war," he sent forward 40,000 men in a frontal attack intended to break Lee's line and drive straight to Richmond. It was a disaster. Lee was firmly entrenched, and within a half hour he had inflicted 7,000 casualties while suffering only 1,500 of his own. Grant compounded the problem by ritualistically stipulating that both commanders mutually seek a truce to attend the wounded and bury the dead. Lee, recognizing that the wounded in the front of his lines were all Union soldiers, insisted that Grant request the truce unilaterally (which Grant refused to do). The upshot of this debacle was that the wounded on the field lay untended for forty-eight hours. All those who were unable to crawl off the field unaided, or who were not individually rescued by a comrade at the peril of his own life, died.

The Federals were now in a fix. Grant had heretofore concluded each battle by sliding around the Confederate right (that is, by moving southeast). To do this once again would be difficult, because the region to which he would move was swampy. Moreover, it would serve no purpose; such a move would leave him occupying the old trenches that McClellan had occupied during the Peninsular Campaign. Richmond would once again be placed in a state of siege, this time behind fortifications that simply could not be carried when occupied by Lee's men.

This solution was as unacceptable politically as it was militarily. It would signify that Grant had taken two months and incurred 50,000 casualties to reach ground that McClellan had occupied at the cost of a small fraction of that number. Unlike McClellan, Grant was fully cognizant of political considerations and realized that this would be intolerable.

Unfortunately, these same factors seemed to foreclose all his options. Any move he made in any direction to outflank Lee would simply drive that general back into the Richmond forts. Any further direct attack would be likely to produce another Cold Harbor, and it was problematical whether either the army's organization or the political consensus behind the war itself could survive that result. Also, Grant was not that kind of general. As the Vicksburg campaign testified, he was best at a campaign of maneuver, where the situation was always fluid, and fleeting opportunities presented themselves seriatim. Siege warfare was not his style.

Grant solved his problem with a masterful tactical movement. Richmond lies on the eastern bank of the James River, whose course forms a flattened letter Z across the state of Virginia. Richmond lies in the center of the diagonal arm (the diagonal runs in the "wrong" direction). The James River is joined by the Appomattox River, flowing from the west and entering at the spot where the James's diagonal becomes its lower horizontal. This junction is named "City Point." Across the rivers from City Point is a peninsula, which lies to the west of the James and the north of the Appomattox, called Bermuda Hundred. Approximately ten miles up the Appomattox, on its southern bank, lies the city of Petersburg. That city is almost due south of Richmond, approximately twenty miles distant.

Petersburg was the transportation hub of the region. A total of five railroads entered it, one from each quadrant of the compass and the fifth from City Point, where a deepwater port was located. The railroad running north to Richmond was the capital's main supply line from the lower south. Only one other railroad entered Richmond directly from the south, this being the Richmond and Danville Railroad extending to the southwest. That area was agricultural. Thus, all that was available via the Richmond and Danville Railroad was foodstuffs, necessary but not sufficient alone to supply a city at war. Other rail lines extended north and west of Richmond, but Grant had already severed these. Thus, to capture Petersburg was the same as capturing Richmond; in either event the capital became untenable, and Lee would be forced to abandon its fortifications and flee into open country. A second major benefit would be the Confederacy's abandonment of the Tredegar Iron Works in Richmond, the Confederacy's only producer of arms and railroad rails. In short, if Petersburg were captured, the surrender of Lee's army and the fall of the Confederate government could reasonably be expected to occur briefly thereafter.

Grant therefore devised a plan to disengage the Army of the Potomac from contact with Lee, bridge both rivers, and seize Petersburg from the south before Lee realized his peril and reacted. There was real risk in this. The Army of the Potomac was not as responsive as Grant's old Army of the Tennessee. It was bureaucratic in its command structure and sluggish and uncoordinated in its movements (it more closely resembled Bragg's old army rather than that of Grant). If matters were not properly handled, the Federals could be strung out for several days over forty miles of roads and bridges and

so be extremely vulnerable to a flank attack. If Lee ever learned of
the movement while it was in progress, such an attack was inevitable.
Still, there was nothing else that could be done; the chance had to
be taken.

The plan was superb. One of the 9th corps's historians called it
"the most brilliant and successful of the war." The plan had to meet
the following criteria: it must screen the army so that Lee would not
detect the movement en route; it must provide for protection against
a flank attack; and it must be timed so that the northernmost corps
would start first and march behind the lines of the corps to its south,
who would remain in battle line until the other passed. Southern-
most units must not start their march before the northern units had
passed in order that traffic jams not occur. However, all movements
should be coordinated so as to be continuous. All in all, it was a tall
order for corps commanders, their staffs, the artillery, and the quartermaster corps.

Grant's plan was carried out as follows. Prior to its inception a cavalry division was sent west on a raid ostensibly to interrupt supplies
coming to Lee from the Shenandoah Valley. Its real purpose was to
divert Lee's attention from his front to his rear. Grant also ordered
that a north-south line of entrenchments be built from the Chickahominy River to the James, the area over which any flank attack by
Lee must pass. Finally, block ships were sunk in the James River, upstream from the prospective bridge site, to prevent Confederate gunboats from interfering with the Union bridging operations.

After these precautions had been completed, the troop movement
started. Grant's northernmost army corps, the 18th, boarded transports that were sent down the York River and up the James to land
them on the Bermuda Hundred peninsula. This brought them both
across the James and closer to Petersburg than any other Federal
force. To reach the city, they needed only to cross the Appomattox,
a much smaller river than the James.

The next corps to the south, the 5th, would march behind those
below it in line to the Chickahominy. Upon crossing that river, they
would enter the newly constructed trenches to guard against a flank
attack. The 2d corps would follow, marching behind the 5th to the
Chickahominy and thence first in line to Wilcox Landing on the

north bank of the James. There, they would be met by a fleet of boats that had been assembled to ferry the corps across the river.

Marching behind the 2d corps would be the 6th corps. They would be followed by the 9th, while the 5th remained as rear guard. The 9th corps would be followed by the army's artillery and supply train. Only after these had completely passed would the 5th corps abandon the entrenchments and follow the rest of the army from the Chickahominy to Wilcox Landing.

The 6th corps would wait at Wilcox Landing until the 2d corps was completely transported across the river. Then they too would start to board the transports. Simultaneously, the army engineers would span the James with a pontoon bridge. As soon as this was completed, the artillery and supply train would start to cross. The two crossings—troops by transport, equipment by bridge—would continue concurrently until all supplies and equipment had crossed. Then any remaining troops would cross by bridge. The key to everything was the pontoon bridge. Without it the army would be in a tight spot. Two corps, ten miles apart, would both be south of the James but be separated from each other by the Appomattox. The remaining three corps would be strung out for several miles on the north bank of the James until ferries could carry them over. All artillery and equipment would be trapped north of the James.

The maneuver began on the evening of June 12. Twenty-four hours later, the 2d corps had been ferried across the James, and the 6th corps was waiting at the landing. The remaining corps reached the landing during the day on the fourteenth. Work on the bridge began at 4:00 P.M. that day. In one sense it was a routine job, simply one more pontoon bridge for experienced engineers to build. This one, though, was special; it was the granddaddy of all pontoon bridges, the biggest one built during the war. The James at Wilcox Landing is almost half a mile wide. It is a swift, deep river, subject to strong tidal currents and upstream flooding.

Bridging a stagnant pond with a pontoon bridge is pretty much a by-the-numbers exercise. Bridging a swift river, however, is treacherous. Things can go very wrong, very fast. Even small mistakes tend to have a cumulative effect and can cause major damage and lost lives.

Work on the bridge started simultaneously from both banks. Four hundred fifty men took part, including our old friend Maj. (now Lt. Col.) Ira Spaulding, the long-suffering deliverer of the Rappahannock pontoons, and his 50th New York engineers.

First, it was necessary to ensure that the bridge would be securely attached to the shore. This involved shoring up the bank with timbers to provide an abutment to which the beginning of the bridge's roadway would be attached. While the abutment was being built, the first pontoon would be either towed or rowed upstream by a six-man "boat party" and anchored to the river bottom. (As all mariners know, the holding capacity of an anchor whose flukes are dug into sand or mud is directly proportional to the length of the anchor line securing it to the boat. There was thus no standard distance upstream from the bridge at which to drop the anchor. The necessary distance would be up to the judgment of the boat party.)

Next, the boat party would permit the pontoon to drift downstream until it was parallel with the abutment. Then, using a boat hook, they would pull the pontoon into the embankment and exit the pontoon to the left of the abutment. Simultaneously, a "balk party" of ten men carrying "balks" would line up to the right of the abutment. (A balk was a timber twenty-five and a half feet long and four and a half inches square.) The balks would ultimately serve as the transverse supports of the bridge's roadway. The balk party would bring five balks, each carried by a team of two men.

A separate "lashing party" of five men would then enter the pontoon as the boat party was leaving. They would be passed one end of each of the five balks by the balk party. They would lash these down to the pontoon, thirty-four inches apart. The far end of balks would be lashed so that each extended six inches over the far side of the first pontoon. When the pontoon was lashed, it would be pushed out into the stream by the lashing party's exiting the boat pushing on the onshore end of the balks. They would then lash these ends to the abutment.

At this point a "chess party" of twenty men would form to the left of the abutment. When the balk and lashing parties were clear, they would bring the "chesses" (planks that would sit on the balks to form the roadway of the bridge). Each chess was fourteen feet long, one foot wide and one and a half inches thick. The chess party would lay these down so that a plank road was built up to the near side of the first pontoon.

While this work was progressing, the boat party would be anchoring the second pontoon and bringing it alongside the first; the balk and lashing parties would fix it in place and lash down the balks; and the chess party would extend the roadway. By the time the third pontoon was in place, "the side rail party" would start its work. This was to lay a top transverse rail over the chess that the side rail party would lash to the balks, thus holding the chess in place. All the foregoing would be completed sequentially, again and again, until the bridge was complete.

When completed, the chess would form a roadway from one shore to the other. The chess would sit on five unbroken parallel lines of balks, each thirty-four inches apart. Each balk would lie across two full pontoons and would extend out six inches beyond on either side. Thus, the junction of the balks would be outside of the pontoons. The distance between the opposite sides of any two pontoons was called a bay and was twenty-four and a half feet wide (that is, the length of a balk less two times six inches). The distance between the adjoining sides of any two pontoons was thirteen feet, ten inches. The width of the roadway between the side rails was eleven feet. Ropes, rather than nails, were used throughout to permit easy disassembly when the bridge was no longer needed.

As the engineers worked, the army and navy offered protection. The 9th corps formed a defensive perimeter of entrenchments around Wilcox Landing, where they remained until all other units had passed. On the south shore, the 2d corps entrenched against a surprise attack on the bridge's southern abutment. Federal ironclads patrolled the James and stood ready to use naval gunfire against any attack that Lee might make on Wilcox Landing. As for the bridge itself, if additional muscle was needed, there were plenty of infantry available to provide it.

As night fell, the engineers reached the middle of the river. Matters then became difficult. The river was very deep and swift, and it was increasingly hard to place new pontoons in position. Moreover, those already in place were suffering a huge strain and could easily lose their moorings. This contingency had been anticipated. Three large naval schooners were standing by. These were sent upstream to drop huge anchors at spots that appeared to offer good holding ground. These vessels were then allowed to drift downstream by paying out their anchor chains until a optimum distance was reached. Chains were then run astern from the anchored ships to several of the midstream pontoons. These secured the pontoons much more effectively than their own pontoon anchors could. Thus, the center of the river was crossed. The two halves of the bridge were joined at 11:00 P.M., but necessary bridge approaches were not completed until four hours later.

Now the transfer of men and material could begin. At dawn on the fifteenth, the artillery and supply train started across. Transports resumed ferrying the infantry as they had done the day before. The remainder of the 6th corps and most of the 5th corps crossed by transport on the fifteenth, while the "train" was crossing the bridge. After the train had completely crossed, one division of the 5th corps and the whole 9th corps crossed via the bridge. As they were crossing, their company officers and noncoms kept exhorting them, "Close up and move smartly, men. We've gotten away from Bobby Lee, and he doesn't know it. Victory and peace are on the other side of this river."

AFTERMATH

Unbelievably, it was true. The 100,000-man Army of the Potomac had disengaged from the Army of Northern Virginia without Lee's becoming aware. Lee had not anticipated the move, nor, when he discovered it, was he able to predict with accuracy where Grant had gone. This unwonted circumstance left Lee anxious and disturbed. The five days June 15–19 were among the worst Lee ever experienced. On one occasion during this period, he actually lost his temper in public, the only time ever so recorded. Lee's anxiety was fully justified.

The first Union general to reach Petersburg, as expected, was William F. "Baldy" Smith, commander of the 18th corps. Smith held that position because of Grant's favor, thanks to his having impressed the army chief by planning and implementing the Cracker

Line at Chattanooga. Smith's corps had originally been part of Ben Butler's (of Baltimore riots fame) Army of the James, which Grant had sent, in May, to invade Virginia between Richmond and Petersburg while Grant's army battled Lee near the Rapidan. Grant was fully aware of Butler's flaws as a military commander but couldn't withstand the politics behind his appointment. He could, at least, seek to provide Butler with competent professional support, and, accordingly, he appointed Smith and another old regular, Gen. Q. A. Gillmore, to command Butler's two army corps.

Grant did not know Smith personally and thus was unaware of his personality quirks. Notably, Smith became obstinate and uncooperative when he believed he was receiving insufficient recognition for his talents. Smith believed that he deserved command of the James's army, and he became resentful when asked to serve as second in command to a political general. As a result his relations with Butler became passive, stubborn, and uncooperative. Butler duly proceeded to make a hash of things, and the relief of pressure that Grant counted on Butler's providing for the Potomac army never materialized. In the end Grant had been forced to extricate and relocate Smith's corps, because Butler had allowed it to become entrapped by a lesser number of Confederates. None of this endeared Smith to Grant. Now, however, Smith was being given a chance not just to redeem himself, but to become "the general who won the war!" All he had to do was to capture Petersburg before Lee could defend it.

Smith crossed the Appomattox on June 15 and, by late morning, approached the "Dimmock Line" of fortifications that completely encircled the city. Here he paused. The fortifications looked even more menacing than those his corps had faced at Cold Harbor only a few days before. Smith wisely decided to conduct a reconnaissance before ordering a frontal attack.

What Smith did not know was that within the fortifications there were only 2,200 men, commanded by Gen. P. G. T. Beauregard. These simply could not be stretched far enough to withstand Smith's 11,000 men, if Smith attacked on a broad front. Nonetheless, Smith proceeded cautiously. He tapped Beauregard's line in several places, and part of it promptly collapsed. One of Smith's brigades succeeded in taking an artillery emplacement and capturing a Confederate battery. Smith's troops discovered in these attacks that the Southern line was lightly held. Particularly heartening to them was the fact that the Confederate battery had been overrun by a brigade of black soldiers. The white soldiers' pleasure was not a sign of interracial harmony; it was just the opposite. With their endemic bias, the white soldiers concluded that if black troops were able to capture the guns, it must mean that the Confederate resistance was minimal. Excited by this thought, Smith's men were prepared that evening to keep applying pressure until they drove all the way into the city.

Beauregard's few men retired in order. They abandoned most of the eastern portion of the Dimmock Line and fell back about a mile to a ridgeline approximately two miles outside city limits. To the south this ridgeline intersected with the southern and western portion of the Dimmock Line. Thus Beauregard shortened his line while preserving encircling entrenchments. Smith advanced to this second line, where he again paused. Those of his officers who had seen earlier how lightly the line was held urged a second assault that they were sure would succeed. Smith, however, demurred. Night was falling, his men were tired and hungry, and Smith did not want to make "the one bad mistake" that might cost him his career. General Winfield Scott Hancock, the best corps commander in the Army of the Potomac, had just arrived on the scene but deferred to Smith's judgment. Smith concluded that enough had been accomplished for one day. He would confer with General Hancock in the morning on how best to proceed. Smith thereby forfeited his claim to the title of "the general who won the war."

Confederate general Beauregard at this moment was frantic. He (correctly) believed that Smith was only the vanguard of a 100,000-man army that would soon confront him with fifty-to-one odds. Beauregard was one of the South's better generals, but President Jefferson Davis detested him and consistently tried to give him rear echelon assignments. In the Confederacy, however, today's rear-echelon had a way of becoming tomorrow's front line, and so Beauregard's talent usually managed to be utilized. Presently his assignment was to command all Confederate forces south of the James (Lee commanded those to the north). South of the James was quickly becoming the place where the action was.

Beauregard immediately started firing off telegrams to Lee urging the latter to move his entire army quickly to the Petersburg trenches. Lee had lost track of Grant on the fourteenth and realized that Beauregard's advice might be correct. Unfortunately, Lee could not be certain. He knew that Beauregard was an excitable man and remembered several "Chicken Little" scares that he had caused in the past. Lee equivocated. He returned to Beauregard one division that Beauregard had previously loaned to him. Otherwise, he kept his army in place.

On the sixteenth Hancock and the 2d corps joined in Smith's attack, but the men were exhausted. The road maps with which the 2d had been provided were badly in error. As a result its troops had marched about twice the distance they should have to reach Petersburg. Hancock himself was also feeling the strain. He had been wounded in the groin at Gettysburg, and the wound had only partially healed. During the day of the fifteenth it had become too painful for him to sit a horse. He had been forced to arrive at Petersburg in an ambulance wagon and to delegate most of his responsibility to his three subordinate division commanders. He was in no condition to take decisive action and continued to permit Smith to remain in overall command of the scene. Smith renewed the attacks on the sixteenth, but due to bad staff work they were late and uncoordinated.

By the sixteenth Beauregard was starting to receive reinforcements. Hoke's division, sent back by Lee, was being fed into the line. Welcome as these 4,000 men were, however, they were still inadequate to hold off two full corps and their expected reinforcements. Beauregard made a desperate decision on June 15. He abandoned the "Howlett Line" and added its 8,000 occupants to the Petersburg defenses, where they, too, were in place by the sixteenth. Thus, when the Union 18th and 2d corps began the second day's attack, Beauregard had increased his on-line strength to 14,000. It was still only half the combined strength of Smith and Hancock, but it held.

The Howlett Line stretched across the base of the Bermuda Hundred peninsula from the James River in the north to the Appomattox River in the south. Its function was to keep Ben Butler's Army of the James penned where Butler's poor generalship had trapped it.

That army now consisted only of Gen. Alfred Terry's 10th corps (Smith's 18th corps having previously been extricated). By evacuating Howlett, Beauregard was unleashing Terry's 10th corps to sever Confederate communications between Petersburg and Richmond and between Lee and Beauregard.

It became a race. Lee was now fully alerted and no longer under any doubt where Grant's army had gone. The Army of Northern Virginia made a forced march south and began to occupy the Petersburg lines during the eighteenth (after again pressing Terry back into Bermuda Hundred on the seventeenth and resealing the Howlett Line).

Meanwhile, the Union's 5th, 6th, and 9th corps were arriving at the Petersburg lines. Throughout the entire five-day period from June 15 to 19, Federals at Petersburg substantially outnumbered Confederates but were unable to put together the coordinated and sustained attack that might have displaced Beauregard and Lee. Finally, on the nineteenth Grant and Meade conceded failure and settled down to a siege. One of the war's great opportunities had been lost.

Someone had to be blamed for this fiasco. Smith was the obvious choice. The general who could have won the war but feared making one bad mistake had made his one bad mistake. In July, Smith was sent home to "await reassignment," which never came.

Hancock's glory days were also over. He struggled until November against the effects of his Gettysburg wound and then asked to be relieved. He finished the war as commander of the Veteran Reserve Corps (a unit composed of convalescent wounded veterans assigned to light duty). Hancock remained in the army after the war, serving as the commander of the Military Department of the East. In 1880 he became the Democratic nominee for president, losing to James Garfield in a close race.

Beauregard had once again performed creditably and deserved the appreciation of his country. Thanks to Davis's continuing animosity, he didn't receive it. He finished the war as commander of the Department of the West, an administrative job with little military responsibility. After the war he became a successful businessman and, on several occasions, turned down offers to command foreign armies. Beauregard's career typifies how consistently bad President

Davis was in his role as commander in chief. With the single exception of his support of R. E. Lee (hardly difficult), his entire record is one of opposing or ignoring talent (Johnston, Beauregard, Cleburne, Breckinridge, Forrest, and Gordon) while steadfastly rewarding incompetence and failure (Bragg, Pemberton, Polk, and Sterling Price).

Lee and Grant were now located where neither wanted to be, locked in a state of siege. For Grant, however, it was but a temporary frustration until Lee could be forced out. For Lee it was the beginning of the end.

CHAPTER XI
"Get Down, You Damn Fool, Before You Get Shot!"

Everyone in the city of Washington, from Abraham Lincoln down to the humblest citizen, was highly sensitive to any threat of Confederate incursion, real or imagined. These fears had been magnified by the Baltimore riots in April 1861 and the city's consequent brief loss of access and telegraphic communication with the North, but this was only a prelude to the crisis that shook the city following the Union army's stunning defeat at the First Battle of Bull Run in July 1861.

The loss at Bull Run can be traced, at least in part, to the aura of myth and legend that had grown around the exploits of the famous minutemen who fought the battles of Lexington and Concord in the opening days of the American Revolution.

Those battles were fought because a British column was advancing on Concord, where, reputedly, the colonists had a supply of gunpowder. At Lexington, armed citizens, standing on the town green, were easily pushed aside after several were killed in a single volley of gunfire. At Concord, colonists stopped the British advance by contesting control of a small bridge. In the aftermath, the minutemen emerged as a fighting force. As the British were leaving Concord (not having found the gunpowder), farmers from the surrounding towns, armed with their hunting rifles, converged on the road down which the column was retiring. Standing behind stone walls and in adjoining woods, they inflicted grievous casualties on the retreating soldiers, turning their retreat into a rout. Only the swift dispatch of a relief column from Boston saved the Redcoats from annihilation. Several weeks later, these same minutemen (so called because they would come at a minute's notice) stood off repeated charges by the British against their fortifications atop Bunker Hill (near Boston).

From these experiences there grew the myth of the invincibility of a citizen militia and the superfluity of a standing army. Because the newly independent Americans detested standing armies (which they associated with British tyranny), the myth was readily believed. Further reinforcing the idea was the propensity of the Founding Fathers to compare the country with the early Roman Republic. An enduring myth of that state had been the story of Cincinnatus, a farmer who, at the request of his compatriots, took command of the Roman state and army, defeated an invading army, then voluntarily gave up the reins of government and "returned to his plow." The lasting power of that myth was attested to by the fact that the postwar organization of Revolutionary veterans was named the "Society of the Cincinnati."

Conveniently overlooked in all of this was the fact that the circumstances of the minutemen's battles were unique. Raw courage in these instances could overcome an absence of training or discipline. During the remainder of the war, however, and notably in the New York and Pennsylvania campaigns of 1776–77, it became obvious that untrained militias could not beat British regulars. It was not until the Continental army received instruction in military drill and tactics from European generals Kosciusko, Pulaski, and Von Steuben that it could maintain discipline during a pitched battle.

The minutemen myth was preserved through the War of 1812, where it caused great damage on both the Canadian front and in the battles around Washington and Baltimore. However, Andrew Jackson's great Bunker Hill–like victory in New Orleans, just as the war was ending, again perpetuated the myth. The Mexican War in the 1840s was hard fought but involved only the regular army and so left the myth unaffected.

So it was that in 1861 neither North nor South thought of military service as a skilled and full-time profession. The South believed that any Southern boy could "wup" ten "paper-collared" Yankees. The North believed that their minutemen would stage one triumphant march to Richmond before which the rebellion would collapse. Northern public opinion and press editorials demanded that such a march begin as soon as possible.

Under such pressure, Lincoln urged Gen. Irwin McDowell, commander of all troops in the Washington area, to start a July offensive as soon as he could get his troops assembled. McDowell protested that the volunteers were too "green" to fight and needed training. The president acknowledged this but contended that the Southern troops were equally green and so the inexperience of both sides should be nullified. He overlooked that, this time, it would be the South that was defending Bunker Hill, while the North would play the role of the Redcoats.

General McDowell tried his best. He assembled a force of approximately 30,000 and marched down the Warrenton Turnpike on a circuitous path toward Richmond. About thirty miles to the southwest, just past Centerville, the army crossed a stone bridge over a stream called Bull Run and confronted General Beauregard and about 20,000 Confederates arrayed on a line of hills facing it. The Confederates also had a second force of about 10,000 under Gen. Joe Johnston that was located fifty miles away in the Shenandoah Valley. Moving against Johnston was a second Federal force under Gen. Robert Patterson, a sixty-nine-year-old veteran who had given good service in the Mexican War and now commanded the Pennsylvania Militia volunteers. Johnston had eluded him for three weeks, but it was hoped that Patterson could at least pin down Johnston so as to avoid his being able to reinforce Beauregard.

McDowell's battle plan was to hold Beauregard in place with 18,000 troops, while sending a 12,000-man flanking force on a wide sweep out to the right. Ultimately, he would trap Beauregard between the jaws of the two converging forces. McDowell could not keep secret his flanking movement, because his force of 12,000 raised a cloud of dust that was easily visible from the Confederate lines. Still, there was little that Beauregard could do but prepare his smaller force to resist simultaneous onslaughts from two directions.

On paper, the plan looked good. The flankers would sweep for five miles and then attack the enemy's left flank, while the remainder of the Federals simultaneously hit their right and center. Unfortunately, Northern staff and field officers were as green as their troops and made a botch of the maneuver. The flankers started at dawn and should have attacked by about 9:00 A.M. In fact, they were not in position until 2:00 P.M. Nonetheless, by midafternoon Beauregard was hardpressed, and McDowell was on the verge of victory. This was the moment when "Stonewall" Jackson got his nickname ("Look, boys, there stands Jackson's brigade like a stone wall. Form on them.").

Back in the valley, Johnston gave the slip to the inept and confused General Patterson. Having been informed by spies of McDowell's advance on Centerville, Johnston loaded his troops on the morning of the battle onto railway flatcars and sent them, via the Manassas Gap Railroad, to the battlefield, where they arrived in stages throughout the afternoon. As the battle progressed, it became apparent that reinforcement was most needed on the left. Later trains were thus ordered to discharge their troops before reaching Manassas Junction. From there a short march would bring them to the battlefield at the exact location where they were needed.

The Federal flankers, who were winning the battle during the early afternoon, progressively saw conditions change as increasing numbers of Johnston's men arrived on their flank. Eventually, they broke and started a reluctant withdrawal from the field. Confederate artillery hastened their retreat. Concurrently, the Federal army's teamsters hitched up their supply wagons and started to leave the field. They were joined by many carriages driven by civilian Washingtonians who had, incredibly, come out to enjoy a summer picnic on the surrounding hills while observing the battle.

Soldiers, teamsters, and civilians now all crowded the roads, creating a massive traffic jam. In its midst a Confederate artillery shell scored a direct hit on a supply wagon just as the wagon was crossing the stone bridge over Bull Run. The wagon's debris jammed the bridge, blocking access by anyone south of the stream. Panic ensued, and the retreat turned into a rout. Soldiers and civilians alike fled back to Washington and didn't stop until they had crossed the Potomac and collapsed, exhausted, in the city's streets and parks. So ended for the North the legend of the minutemen. The South would have a similar revelation the following spring at the Battle of Shiloh.

The citizens of Washington and the War Department were horrified by this breakdown of their army, which had left them defenseless against any incursion by even a small force of Confederates. They vowed that they would never again be without protection, regardless of the state of their field army, and so they determined to build a system of fortifications that could withstand any attack.

The chief engineer of the Military Department of Washington at the time was John Gross Barnard, an 1833 West Point graduate (at age eighteen) and one of the most prominent men of the prewar army. As an army engineer he had designed and built fortifications on all seacoasts and the Great Lakes, and he had built the fortifications of Tampico City during the Mexican War. Now he set to work on the fortifications that would encircle Washington.

One should not visualize these as an enormous medieval stone castle with a continuous wall around the city. Rather they consisted of a series of individual forts spaced half a mile apart. The forts were created from earthen embankments. These might cover either a masonry foundation or a natural rock formation, if such were conveniently located on the site of the intended fort.

Each fort would be placed on whatever hill or high ground commanded its immediate vicinity. Moreover, the forts would be so located that an attack on any of them would be resisted by converging cannon fire from three installations—the fort itself, the fort on its left, and the fort on its right.

No entrenchments were built to link the forts, but the spaces in between were covered with obstacles, particularly where roads entered these spaces. The obstacles consisted either of felled trees with interlocking branches or logs studded with pointed stakes known as chevaux-de-frise. A variant of this was a fraise, also a defense of pointed sticks, these being fastened into the ground so as to stick out, chest high, from the incline of sloping land. Finally there were gabions, hollow cylinders of wicker filled with earth. These constituted portable breastworks behind which infantry could stand.

Altogether, 60 forts and their intervening obstacles formed a square with a perimeter of 33 miles, bisected by the Potomac River. A garrison of 30,000 men tending 762 field guns and 74 mortars manned the works.

Work on the fortresses on the Maryland side of the Potomac proceeded rapidly during the last half of 1861; but work could not begin on the opposite side, because the Confederates then controlled Alexandria and the south bank of the lower Potomac. That obstacle was overcome by early 1862, and the fortifications were then extended on the Virginia side in a chevron extending from the Chain Bridge (at Georgetown) to Forts Ellsworth and Lyon, which covered Alexandria. The works around Washington were thus complete, with all points of access guarded.

The fortifications were manned by regiments originally recruited, state by state, as "heavy artillery." This distinguished them from the "field artillery," who made up the movable gun batteries that were assigned to specific armies and who traveled and fought with those armies in their campaigns. The "Heavies" were a force unto themselves and manned the larger cannons that were either in static fortifications, such as those of Washington, or those belonging to the "siege train." The siege train constituted the army's heaviest cannons, howitzers, and mortars. These could be moved only by ship or railcar. If a city were placed under siege (such as Yorktown during the Peninsular Campaign and subsequently Petersburg), the siege trains would be transported to fixed emplacements and there dug in. Thenceforth, they would pour down a continuous stream of heavy shells to disrupt and demoralize the besieged city and its defenders.

The heavy artillery regiments constituted an ideal vehicle for those Northern stalwarts who wished to serve their country (and avoid the opprobrium at home of being deemed a shirker or a coward) but who feared death or mutilation on the battlefield. Consequently, their regimental recruitment quotas were always oversubscribed. Frequently, some degree of political "pull" was required to enlist in such a regiment, even as a private.

The wisdom of the forts' construction seemed to be demonstrated almost immediately by the Northern loss of the Second Battle of Bull Run. Although the tactics of this battle varied from the first, the outcome was identical in all respects—a panic-stricken flight by the Federals from the battlefield to Washington. This time, however, the forts stood as a deterrent to any pursuit by the Confederate army. Whether this fact or the battle of Chantilly was decisive in thwarting any such pursuit cannot be determined, but no attack on any of the forts was attempted.

For two years thereafter the forts remained manned and ready but unthreatened. During this time the armies marched and counter-marched on the city's threshold on their way to the battles of Anti-etam, Fredericksburg, Chancellorsville, and Gettysburg, but no Southern army even feinted in the direction of Washington. It is in-teresting to speculate what might have happened if either the Con-federates had won the Battle of Gettysburg or had avoided battle by marching east, thereby "sliding across the top" of the Northern army. In such a case, they almost certainly would have raided Harrisburg, putting the Pennsylvania state government to flight and destroying supplies and railroad lines. Where they would have gone after that remains conjectural.

One thing is virtually certain. They would not have attempted to raid Washington. To do so would have put them between the Wash-ington forts and Meade's army, an untenable spot. In fact, there would have been few good options for a victorious Lee. As Lincoln recognized, Lee's northern invasions presented the North with op-portunity, not danger. Any damage that Lee could do would be re-paired and restored quickly, but Lee's army would be vulnerable to encirclement and entrapment for the entire time that it was above the Mason-Dixon Line. Lee was living on borrowed time on each oc-casion when he came north, and he would inevitably retire quickly from any such foray. Until Grant, Lincoln's generals could never comprehend this point. Thus, to Lincoln's intense frustration, the fruits of victory at both Antietam and Gettysburg were thrown away.

By May 1864, however, strategic circumstances would change. Grant needed large numbers of infantry to fill out the ranks of the Army of the Potomac, which had been depleted at Chancellorsville and Gettysburg. The gravity of his problem was compounded by the fact that most of his veterans would complete their three-year en-listments in June and July, and nothing could force them to reenlist against their will. Grant also knew that casualties during his prospec-tive Overland Campaign would be severe.

The commanding general realized that he could not count on a new surge of volunteers. By now, knowledge of the reality of war was widely disseminated, and ardent young men thought twice before en-listing. A military draft law was in operation, but it was so badly designed that one could not have intentionally created a more ineffi-cient and inequitable system. The draft ultimately depended upon a series of "bounties" to be paid either by the government to a prospective recruit or by a draftee to a "substitute" whom he would pay to replace him in the ranks. The system succeeded mostly in re-cruiting "bounty jumpers"—recruits who would sign up and collect the bounty, then immediately desert. They would repeat the process again and again, until they were caught and imprisoned. Such men at best would be of limited value and would certainly not replace trained veterans.

To help overcome his difficulty, Grant cast his eye on those thou-sands of Heavies who were standing essentially idle in the Washing-ton fortifications. Other generals had eyed them, but Grant was the first who had the clout to get them transferred.

The Heavies, who had been sleeping between clean sheets and en-joying great quantities of good food, were received with merciless glee by the infantry veterans who had been sleeping for three years in flooded ditches in a state of permanent exhaustion and terror. The veterans' favorite trick was to cover with a blanket some particularly appalling corpse lying by the side of the road. Then, when a com-pany of Heavies passed by, the veterans would uncover the corpse and observe, "Look, there lies Somebody's Darling." ("Somebody's Dar-ling" was a particularly lachrymose ballad then popular in both the North and South.) The Heavies would, of course, usually lose their lunch after such an encounter. A variant was to pin on the same corpse a label reading "Future billet of the 1st N. Y. Heavy Artillery," or the like. This produced the same satisfying result.

The size of the Army of the Potomac was thus swelled by 30,000, seemingly with little risk to Washington's security. After all, had not General Grant provided for two ancillary offensives, one in the Shenandoah Valley, the second on the James, to supplement his own titanic struggle with Lee? Surely the Confederates would not have the capacity to resist all three offensives and simultaneously mount an attack on Washington. As poet Robert Burns cautioned, however, the best-laid plans of mice and men have a tendency to go astray.

In this case, by the middle of June, Lee managed to neutralize But-ler's Army of the James and to confront Grant across a defensive line

stretching from the James near Richmond and thence south and
west of Petersburg so as to guard his vital arteries from the south—
the Weldon and the Southside Railroads and the Boydton Plank
Road. Although this expedient temporarily preserved both Lee's
army and the capital, it was in the long run a strategy that would
doom Lee and the Confederacy. Over time, Grant had access to effectively unlimited resources of men and materials. Lee didn't.
Grant therefore could keep stretching the line until Lee broke. It was
inevitable. The only question was how much time and blood it
would cost.

Lee was forced to plan a counteroffensive. But how and where?
He fell back on a stratagem that had served the Confederacy well
since the days of Stonewall Jackson. Go on the offensive in the
Shenandoah Valley, push aside the Federal force under Gen. David
Hunter, and make trouble in Maryland. To do this, he picked Gen.
Jubal Early and sent him to the valley with an army of 14,000, a third
of Lee's total force.

Early was an abrasive and hard-drinking old regular who nonetheless had compiled an effective war record and was well regarded by
his men. It was his good fortune to have as his opposing Union commander Gen. David Hunter, one of the few remaining West Pointers with a mediocre record who still held a position of responsibility in the Northern army. Early and Hunter met at Lynchburg at the
southern end of the Shenandoah Valley. Early repulsed Hunter's
attack and then pursued so closely that Hunter was put to flight
into the West Virginia mountains. This left the valley open to Early's
advance.

Throughout the war the valley had been a thorn in the side of the
Union. It acted as the granary of the Confederacy, supplying much-
needed rations to Lee's army, and its geographic orientation was
southwest to northeast. This meant that whenever a Confederate
army marched up the valley, it threatened Washington, Baltimore,
and Philadelphia together with the main line of the Baltimore and
Ohio Railroad, a vital Northern supply route. When a Northern army
marched down the valley, it went effectively nowhere and temporarily removed itself from the war. Early proceeded once again to
demonstrate the validity of this strategic circumstance.

Unopposed, the Confederates quickly marched up the valley to Winchester. There Early divided his army, sending a small force north to conquer Harper's Ferry and disrupt the Baltimore and Ohio Railroad. A second force, composed of cavalry, was sent to attempt to free the 18,000 Confederate prisoners held at Point Lookout (a peninsula formed by the Potomac's entrance into Chesapeake Bay). The main body of the army marched east toward Washington.

It was met on the banks of the Monacacy River near Frederick, Maryland, by an army of about 5,000 Federals, many of whom were state militia. The core of this force was the 6th corps division of Gen. James Ricketts, sent north by Grant after Hunter retreated. General Lew Wallace (commander of the Baltimore district and future author of *Ben Hur*) assumed command of the Union force. Though heavily outnumbered, Wallace's force held for a day against sustained attacks until it was flanked and forced to retreat. Early proceeded toward Washington.

The Confederates approached the city from the north down the road guarded by Fort Stevens, which was now, of course, stripped of its previous complement of heavy artillerists. The War Department attempted to replace them by ordering a variety of quartermasters, telegraphers, payroll clerks, et cetera, to man the fortifications, but no one doubted what would happen if those men ever had to face Early's army. The North's main reliance was upon the remaining divisions of the 6th corps whom Grant had ordered to follow Ricketts when it became apparent that Early's threat was real.

Early's army arrived in front of Fort Stevens on the afternoon of July 11. The men were choked with dust and exhausted after a forced march. Early decided to hold off for the night and attack in the morning, when his men were fresh. During the evening of the eleventh and the morning of the twelfth, however, the rest of the 6th corps arrived at the Washington docks and marched to the fort. Thus, when Early attacked on the twelfth, most of the 6th corps was there to meet him. The attack was barely launched when Early realized that he had lost the race. Faced with converging cannon fire from Fort Stevens in front and Forts DeRussy and Slocum on their flanks, plus sustained rifle fire from obviously trained infantry, the Confederates realized that their only option was prompt withdrawal.

By the middle of the afternoon they were gone, headed back to the Shenandoah Valley. General Lew Wallace and Ricketts's division had spared the city by gaining one all-important day. Joining Early's men were the survivors of the cavalry raid that had failed to free the prisoners at Point Lookout.

During the course of this encounter, a lanky civilian intruded upon Fort Stevens. At first, Abraham Lincoln maintained a judicious distance, but never having seen action before, he came progressively closer to the ramparts. Finally, his curiosity got the better of him, and he craned his neck to peer over the ramparts at the attacking force.

While this was occurring, the closest army officer to the president was a young captain of the 20th Massachusetts regiment. The captain, engaged in positioning his company, saw the civilian only peripherally and was unable to recognize him. It was apparent, however, that the civilian was oblivious to danger, even after a soldier was killed not more than three feet away from him. Finally, the young officer yelled out, "Get down, you damn fool, do you want to have your head shot off?" Not until a startled Abraham Lincoln hit the dirt did young captain Oliver Wendell Holmes realize to whom he had just given his command.

AFTERMATH

Following Early's retreat, Grant appointed his favorite lieutenant, Gen. Philip Sheridan, to wipe out all Confederate resistance in the valley and to burn its harvest and farm machinery. Grant's goal was described in colorful (if cold-blooded) language: "I want to leave it so that even a crow flying over it will have to bring its own provender." A substantial army composed of the entire 6th corps, General Emory's corps (General Franklin's troops from the Red River campaign), and General Crook's corps (formerly David Hunter's Army of West Virginia) together with Custer's and Merritt's cavalry divisions was given to him for this purpose.

At first, Sheridan fell back before the Confederates, causing Early to think he was just another timorous Yankee general. Early pursued, only to be attacked and beaten at the third battle of Winchester and then beaten twice more in rapid succession. By the end of October, the campaign was over. Early's army had been decisively beaten and scattered, and all its equipment was either captured or destroyed. The army was never re-formed, although some elements did find their way back to Lee. The Union victory was a combined effort of both the Union infantry and cavalry. The latter had finally proved itself superior to the Southern cavalry.

Sheridan carried out Grant's order to burn all crops, machinery, and outbuildings. It would take the valley several years after the war to recover fully.

Early fled the country for Cuba and Canada at war's end. In 1869 he returned to Lynchburg, Virginia, where he resumed the practice of law. He died in 1894, still "unreconstructed."

Sheridan commanded in the west during the Indian wars and ultimately became commanding general of the armies. Emory, Crook, Merritt, and Custer all remained in the army, the latter three serving in the Indian wars. Custer achieved fame because of his "last stand," but Merritt went on to become superintendent of West Point and head of the Philippine expedition in the Spanish-American War.

The story of the "Heavies" ultimately became tragic. They were thrust as untrained infantry onto a battleground that evolved too far from its Bull Run origins for them to be able to understand. Consequently, unlike the veterans, they did not know when to tacitly resist when ordered to storm an impregnable rampart or even to lie down and take cover rather than to stand and fight on open ground. The battlefields of the Overland Campaign and of Petersburg all have suitable memorials at places where one or another heavy artillery regiment gloriously (but needlessly) took 60 to 70 percent casualties in a single afternoon.

Captain Oliver Wendell Holmes went on to become one of the most long-lived and best-regarded justices of the U.S. Supreme Court. It would be sixty years before he would lay claim to the "damn fool" remark. (It is suspected that the remark was actually made by one of the enlisted men in his command, but then it wouldn't be much of a story.)

CHAPTER XII
We Look Like Men of War

General Grant was not a man who was much given to reflection and introspection. In fact, one of the strongest aspects of his character was his ability not to let setbacks and missed opportunities break his concentration or divert him from his purpose. (Before the evening of the first day of the Battle of Shiloh, the Union army had been forced to retreat to a small pocket with its back to the Tennessee River. As Grant and Sherman stood in this constricted area looking out over the encircling Confederate campfires, Sherman observed, "Well, general, we've had the devil's own day, haven't we?" Grant responded, "Yep, lick 'em tomorrow, though." That promise and its fulfillment typify Grant's character.)

By late June 1864, however, Grant's patience was being sorely tried. No matter whether he attempted to control the Army of the Potomac directly or through Meade, he seemed unable to cause it to move with sufficient alacrity to capitalize on its opportunities. Thus, the great flanking attack on Petersburg had failed, and the army was now forced to conduct a siege. Coupled with this was the abject failure of subordinate commanders such as Ben Butler and David Hunter to properly execute their portions of the master strategic plan. Their failure had forced Grant into more of a head-to-head confrontation with Lee than he would have preferred. Finally, there was the astounding pertinacity of Lee himself. The old lion had been wounded during the past several months and had lost his offensive punch, but as Grant was learning to his chagrin, a cornered animal is both wily and dangerous.

Grant's impatience was more than just psychological. It was also political. There was more at stake than his personal gratification and future ambition. A real possibility existed that the stalemate at Petersburg (coupled with the concurrent stalling of Sherman's drive on Atlanta) would cause war weariness to rise to the point where the North might seek a peace involving Southern separation. Certainly the North would be unwilling to indefinitely sustain casualties at the rate of the Overland Campaign's (1,000 men per day in the Army of the Potomac alone).

Lincoln, although remaining steadfastly supportive of Grant and Sherman, was fearful of this result. During July he prepared a memo, whose envelope he asked his cabinet officers to sign, in which he stated his fears that he would lose the election in November. In that event, the memo continued, he and the president-elect must cooperate to win the war before March 1865, because the president-elect would have won the election on a platform that would make winning the war thereafter impossible. Such a possibility was also apparent to Davis and Lee. It was their last rational basis for continuance of the war.

Grant therefore needed a dramatic means of breaking the deadlock and capturing Petersburg. There was no point in considering a frontal attack. That would produce another Cold Harbor and be suicidal. A successful flank attack around Lee's right would do the trick, but Lee had the interior lines. If Grant were to send a massive encircling force to his left, it could be successfully countered by Lee's bending his right side to the south. This might cause Grant to weaken his center and so invite a counterattack that could split his army in two. There was no obvious solution. All Grant could do was to keep gradually extending his line to the west until, finally, his superior numbers forced Lee's line to break. There was no doubt that this strategy would ultimately succeed, but it would take time. Time was the one resource that Grant didn't have.

While Grant and Meade pondered these matters, a chance remark between two enlisted men triggered an idea in the mind of their regimental commander that would eventually find its way to the commanding general. The regimental officer was Lt. Col. Henry Pleasants, a civil engineer and commanding officer of the 48th Pennsylvania infantry.

The 48th had been recruited in the coal country of Schuylkill County, Pennsylvania, and many of its members were formerly coal miners. The conversation that Colonel Pleasants overheard was between two such miners who were examining a Confederate fortification directly opposite their position in the Union line. One of the miners remarked that they could blow that fort away by digging a tunnel underneath it and planting explosives at the end of the tunnel. That thought intrigued Colonel Pleasants and started an increasing preoccupation that eventually became an obsession. That the thought ever occurred to anyone, however, was the result of a peculiar coincidence. Once again fate selected to forever illuminate an otherwise totally obscure part of the landscape.

The Confederates were under heavy pressure from Smith's and Hancock's corps during their retreat from the Dimmock Line in early June and had fallen back to the last possible ridge to the east of Petersburg. They then had no alternative but to fortify this line and hold it; an in-depth defense was impossible. Moreover, because the Federals had hard-pressed the defenders, the distance between the two sides was only several hundred yards wide. Both sides had cleared the ground in between of all trees and bushes so as to provide clear fields of fire. Thus, almost everywhere on the line, the possibility was nil of digging a 500-foot mine shaft without being observed by the enemy.

There was, however, one exception to this state of affairs. There was a section of the Confederate line to the southeast of the city known as Elliot's Salient. At this spot a deep ravine separated the two lines. The slope of its bank was gentle on the eastern (Federal) side but somewhat steeper on the western (Confederate). Poor Creek ran through its bottom. Scrub brush, which provided limited cover, still grew on the banks of the creek, but above it the eastern and the western slopes were clear. The Federals posted several artillery batteries on the eastern edge. The Confederates had built a major earthwork fortification on the western crest.

During the June 15–19 offensive, Federal forces had stormed across Poor Creek and established an infantry line at the foot of the western slope. Thus, the opposing lines here abutted by no more than 500 feet. Because of the slope, it was not easy for the Confederates to observe the infantry entrenchments, although they could clearly see the Northern works on the opposite side. The two miners that Pleasants had overheard had been standing in the infantry trench and looking up through its firing slit at the Confederate fort on the crest. It was pure happenstance that a regiment of coal miners chanced to be assigned to this particular area, where their talents could be used to good advantage.

Elliot's Salient was unique in another way. It was the defensive work that protected the suburb of Blandford and the Petersburg town cemetery. These were located on high ground that overlooked downtown Petersburg. If Union artillery could be placed at the salient, it could dominate Petersburg as far as the banks of the Appomattox River and all road and railway connections into the city. Petersburg would become untenable, and its abandonment by Lee would be imperative. This would force the evacuation of Richmond by the Confederate government. Once the Union forces were past the salient, a half-mile advance up a gentle hill would bring them to these commanding heights. Thus, the removal of the fort on the crest would be the single most tactically advantageous move that the Union could make.

The more Colonel Pleasants considered the possibility of undermining the salient, the more excited he became. Finally, he approached his division commander, Gen. Robert Potter, and enlisted his support. The two then presented the idea to their corps commander, none other than Gen. Ambrose Burnside, once more restored to a command of great responsibility. Pleasants advised Burnside that the mine entrance would be sheltered from Confederate view and would slope uphill, thus eliminating drainage problems. Although the shaft would be more than 500 feet long, Pleasants was sure that it could be ventilated.

Burnside said he would discuss the idea with the army commander, General Meade. Meade liked the idea in principle, because it offered an alternative to a stalemate, but his West Point training cautioned him that 500 feet was beyond the existing state of technology for tunneling. He called in his military engineers for a consultation. The engineers dismissed the whole suggestion. Yes, mining an enemy fortification was an accepted siege technique, but 500 feet was simply too long. A shaft of that length could not be ventilated and would probably collapse on the miners.

Meade told Burnside that he appreciated his initiative (which he expected of a corps commander) but that the idea was impractical. Meade advised Burnside to use his ingenuity in a different manner. However, Meade gave Burnside implicit permission to get started, although it was clear that Meade was authorizing what he thought would be a make-work project to keep otherwise idle men busy. He offered no logistic aid to support Pleasants's efforts. Burnside reported this to Potter and Pleasants but told them that they had his support and should commence work. Meade also mentioned the idea casually to Grant, but he and Grant continued to think of it as a long shot.

With this limited backing, Pleasants went to work. Because he was receiving no official cooperation, all arrangements had to be improvised. There were plenty of picks and shovels, but the picks were of the wrong shape. Pleasants, therefore, had to induce 9th corps blacksmiths to recast his pick blades to suit his purpose. We do not know what blandishments were offered, but some must have been necessary. There is an old army tradition (which probably originated before the Punic Wars) that no soldier ever provides unofficial services without something in exchange.

Pleasants appointed a pit boss and designated miners to work in shifts around the clock. He had three main problems to confront. First, he must remove the excavated dirt and dispose of it so it would not be seen by Confederate observers. For this purpose he was to receive wheelbarrows and sandbags from headquarters, but these never materialized. Pleasants therefore collected hardtack cracker boxes, reinforced these with barrel hoops, and attached handles. Disposal parties would fill these boxes and drag them to the foot of the ravine. There, the dirt would be dumped and branches would be laid on top to conceal it.

Second, there was the problem of obtaining the huge number of cut timbers that were needed to shore up the tunnel. For this purpose a preexisting railroad bridge in the ravine was torn down, and all its timbers were used. Additional timbers were shaped in an abandoned sawmill that Pleasants discovered about five miles behind the lines. He prevailed upon Burnside to allow a squad of men to be detached to run the mill and to handle the horses and wagons that were needed to bring the timbers to the tunnel entrance. The project had by now grown to the point that practically all the men in the 48th Pennsylvania performed some function connected with it.

There remained the bugaboo of ventilation. Here, Colonel Pleasants's plan was simple but ingenious. Once the mine shaft reached a certain distance, Pleasants had a vertical shaft sunk to intercept a small alcove to the side of the main tunnel. He next prepared a square wooden tube to extend from a point beyond the tunnel entrance to the working face of the mine shaft. Then he sealed the entrance to the mine so that air could enter only through the wooden tube. Acting on the principle that hot air rises, he kept a fire burning continuously in the alcove. As the fire burned, it sucked stale air out of the tunnel and sent it up the vertical shaft. Fresh air flowed in through the wooden tube to fill the vacuum so created. The working end of the mine remained ventilated, regardless of how far the shaft progressed, simply by extending the wooden tube.

With these problems solved, the excavation developed into a day-in, day-out occupation. Remarkably, in spite of the now apparent feasibility of the project, neither Meade and his engineers nor Grant seemed able to develop any enthusiasm for it. When Pleasants tried to obtain a theodolite, an instrument to be used for triangulating the exact position of the fort, the engineers turned a deaf ear. Pleasants's requisitions kept getting "lost." Ultimately, Burnside had to write to a civilian friend residing in Washington to obtain the necessary instrument.

Two potential hazards remained. The Confederates might see the smoke rising from the ventilation shaft and wonder about its source. The Confederates might also suspect the existence of a mine if they heard mysterious underground noises. Countermines would then be sunk in order to locate it.

Smoke turned out not to be of consequence. There were several reasons for soldiers to build fires, even in the summertime, such as cooking, blacksmith forges, and lead ball preparation. These did not invite suspicion. Just to be safe, however, Pleasants arranged to build several random campfires in the area simply to accustom the Confederates to the presence of round-the-clock smoke. The stratagem worked. Confederate battle reports never mentioned that the South's suspicions were aroused by the presence of smoke plumes.

The Confederates did notice odd noises within their works that seemed to come from underground. They also observed that the opposing sector of the line seemed abnormally quiet. They thus conceived of the possibility of a mine, although Southern engineers, like their Northern counterparts, dismissed the idea as infeasible. The Confederate commander of the fort was not satisfied. To be certain he ordered the digging of several vertical shafts to intercept any horizontal tunnel. The Union was in luck. None of the several shafts intercepted the tunnel. Reassured, the Confederates abandoned digging and resumed their day-to-day occupations.

When Burnside observed that work was proceeding satisfactorily, he undertook to devise an attack plan that would capitalize on the explosion. Burnside's 9th corps was composed of four divisions. One of these would be used to spearhead the assault, and the remaining forces would be used in its support. Three of the divisions had been engaged throughout the Overland Campaign and clearly showed the effects of a war of attrition. The fourth division, however, had seen little action and was close to full strength. Designation of the latter as the assault division seemed the obvious choice, but there was one big problem. The fourth division, under Gen. Edward Ferrero, consisted entirely of black troops. The other divisions were white.

Burnside, to his credit, chose the fourth division to lead the attack based on its numerical strength and readiness, and he ignored its racial composition. Given the pervasive prejudice that then existed, the other three divisions probably would have questioned the black troops' capability to lead an attack. If, however, they had been asked the color they preferred for the resulting corpses, there is no doubt how they would have responded. Griping, therefore, was at a minimum. Ferrero's division was sent to the rear to train for its new mission.

There the men developed that sense of pride that goes with knowing that one has been entrusted with a special and vitally important responsibility. A sign of that pride was a song that they sang as they trained, the chorus of which was:

> *We look like men a marchin' on*
> *We look like men of war.*

The plan was for them to go "over the top" of the infantry trench as soon as the mine exploded and then charge uphill to fan out on either side of the newly formed crater. Those troops that were on the extreme left and right were to make a ninety-degree turn at the crater and to capture the adjoining Confederate trenches. The main body of the division, at the center of the line, was to continue the forward advance beyond the crater, bearing to the right. This would lead them to Blandford and the summit of Cemetery Hill. There, they were to hold their ground until the supporting divisions of the 9th corps came up. On paper, the plan seemed flawless, with the added virtue of being unambiguous.

While this plan was in preparation, Burnside again approached Grant and Meade for final permission to mine the fort. His case was now stronger; it was apparent that the shaft would in fact reach the Confederate line in spite of the engineers' naysaying. Neither Grant nor Meade was hidebound. They were content to concede that they had been in error, and both generals now agreed to the attack. Meade authorized that it be made on July 30 and that the entire 9th corps be used. Grant further ordered the 2d corps to create a diversion by making a feint attack near Richmond. That would induce Lee to strengthen his northern flank by pulling troops away from Petersburg and should thus reduce resistance at Elliot's Salient.

The feint went as planned. By July 29, 1864, Hancock's 2d corps had returned to its Petersburg lines, having successfully diverted half of Lee's available force to the north. The mine was undiscovered by the Confederates and had been packed with blasting powder. Ferrero's troops had been drilled incessantly and were at a peak of readiness. Then, less than twenty-four hours prior to the scheduled attack, Meade had a last-minute reservation that, on reflection, Grant supported. Meade instructed Burnside to substitute one of the white divisions for Ferrero's as the spearhead of the attack. Burn-

side protested that it was too late to make such a change, but Meade
was adamant.

It all seemed logical, but it was to be their collective undoing.
Meade's decision was based upon political rather than military considerations. By mid-1864, black troops had been recruited in large
numbers and were well on their way toward attaining the level of
180,000 that they would reach by the war's end. Normally, however,
they were not used in active combat because of the then generally
accepted conception that blacks were timorous and unaggressive. No
one really knew how they would behave under fire, particularly if they
were leading an attack.

Meade's concern was that the high command not appear to be using black troops as "cannon fodder" in hopeless situations. It would
be catastrophic to the army's political support if such a concept
should gain credence among radical Republican congressmen or the
leaders of the abolition movement. Two more vocal and strident ide-
ological interest groups could not have been found. Meade was not
as sanguine as Burnside that the mine explosion would ensure success. Moreover, he was aware that Southerners bitterly resented the
recruitment of their former slaves into the Union army. Black troops,
if surrounded, could expect no quarter and would not be taken prisoner. Thus, if a Union general were to order thousands of black
troops into a battle where they might become entrapped, he was
inviting atrocities on a massive scale. Ferrero's division contained
4,300 men.

This reasoning was very logical and persuasive to Meade and
Grant, but the decision totally unnerved Burnside. Until now his behavior as a corps commander had been exemplary. From here on,
however, the Union cause would have been better served if he had
folded his tent and headed home to Rhode Island. Burnside did not
fold his tent, but he did lose his ability (such as it was) to make critical judgments. Meade had deflated him to the point that he could
no longer make rational decisions.

His first subsequent action was to convene a council of war with
his four division commanders. After announcing Meade's decision,
he invited the three remaining generals to draw straws to determine
who should lead the attack. Drawing straws might have been ap-

propriate if the remaining divisions were each ably led, contained equivalent numbers of battle-wise veterans, and had each suffered equal amounts of recent battle casualties. Such was not the case. Two of the divisions were equal to any in the Army of the Potomac and were commanded by experienced officers, Gen. Robert Potter (to whom Pleasants had originally submitted his idea) and Gen. Orlando Willcox. The third division was commanded by Gen. James Ledlie. Both it and its commander were reputed to be among the weakest in the entire army. As fate would have it, the short straw was drawn by Ledlie.

Ledlie's troops consisted primarily of heavy artillery regiments that Grant had released from the Washington fortifications. Although the "Heavies" had successfully made the adjustment to combat condition in other army corps (to the point of foolhardiness in some cases), those regiments in Ledlie's division were not well regarded. In fact, the entire division was gun-shy, thanks in large part to Ledlie's having volunteered them for a suicidal charge against Lee's fortifications at the North Anna River. It hadn't taken a genius to realize that Ledlie's main consideration had been personal glorification, not the men's welfare. Ledlie himself was without military experience and had spent most of the war rising to command a New York heavy regiment. He was not only incompetent but was also an alcoholic and a coward. The latter trait distinguished him from his peers, even if the former two flaws were commonplace. His normal approach to a battle was to hide somewhere in the rear and drink himself into oblivion. This, of course, was well known to his men but seemed to have escaped the attention of General Burnside.

So it was that on the day before the planned attack, and to their mutual amazement and consternation, Ferrero's men were withdrawn from the front line and Ledlie's men were sent forward to replace them. Neither were instructed in their new roles. Ferrero's men were not told that they had been replaced. The mine's existence was confirmed to Ledlie's men (theretofore it was only a rumor), but they were simply advised to storm the opposite line immediately following the blast and then to follow the orders of their field officers.

Detonation of the explosion was scheduled for 3:30 A.M. on July 30, 1864. Pleasants was supposed to receive a "galvanic" detonator from army headquarters. It too never materialized. Pleasants improvised by splicing lengths of conventional fuse until he had a cord several hundred feet long. This was attached to 320 kegs, aggregating 4 tons, of blasting power that were arrayed in a lateral gallery stretching under the Confederate fort. Sandbags were placed between the kegs and at the end of the mine shaft to prevent a blowback.

Shortly before 3:30 A.M., the fuse was lit; 3:30 arrived but nothing happened. Then 4:00 A.M. and finally 4:15 A.M. arrived, still without any explosion. It was clear that the fuse had failed. Sergeant Harry Reese, the pit boss, went in at great personal risk, respliced the fuse at the break, relit it, and just managed to escape the tunnel before the mine exploded at 4:45 A.M.

Many soldiers who were present spent the rest of their lives trying to describe what happened next. There was a deep rumble, and the hill in front of them seemed slowly to rise. Suddenly, there seemed to be a volcanic eruption. Fire leapt out of the earth. Men, cannons, and equipment were thrown in every direction as the whole top of the hill seemed to lift into the air and hover above the attacking force. The Union troops were terrified. Looking up, they thought they were about to be buried under tons of earth. They ran screaming to the rear, and a quarter of an hour passed before they could be brought back in line.

Those Confederates who had not been blown up were equally terrified. They too abandoned their positions on either side of the newly formed crater and fled for their lives. Thus, at 5:00 A.M. there existed a hole in the Confederate line that was 500 yards wide. All the 9th corps had to do was charge through it, and Petersburg would fall. One thing, however, was certain. They had to move fast and purposefully. The Confederates would not remain stunned forever.

Unfortunately for the Union, Murphy's Law remained in full force and effect. First, it was discovered that there were no steps or ladders at the bottom of the front-line trenches. Heavily laden soldiers simply could not get out. Eventually, improvised ladders of bayonets stuck into trench walls or piled sandbags permitted egress, but it was slow, and valuable time was squandered. Next, supporting troops behind the first attack wave were instructed to approach their own front line via the covered ways (sheltered approach trenches). This caused massive traffic jams and was unnecessary, because few Confederates were then firing into the ravine. A direct march from the rear to the front line would have been reasonably safe and much faster.

Little by little, Ledlie's men got out of their trenches and struggled to the top of the ravine. There, they discovered a hole more than 100 feet long, 60 feet wide, and more than 30 feet deep. Inside it was an incredible hodgepodge of half-buried men and equipment. Ledlie's men, unlike Ferrero's, had not been told that they were to ignore the crater and to proceed around it to gain the high ground. The one man who did know the plan and who could have given them on the spot instruction, General Ledlie, was nowhere in evidence. He was instead hiding in a bomb shelter behind the Union line, bottle in hand. (Here he was later joined by General Ferrero, who also decided to desert his troops at a critical moment.)

Ledlie's troops, receiving no orders, stopped at the edge of the crater and gawked. After a while, many descended into it and started to pull out buried men and equipment. While Ledlie's first brigade was plunging into the crater, his second brigade came up. Its officers urged them to form a defensive line on the far side, but most of them also climbed down into the crater. Thus, in the critical early moments, Ledlie's division was totally disorganized and concentrated within the crater.

Finally, some of Potter's and Willcox's support troops came up. Slowly, they occupied the abandoned Confederate trenches and then attempted to resume the advance. The situation by now was much different than it had been a half hour before. Confederate infantry and artillery had now begun to re-form a few hundred yards behind their original line. Gaining strength as time went on, these forces now succeeded in pinning down the Federals. By 7:00 A.M. the Federal advance was stalled at the far edge of the crater.

Back at headquarters, Meade kept demanding to know from Burnside what progress was being made. Burnside did not know. He had no concept of the status of the battle. As at Fredericksburg, all he could think to do was to throw in ever larger numbers of men. He accordingly asked Generals Ord and Warren, the corps commanders on either side of his troops, to make supporting attacks.

Both tried, but Burnside's rear was so clogged that nothing could get through. Now, when all opportunity was gone, Burnside ordered Ferrero's black division into action.

Ferrero's division entered the battle at 7:30 A.M. By then the Confederates had reoccupied portions of their original line, from which they now fired as these troops were scaling the ravine. When they reached the crater, they skirted it to the right, as ordered, and attempted to advance to Cemetery Hill. By now this was hopeless. The hill was crowded with Confederates who not only stopped the charge but drove the men back into the captured trenches to the right of the crater. No safety could be found there. Conditions in the trenches were so crowded that no defense could be organized. The Confederates were pouring withering rifle volleys into this constricted group, and Confederate mortars and enfilading cannons had also found the range. The trenches could not be held. Ferrero's men were forced back into the crater itself.

By midmorning, Grant and Meade resigned themselves to failure and ordered Burnside to withdraw his men. Burnside, however, still believed that success was possible. The recall was not sounded. All that the delay accomplished was to increase the butcher's bill and add to the prisoner list. The battle finally ended about midafternoon.

The North reported casualties of 3,800 men. Of these, more than a third were in Ferrero's division. Grant observed in his official report that it was "the saddest affair I have witnessed in the war. Such an opportunity for carrying fortifications I have never seen and do not expect again to have."

AFTERMATH

The failure of the crater attack spelled the end of Grant's offensive to break through the Confederate lines around Petersburg. General Lee also clearly wished to break out of his trench line and return to a battle plan of entrapment and counteroffensive. That alone would offer the South some possibility of actually defeating Grant's army. Such a strategy, however, was impossible; retaining Petersburg was Lee's only means of defending Richmond. To attempt it would also involve the risk of being overwhelmed by Grant's larger force as Lee attempted to break contact. Much as Grant and Lee both sought to avoid a state of siege, they were locked into it, in spite of the fact that Lee's army was by no means encircled.

Grant's strategy for conducting the siege was twofold: use heavy siege artillery to pulverize Confederate emplacements to the south and east of Petersburg (as well as to make the city itself uninhabitable), and extend the Union line to the west and northwest until all of Petersburg's supply routes were cut.

The siege artillery consisted principally of heavy howitzers and mortars. Both fired large explosive shells that were triggered by a length of burning fuse. Fuse lengths were cut by the artillery men to correspond to desired ranges. In both cases the shape of the shells' trajectory was an arc, so that the shells would descend from an altitude above whatever lateral ramparts protected the intended target. A howitzer's trajectory subtended an angle of arc of approximately thirty degrees. The subtended angle of a mortar shell's flight was upward of forty-five degrees. It was not easy to manually aim either a heavy howitzer or a mortar. Thus, both were customarily employed from permanent emplacements against stationary targets (such as a fort) whose range and bearing had previously been triangulated.

Mortars were squat, heavy-walled cylinders suspended by pivots from their supports. They varied in size from large to enormous. The smaller "coehorn" mortars had a bore of as little as 4.5 inches and shot a 20-pound shell. The largest mortar of the war, used at Petersburg, was the "Dictator," which cast a 220-pound bomb out of a 13-inch bore for a range of more than 2 miles. Larger mortars were mounted on flatcars so that they could be moved anywhere that a railway siding could be placed.

Howitzers were smaller. A field artillery model usually threw either a 10- or 18-pound shell or canister. The siege version had an 8-inch bore and could cast a 50-pound shell for 1,200 yards. Howitzers resembled ordinary cannons except their barrels were shorter and their elevation was higher.

The installation of the siege guns at Petersburg was easier than at Yorktown two years earlier. There, barges had brought the weapons to a proximate landing site along the York River; from there the weapons were hauled by teams of men and animals to their intended emplacements. In Petersburg the combination of existing water and rail facilities made movement and emplacement easier. Even a piece as cumbersome as the Dictator could be brought up the James by ship for landing at the deepwater terminal of City Point. There, it would be off-loaded onto a railway flatcar that rested on a siding by the dock. The weapon could then be transported to its approximate position by the U.S. Military Railroad. The flatcar, upon arrival at its destination, would be switched onto a newly constructed siding, then brought to its place of installation.

The mortar normally would remain permanently on its flatcar, which would act as a firing platform and recoil arrester. Manual labor was thus largely eliminated. Although labor would be used to build the revetments within which the weapon could be housed, even this was frequently unnecessary. The mortar could often be located behind the reverse slope of a hill because its trajectory was high enough to permit the shell to pass over the top of the hill after firing. The hill itself became the mortar's revetment.

One of the main problems associated with emplacing mortars was to provide for their firing recoil. For cannons and howitzers, this simply entailed ensuring that there was adequate space behind the weapon and some means of arresting its backward movement and returning it to its firing position. The direction of a mortar's recoil was downward as well as backward. Unless the base of the mortar was strongly reinforced and provided with some means of absorbing impact, the base would invariably be destroyed. No ordinary flatcar would serve. Reinforced cars and rails had to be designed and produced.

Upon the arrival of siege artillery, Grant opened an eight-month barrage against opposing entrenchments and supply dumps. No doubt some shells were also fired indiscriminately as a weapon of terror to induce the citizenry to panic and flee. It didn't work. In time, Petersburg's residents became so blasé that they would proceed on their errands about the city even as an artillery barrage was in progress.

Grant's strategic purpose was to choke off supplies. Petersburg was a transportation hub, but some of its supply routes were already in Union hands. Thus, the road and railroad to Norfolk were useless to the South, as was the City Point Railroad. The Jerusalem Plank

Road, the city's main north-south highway, became a no-man's-land a few miles south of the city. Thus, it was of no value as a supply route. Lee's capacity to endure rested on the preservation of his three remaining routes: two railways and a road. The two railroads were the Weldon Railroad, which entered from the south and connected the city with North Carolina, and the Southside Railroad, which entered the city from Lynchburg to the west. Between the two ran the Boydton Plank Road, which exited Petersburg to the southwest but later curved south.

The Weldon Railroad was under Confederate control up to a point about twenty miles south of the city. Beyond that it was still within Confederate territory prior to August but was subject to increasing "smash-'em-up" Federal raids. By the end of August, Union infantry had gained a permanent foothold on the Weldon and finally severed its link to the city. Lee countered by off-loading freight from northbound trains at the northernmost station under his remaining control and transferring it to wagons. These were then sent westward down local roads until the junction with the Boydton Plank Road. The wagons would then proceed down Boydton to the city. Thus, by September, Lee's reliable routes had been reduced to two fragile arteries, the Boydton Plank Road and the Southside Railroad. These had to be defended at all costs.

One of the few beneficial results of the battle of the crater was the shaking up of the Union high command. Burnside had blundered once too often. After the battle he was relieved of command of the 9th corps and sent home to Rhode Island to "await orders." These never came. Burnside resigned from the army on April 15, 1865.

Burnside's disastrous military career typifies the strange hankering for military glory that throughout the North gripped otherwise contented and successful civilians. A few, such as John Logan, Joshua Chamberlain, and Benjamin Grierson, discovered a natural military talent and served their country well. Most, such as Burnside and "Commissary" Banks, provided more inadvertent comfort to the enemy than assistance to their own cause. Burnside was otherwise a successful and capable man. He was the inventor of the Burnside carbine and owner and president of the company that produced it. After the war, he served three terms as governor of Rhode Island and was an incumbent U.S. senator when he died in 1881. It is ironic that a man who so much sought glory is today remembered chiefly for his facial hair, that is, sideburns.

It remains a mystery how General Ledlie survived his previous repeated string of failures so as to still remain in command of a division in July 1864. The crater, however, finally proved his undoing. After the battle he was faulted by a court of inquiry and personally read out of the army by Gen. Meade. Nonetheless, he later prospered as a civil engineer and died in 1882.

General Meade's position became increasingly awkward as the Overland Campaign progressed. Grant seemed to constantly intrude on his prerogatives as commander of the Army of the Potomac. Grant personally liked Meade and found him an exemplar of soldierly virtue. He certainly meant him no harm. What Grant could not tolerate, however, was the lack of accountability that was the hallmark of the Potomac army (of which Meade was a product). Grant thus relied increasingly on generals in whom he had full trust, notably Sheridan, and for practical purposes relegated Meade to a chief-of-staff function. Meade bore it with patience. After the war he served with fairness and compassion as a military governor of Georgia. He died in 1872.

The Confederate general who rallied the Southern forces and sealed the breach in the line was William Mahone, a Virginian and Petersburg resident. Mahone's reputation had been rising throughout the Overland Campaign, and Lee was increasingly using his brigade as shock troops. Because of Mahone's success at the crater, he was promoted to major general and given command of a division, which command he retained until Appomattox. After the war, he became active in Virginia politics and was elected to the U.S. Senate in 1880. He died in 1895.

Ferrero somehow escaped inquiry in spite of his dereliction of duty at the crater. Although his division served diligently until the end of the war, it was never again able to attain that special spirit that the French call élan, and it was never again heard singing its special marching song.

With the departure of Burnside, Ledlie, and Ben Butler (whose relief occurred in November 1864), the modern adaptation of the legend of Cincinnatus and the minutemen came to an end. Never again would the U.S. Army appoint amateurs to lead field armies into battle. This was reflective not just of common sense but also of the changing nature of society as a whole. A new class of professionals was arising in business, government, and academia. West Point ceased to be principally an engineering school and became in fact what it had always been in theory, a college to train men in the profession of war. The dawn of specialization had arrived, and the nation and the world would henceforth follow that course at an accelerating pace.

CHAPTER XIII

That's When I Knew We Were Beaten

By mid-August 1864, life for the ordinary soldier and junior officer in the Army of the Potomac had become a humdrum routine of ever-increasing boredom. This had its advantages. At least the soldiers did not have to steel themselves each morning to the prospect of that day possibly being their last. One should not, however, conclude that the men were beyond harm behind their fortifications. The opposing lines remained very close, and irregular fire emanated from the trenches on either side. Picket duty was most feared. This involved standing guard as part of a thin line of skirmishers in rifle pits dug in the no-man's-land between the lines. One could easily be picked off when so exposed. Even more dangerous was running the gauntlet of covered ways to get to and from one's picket post.

The purpose of pickets was to give early warning of an enemy attack. Soldiers were more apt to conclude that it was an attempt to propitiate the daily appetite of some bloodthirsty god, so senseless did it seem. Pickets on both sides learned early that nothing would be gained from shooting one another, so they usually arranged informal cease-fires among themselves. Both sides equally detested sharpshooters acting as snipers. To the common soldier such men were no better than cold-blooded murderers. They were shunned by their own comrades, and if captured and identified they were apt to be lynched.

As a result of both picket duty and random rifle and artillery fire, casualties continued to be incurred on a slow but steady daily basis. Moreover, engagements kept occurring at either end of the opposing fortifications as the two sides shifted and extended their lines. Finally, the army's old nemesis, disease, returned with a vengeance. The soldiers were living in crowded earthworks that were lacking in sanitation and were infested with lice and vermin. The soldiers were unable to bathe for weeks at a time and were exposed to weather ranging from baking heat to freezing cold. Every imaginable form of illness became endemic. This provided Grant with another reason, if any more were needed, to break the siege.

Grant still retained the initiative but had given up the illusion that one grand maneuver would produce sweeping victory. The battle would now be carried on in increments, with Grant following a localized version of Gen. Winfield Scott's Anaconda plan. Little by little, Lee must be choked until he strangled. Only then would he leave his works and head for open country, where Grant would be capable of delivering a coup de grâce.

Grant's advance in late June had temporarily severed the Weldon Railroad, but Confederate General A. P. Hill found a gap between the two attacking Union corps. Hancock's 2d corps was caught in the flank and thrown back with heavy casualties. This not only temporarily restored the line to the South, but it also illustrated how badly the Union army was being used up. When the 2d crossed the Rapidan in May, it had been the army's best corps. Since then, it had suffered almost a complete turnover. Now it retreated in panic with only minimal provocation. It needed total reorganization.

At the end of August, General Warren's 5th corps was ordered to gain permanent control of the railroad. They succeeded. Lee was left with only two arteries, the Boydton Plank Road and the Southside Railroad.

Grant now fell back on a tactic that he had first used during the battle of the crater: feint in front of Richmond to pull Lee's forces to the northeast, then open an assault on the weakened western flank to break Lee's supply lines. Grant tried this twice during September and October 1864 with offensives at Peebles Farm and the Vaughan

Road. In both cases, Lee's Boydton Plank Road defenses were threatened but held. Lee entered the winter months with his remaining
supply lines intact but increasingly in jeopardy.

The protracted stalemate at Petersburg, with its ever-increasing ca-
sualty list, was not aiding Lincoln's election campaign. In fact, the
successes that later enabled Lincoln to gain a renewed mandate for
continuation of the war came entirely from outside Petersburg. At
last, the North was awakening to the thought that the war would not
be decided in Tidewater Virginia but in the "west."

The first such indication came in early August from Admiral Farragut's victory at Mobile Bay, Alabama. Mobile was the last active Confederate port on the Gulf Coast. It stood at the head of an enclosed
bay guarded by a series of barrier islands. Because of this geography,
there were many small unguarded channels leading into the bay that
blockade runners could use. Beyond the barrier islands, the bay itself was Confederate controlled and provided runners with safe passage. Thus, considerable freight was continuing to reach Mobile in
spite of the Federal blockade.

Farragut assembled a fleet of fourteen wooden warships and four
ironclads and again raised his flag on the USS *Hartford.* The fleet
could enter the bay only up a narrow channel past a minefield (the
mines were referred to as "torpedoes") on their left and Fort Morgan and the docked Southern ironclad *Tennessee* on their right. As
the fleet proceeded up the channel, the Federal ironclad *Tecumseh*
struck a mine and sank. The vessels then slowed and milled about
uncertainly while Fort Morgan raked them with fire. Farragut, seizing the moment, cried out, "Damn the torpedoes! Full speed ahead!"
and steered *Hartford* to the head of the column of ships. These then
entered the bay without further loss.

Upon the fleet's arrival the CSS *Tennessee* steamed to intercept it
against odds of seventeen to one. Although her armor could not be
penetrated, she lost her funnel. This reduced the vacuum in her engines and lessened her motor power. She next had her steering shot
away. Helplessly adrift, she was forced to surrender to Farragut.
Shortly thereafter, Fort Morgan also surrendered.

Farragut now controlled the bay. The South still held Mobile, but
that didn't matter. It could no longer be used as a port. After a spring

in which the North experienced mayhem, stalemate, and frustration, Farragut's victory had a dramatic impact. He was lionized throughout the Northern states.

Next, dramatic word was received that on September 1 Sherman had broken the two-month siege of Atlanta and occupied the city. His situation had resembled that of Grant. Notably, Atlanta was a transportation hub with railroads reaching the city from the northeast, southeast, southwest, and northwest, respectively. Throughout the summer, Sherman had contested Bragg's former army (now under Gen. Joe Johnston) for control of northern Georgia and had advanced down the Western and Atlantic Railroad from Chattanooga to the gates of the city. Johnston's army (only half the size of Sherman's) had carried out a skillful retreat but finally stood on the banks of the last natural barrier before Atlanta, the Chattahoochee River. President Jefferson Davis was fed up with Johnston's policy of retreat. When Johnston fell back beyond this last line, Davis replaced him with J. B. Hood, a general known for head-down frontal assaults while posted as a division commander under Lee.

Sherman could not take Atlanta by frontal attack. So, like Grant, he sought to cut the three remaining railroads that supplied the city. In this, he was inadvertently assisted by Hood's taking the offensive. In three furious attacks against segments of Sherman's army, Hood successively lost control of each of the city's three remaining railroads. When these were gone, he was forced to abandon the city.

Finally, a heroic story of peril, rescue, and ultimate triumph was received from the Shenandoah Valley. In July, Gen. Jubal Early's army had been turned away from Washington only by the last-minute intervention of the Potomac army's 6th corps. To counter this threat Grant then ordered an increased force of infantry and cavalry, under Gen. Philip Sheridan, to drive Early from the valley and to destroy that region's capacity to produce foodstuffs. Sheridan spent a month in organization. Then in late September he inflicted two major setbacks on Early, at Winchester and Fisher's Hill.

Early, though defeated, had not been driven from the field. In mid-October, he discovered a means of outflanking "Little Phil's" line at Cedar Creek and struck it while Sheridan himself was in the city of Winchester, some twenty miles away. By noon, Early's attack had

routed all but one division of the Union army. Then Early paused
(against the advice of his deputy) to consolidate his gains.

While this was occurring, Sheridan was riding pell-mell from
Winchester to the battlefield, rallying his retreating army ("God
damn you! Don't cheer me. Fight!"). By midafternoon he restored
his formations and delivered a pulverizing counterattack. Early's
army lost its equipment and was driven from the valley. It never recovered (although some of its units later rejoined Lee's army).
Sheridan was acclaimed, and a poem, "Sheridan's Ride," popularized
his feat throughout the North. (Sheridan observed prosaically that
the poet seemed more interested in his horse than in him.)

Farragut's, Sherman's, and Sheridan's triumphs revitalized Lincoln's election campaign. In November, he beat the Democratic
nominee, General McClellan, by obtaining 55 percent of the popular vote and practically all that of the electoral college. Further evidencing Northern resolve, the soldiers' vote went overwhelmingly for
Lincoln. In several states it provided the winning margin. The
South's last hope was gone.

Simultaneously, the Petersburg campaign ground on and took on
an air of permanence. During the summer Grant established his field
headquarters at City Point, Virginia, at the confluence of the James
and Appomattox Rivers. Declining accommodation in a prewar
mansion, he set up his living quarters and office in a small wooden
cabin near the docks. Thereafter, the general's staff, together with
quartermaster, legal, and medical officers assigned to the base, established their offices in a tent city on the lawn adjoining the general's cabin.

By early October, the first nip of approaching winter was in the
air, and tent living was becoming uncomfortable. No one, however,
dared approach the general in chief to obtain authorization to erect
winter cabins; to do so would be to acknowledge that the siege would
not be lifted before spring. Thus, the staff shivered until November,
when Grant went to Washington for consultations. Upon his return
the following week, the commanding general discovered that the
tents had vanished. They had been replaced by neat rows of wooden
cabins similar to his own.

City Point facilities before the war had consisted of the modest dockage needed to load the tobacco, cotton, and corn grown in the Petersburg region for export. By September 1864, the docks had vastly expanded, and City Point became the busiest port in the United States. A single pier lined the James for more than a mile. Every day approximately 40 steamboats, 75 sailing vessels, and 100 barges used that dock. At the head of the pier was a rail yard from which several rail sidings descended down its entire length. The pier was bordered by commissary, quartermaster, and ordnance warehouses. An engine roundhouse and repair shed adjoined the rail yard.

City Point also provided many other necessary facilities, including a 200-acre tent hospital, a medical evacuation pier, the regional head-quarters of the U.S. Sanitary Commission, a courthouse and jail, a facility for exchanging prisoners of war, a post office, offices for the chaplain corps and the U.S. Christian Commission, and a telegraph office with a direct line to Washington. Bakeries, forges, wagon re-pair shops, and barracks for the garrison rounded out the complex. The whole installation was ringed by trenches that were permanently manned by an assigned garrison.

The complex was too vast and too crucial for the Confederates not to attempt sabotage. This might also bring them the added benefit of the death or injury of General Grant or his staff. Thus, on August 9, 1864, an ammunition barge, on which two Confederate spies had planted a time bomb, exploded while the barge was alongside the loading pier. Forty-three people were killed and 126 injured. Great damage was also done to the dock and adjoining warehouses. How-ever, neither Grant nor any senior staff member was injured, nor was the port's cargo-handling capacity significantly impaired. Within days the installation was back in full operation. The explosion was thought to be accidental. Confederate involvement was not realized until the confession of one of the Southern operatives many years later.

Before the war the City Point Railroad right-of-way ran for ten miles to the terminal of the Southside Railroad in Petersburg. By mid-June 80 percent of that trackage was in Union hands, but it was in very poor condition and had been laid in the Southern gauge rather than the Union's standard gauge. To expedite matters, most of the rails that the army relaid were salvaged from the Richmond and York River Railroad (McClellan's old supply line).

By July 7, 1864, train service was resumed to Pitkin Station (immediately behind the eastern portion of the Union fortifications), and the line was made part of the USMRR system under the overall charge of Gen. D. C. McCallum. The superintendent of the Alexandria district, which was now enlarged to include Petersburg, was his son, J. McCallum. Chief engineer and head of construction for the district was J. J. Moore, who was detailed to survey a new route to extend the line to the south and west of the city. In September, nine miles of track were laid as far as Yellow House, the 5th corps' headquarters to the west of the Weldon Railroad. In November, the line was extended farther west to Peebles Farm, a grand total of twenty-one miles from City Point. A southward branch line was added in December.

There were many "stations" along the line. These consisted mostly of supply dumps, troop disembarkation points, medical transport areas, or coffin loading locations. The line was characterized by short, steep grades. One observer compared the progress of its trains to that of a fly crawling over a washboard. At its peak it was handling an average of eighteen trains a day, each with fifteen to twenty-five cars. Its most famous passengers were President and Mrs. Lincoln.

By December, major military activity ceased, not to be resumed until February. Within the city the civilian population made an effort to preserve some semblance of holiday gaiety. "Starvation balls" (at which nothing but cold water was served) became the social events of the season. A large number of civilians remained in town in spite of the danger. Their reasons were primarily economic—their income and wealth were derived from the city. To leave meant impoverishment and probably homelessness, unless they had relatives living elsewhere. Bad as conditions were in town, homelessness in the latter days of the Confederacy was much worse.

In February, Grant resumed his attacks at Hatcher's Run and the White Oak Road, these being additional attempts to capture the Boydton Plank Road. Southern counterattacks temporarily prevented its loss, but Lee was stretched to his limit. Grant's next move was obvious: send a force south and west to Dinwiddie Court House and then march north to cut the Southside Railroad to the west of the existing trench lines. Being deprived of both the railroad and the Boydton Plank Road, Lee (and Richmond) would be cut off.

The troops to do this were at hand. Sheridan's decisive October battle of Cedar Creek (coupled with a follow-up victory against its survivors on March 2, 1865) had scattered Jubal Early's army in the Shenandoah Valley and so freed Sheridan to return his army to Grant. Ever the realist, Lee resigned himself to the loss of both Petersburg and Richmond and concentrated on his only remaining option, the withdrawal of the Army of Northern Virginia before Sheridan rejoined Grant.

Lee knew that Grant had posted most of his offensive power at the two ends of his line, that is, to the north directly confronting Richmond and to the west near Dinwiddie Court House. Lee presumed that Grant's line to the east of the city was thin and manned by second echelon troops. Therefore, Lee devised a plan that would amass portions of all three of his infantry corps and a division of cavalry to punch through the center of the Union line. All told, 11,500 men would make the direct assault, with another 8,200 in reserve. This was to be an all-or-nothing offensive that would utilize the entirety of Lee's remaining strength. The corps of Gen. John B. Gordon, a young officer who had risen to high Confederate rank after the first generation of generals was incapacitated, provided most of the attack force. Gordon himself was placed in overall charge.

The plan called for the capture of Fort Stedman, an earthwork to the east of the city and somewhat north of the crater battlefield. This would be followed by the capture of three smaller forts that were thought to be immediately to Fort Stedman's rear. When a gap in the Union line was firmly established, support forces would seize the trenches to the right and left of the opening, while the remainder of Lee's army passed through the hole and headed south.

Everything was carefully planned. First, a company of axmen was to be sent forward to clear away the abatis (pointed stakes) and other obstacles between the two lines. This was to be followed by a 100-man strike force to storm Fort Stedman, on whose heels were to follow the three additional 100-man forces needed to capture the three satellite forts. An artillery barrage and mass attack would follow when the several forts were taken. If all went as planned, the Northern army would be sufficiently stunned to enable Lee to gain the lead he needed to unite his army with that of Gen. Joe Johnston in North Carolina.

Every contigency that could be anticipated was analyzed. Gordon left nothing to chance and tried to capitalize on every advantage. The following detail is illustrative. As Confederate fortunes waned during the winter, there was an increasing number of deserters who daily entered the Union lines. In time, a tacit code was implemented. If a Confederate was observed trailing his rifle stock along the ground, this meant that he was deserting and so should not be fired upon. Gordon therefore ordered his axmen to trail arms when they approached the Union lines so that their real purpose would not be discovered.

At 3:00 A.M. on March 25, 1865, all was ready. The attack was about to begin when a poignant moment occurred. Earlier that night the Confederate axmen had been noisy in removing obstructions, and a Federal picket had called out: "Hello there, Johnny Reb, why are you making all that fuss over there?"

General Gordon was nonplussed, but an alert private at his side called back: "Never mind us, Yank; lie down and go to sleep. We are just gathering a little corn. You know our rations are mighty short!"

The Yankee picket responded, "All right, Johnny, go get your corn. I won't shoot at you."

The Confederate troops breathed a collective sigh of relief and went back to work. Later, when the attack was to commence, Gordon ordered a cannon signaling the charge to be fired. The same private who had responded earlier to the Federal picket now hesitated to fire the signal cannon and called out, "Look out for yourself now, Yank, we're going to shell the woods."

This debt of honor to his Yankee counterpart having been paid, the private fired the signal. Gordon later commented that he was moved by these acts of chivalry by both sides as much as by any other minor incident of the war.

Bang! Bang! Two shots were fired, and the 100-man strike force charged, with the 300 remaining assault troops following immediately behind. They soon achieved their initial objective. Fort Stedman was overrun, as were Federal artillery batteries X and XI to its immediate right and left.

The Confederates had succeeded in driving a hole in the Union line but had now reached their high-water mark. Things started to go wrong. First, the three satellite forts that the Confederates had planned to capture did not exist. There was thus no way to advance by moving from strongpoint to strongpoint. Second, the commotion at Fort Stedman had alerted the two adjoining Union forts, McGilvery and Haskell. Their suspicions were confirmed when they observed soldiers within Fort Stedman firing a captured cannon in the "wrong" direction. Both Union forts swiftly loaded their guns with canister and turned them ninety degrees in anticipation of being attacked. Finally, it became apparent that the Union line was defended in depth. Behind the front line lay a reserve division whose function was to seal any breakthroughs in this sector.

Once again, there is an almost Greek sense of destiny's having sought retribution. The troops who manned Fort Stedman were from Willcox's division of Burnside's ill-fated 9th corps. The reserve division was Ledlie's former third division, now commanded by General Hartranft, a competent veteran of the eastern campaigns. The reserve division was now filled with new Pennsylvania regiments that had been recruited to replace the many casualties that Ledlie incurred at the crater. Together, the two forts and Hartranft's division sealed the breach. The Confederates held their captured ground but could go no farther.

The game was lost. Lee's plan required that his army break free and escape while the North was still stunned. Now the South could do nothing but wait in the captured entrenchments until the North mustered overwhelming force against them. At 8:00 A.M. on March 25, Lee gave up and recalled his men. The Army of Northern Virginia had just mounted its last offensive. Lee had lost 4,000 men (killed, wounded, or captured) without any tangible gain. His remaining options were few and forlorn.

Captain R. D. Funkhouser of a Virginia regiment had been fighting all morning. Toward 8:00 A.M. he tried to lead several of his men back to the Confederate lines but was stunned by an artillery shell and captured. Brought to the rear of the Union line, he was amazed to see President Lincoln (who had arrived that morning on the City Point Railroad) calmly reviewing troops as if nothing unusual had occurred that day. All around the captain was the usual hustle-bustle of supplies being unloaded, blacksmiths working at forges, and chaplains leading prayer services. Funkhouser took a searching look at this purposeful but tranquil scene that had barely been interrupted by the Confederacy's maximum effort. He and his fellow prisoners were forced to agree that the Confederacy was beaten and its cause was lost.

AFTERMATH

As Lee had feared, Sheridan returned approximately 25,000 cavalry and infantry to Grant on March 28, 1865, after having captured earlier in the month most of Jubal Early's last remaining 2,000 men. Grant promptly put Sheridan in charge of the western segment of his line, with instructions to outflank Lee and to sever the Southside Railroad. He was given two infantry corps and three cavalry divisions to accomplish this. Lee could concentrate less than half that number to oppose him.

The decisive battle came on April 1, 1865, at a country crossroad west of Petersburg called Five Forks. (Five roads converged at the crossroad, giving the spot strategic significance—all east-west or north-south traffic in the locality had to pass through it.) The Confederates had amassed five thin divisions of infantry and dismounted cavalry and entrenched them on an east-west line through the intersection along the White Oak Road. The defenders were under the local command of General Pickett (of Gettysburg fame).

Two roads entered the crossroad from a southerly direction: one from the south, the other from the southeast. Sheridan's cavalry (mostly dismounted) under Generals Custer and Devin approached up the southern road toward a face-to-face confrontation with Pickett. It was assumed by Sheridan that General Warren's 5th infantry corps was moving up the southeasterly road toward the Forks. (General Warren was another Gettysburg hero. It was his timely decision to station troops atop Little Round Top that kept the Union army from being outflanked.)

General Sheridan's plan was to have his dismounted cavalry pin down Pickett's forces by frontal assault. General Warren's corps, as it arrived, would then hit the Confederate left flank and roll up Pickett from the Federal right to left. This would uncover the road leading north from the crossroad. One mile to the north, this road intersected the Southside Railroad. If Sheridan reached that intersection, Lee's last connection would be closed. Lee accordingly ordered Pickett to hold Five Forks at all cost.

Pickett posted his men and decided to protect his left flank (which was "in the air") by angling it to the north (that is, refusing the left). Satisfied with his dispositions, he received a courier from "Rooney" Lee, General Lee's son, who commanded the dismounted cavalry division on Pickett's right flank. Rooney Lee was inviting Pickett to a "shad bake" luncheon behind the lines. Given the state of the Confederate commissary, this was a real treat. Pickett readily accepted, after having convinced himself that no action would occur that afternoon. He compounded his mistake by not informing his second in command of his whereabouts.

Sheridan's cavalry arrived at the Forks early in the afternoon and formed a battle line. Sheridan, who under the best of circumstances had a "short fuse," awaited Warren's arrival with mounting impatience. His mood was not improved by mulling over his previous judgment, formed during the Overland Campaign, that Warren was a timorous dawdler—in Sheridan's eyes, a typical Army of the Potomac general. Finally, when 4:00 P.M. arrived without Warren's having come up, Sheridan would wait no longer and attacked with his cavalry alone.

Warren, in fact, had come up. Instead of arriving at the Forks, however, he came up a road about a mile to the east. Warren then crossed the White Oak Road and attacked, but he missed Pickett's left flank, which was located a half mile to his west on the far side of some intervening woods. Warren's first and second divisions thus marched north into a vacuum. His last division, however, heard firing to its left and made a ninety-degree turn. Within a few minutes they were engaged in a firefight with Pickett's "refused" left flank. Warren heard this firing coming from his left rear and realized his mistake. He then turned the leading divisions ninety degrees and marched left.

What had begun as a blunder now became a tactical master stroke. Warren had marched far enough north not only to outflank Pickett's refused flank but also to have gone north of the Confederate division that Pickett had stationed at his rear in reserve. Thus, Warren's attack brought about a grand envelopment that hit Pickett in both his left and rear. The left side of Pickett's line collapsed under the assault.

While this was transpiring, Pickett and Rooney Lee were enjoying their shad bake. This occurred only a mile behind the line, but it appeared that its location was in an acoustical shadow. Thus, Pickett and Lee didn't hear battle sounds until they became overwhelming. They also had not been notified that action had commenced, since their whereabouts were unknown. When they finally returned to the battle line, the battle was already lost. They did succeed in mounting a last-ditch defense. This permitted some additional Confederates to escape to the west and north and so to avoid capture, but this was a small consolation.

General Warren, at the head of his first division, arrived at the crossroad toward evening expecting Sheridan's praise for the decisive role that the 5th corps had played in the action. Instead, Sheridan dressed him down like a West Point plebe for delay and ineptitude that might have caused the loss of the battle. Then and there, Little Phil relieved Warren of his command and instructed him to report back to Meade for reassignment.

Warren was aghast. He could see that Sheridan was totally enraged, and he begged him to defer his order until he had calmed down and had a chance to reconsider the matter dispassionately. Sheridan categorically refused and told him to turn over his command to General Griffin and to depart the field. April 1 had proved to be a bad day for Gettysburg heroes.

The battle of Five Forks was decisive. Lee's flank was turned, and Petersburg had become indefensible. In a week's time, Lee had incurred more than 10,000 casualties, and thousands more (Pickett's survivors) were cut off from the rest of the army. In desperation Lee worked to extricate his remaining 35,000-man army. Only a suicidal "hold at any cost" defense by two Confederate forts to the west of the city gained the necessary hours for Lee's men to cross the Appomattox River and withdraw first to the north and then to the west. The army marched all night with neither sleep nor food to gain time. It worked. By morning Lee had a twelve-hour head start.

Lee's plan was to reassemble his scattered corps at Amelia Court House on the Richmond and Danville Railroad about fifty miles west of Petersburg. In his final telegram to the Confederate War Department that recommended the Confederate government's evacuation from Richmond, Lee had also asked the department to send rations by rail to Amelia to await the army's arrival. When Lee's forces arrived at Amelia the following morning, they discovered that the requested freight cars had arrived but that they were filled with miscellaneous equipment that was of no value to the army. The chaos of Richmond's last days had caused the government to dispatch railcars indiscriminately without first removing their contents.

Lee's men had not eaten in two days. The general had no choice but to send his wagons into the countryside around Amelia seeking foodstuffs. In the process he sacrificed his head start. This allowed Sheridan to seize the key rail junction of Burkeville. Lee's way south was blocked. Disaster now followed disaster. Lee recrossed the Appomattox River and turned west, but a miscue caused the loss on April 6 of 8,000 men, fully one-fourth of his remaining army, at Sayler's Creek. Lee's hungry, exhausted remnant struggled on until it was surrounded in the fields near Appomattox Court House. Lee's options had finally run out.

Lee sent an emissary to Grant requesting terms. Grant had suffered all the previous night from a fierce migraine headache, which instantly disappeared when Lee's message arrived. The two agreed to meet at the village of Appomattox Court House. One of Grant's staff selected the modest brick home of farmer Wilmer Mclean as the site for their meeting.

Here arose another of those weird coincidences with which the Civil War abounds. Farmer Mclean originally lived on the banks of Bull Run in Manassas Junction, Virginia. After the First Battle of Bull Run, he decided to move his family to a place where "the sound of battle would never reach them." He chose the totally unstrategic hamlet of Appomattox Court House, but he could not escape destiny. The war that began in Mclean's backyard ended in his front parlor. The name of this perfectly ordinary and obscure citizen is now forever inscribed in the annals of American history, and his home has become a national shrine.

Lee arrived first in full dress uniform followed by Grant who was embarrassed by his muddy trousers and boots. They reminisced briefly about meeting each other during the Mexican War and then turned to business. Grant's terms were simple and generous. The Confederates were to be paroled, their arms and insignia (not including officers' horses and side arms) were to be stacked and surrendered, and the men were to return to their homes, "there not to be disturbed by the United States authorities as long as they observe their paroles and the laws in force where they may reside." By these mighty words Grant forever slammed the door on any campaign of revenge or retribution that some ambitious politician might try to launch against their now defenseless foes. Lee read the proposed terms and thanked Grant for their generosity. He observed, however, that, as written, they did not permit enlisted men (who in the Confederacy owned their own horses) to recover their animals, which they would need for plowing. Grant advised that he could not change the written terms but would nonetheless permit all Confederate soldiers who claimed a horse or mule to take one.

As the two emerged onto the Mclean porch, they heard cheers start to rise from the Union troops. Grant immediately ordered it stopped, stating, "The war is over, the rebels are our countrymen again, and the best sign of rejoicing after the victory will be to abstain from all demonstrations." This was the finest moment of Grant's life. Even though the luster of his name was tarnished by his later presidency, his behavior at Appomattox deserves the undying gratitude of the nation. Lee too rose to the occasion and deserves our admiration. His final address to his troops firmly discouraged any band of Confederates from going underground and conducting guerrilla warfare.

Only one ceremony remained, and for the Confederates it would be the hardest. They must stack and surrender their weapons, regimental insignia, and battle flags so that these might never again be used as a source of inspiration to future demagogues or separatists. General Joshua L. Chamberlain, the valiant savior of Little Round

Top at Gettysburg, was given the honor of commanding the Union troops at the ceremony. The ceremony would entail the Union forces lining either side of a wide path down which the Confederate formations must pass. General Chamberlain would be mounted at the head of the Union line. General John Gordon, also on horseback, would lead the Confederate infantry regiments.

After their breakfast (on rations provided them by General Grant), the Confederates dismally formed up and started their slow march toward the waiting Yankees. Both General Gordon and his men had their heads down with expressions of great dejection on their faces. General Chamberlain was moved to compassion at the sight of these proud and resolute men brought to such low estate by their absolute devotion to their cause. These men were Lee's finest, the men whom no amount of suffering, hardship, or privation could induce to desert.

Chamberlain could not let the moment pass without some form of recognition. As General Gordon approached at the head of his column, Chamberlain ordered the salute: not the formal "present arms" display but the more informal rifle salute by which comrades acknowledge each other. Chamberlain himself raised his sword in salute. Gordon, with eyes downcast, heard the jingling of uniform fittings and observed Chamberlain out of the corner of his eye. Instantly alerted, Gordon sat erect in his saddle and with one fluid motion drew his sword, raised it above his head, and bowed deeply to Chamberlain. He simultaneously gave the order to return the salute to the Confederate infantry behind him. Silently, heads erect and eyes forward, rank on rank of Confederate soldiers gravely returned the salute that regiment upon regiment of Federals delivered.

This was one of the great tableaux of American history. A close acquaintance and veteran leader of many a battlefield tour observed as we were standing on the site of "Surrender Triangle," where it all occurred, that if he could miraculously be transported back to the Civil War epoch for only one moment in time, this was the time and place that he would choose. I share his sentiments.

It is true that, after Appomattox, small Confederate armies under Johnston, Taylor, and Kirby Smith still remained in the field, but their time there would be brief. Victory had been achieved, and all that generals and privates could do to start the healing process had been accomplished. Now it was up to the citizenry and their political leaders.

After the war General Lee turned down many offers of prestigious jobs and accepted the post of president of small Washington College (now Washington and Lee) in Lexington, Virginia. Throughout the remaining five years of his life, he threw his tremendous influence into the reconciliation of the sections, urging Southerners to put aside bitterness and again become loyal Americans. Ironically, he himself was never pardoned. Neither was his citizenship restored nor his property returned. The grounds of the Lee estate now make up Arlington National Cemetery.

Grant, of course, went on to become the eighteenth U.S. president. High hopes were held for his presidency because his intentions toward Native Americans, blacks, and Southerners were enlightened and generous. However, two traits that had served him well during the war now played him false. He was too loyal to his friends and favorites, some of whom now betrayed him. He was also too determined never to fail, particularly monetarily. This led him to associate with unsavory business elements and to oversee (but not participate in) corruption. Never a good businessman, he failed in his investments, and he was reduced to relying on the charity of associates and admirers. Finally, fighting a last heroic battle against throat cancer, he completed his memoirs (and thus provided for his widow) just before his death in July 1885.

Grant created a dynasty of generals in chief that lasted through the Spanish-American War. He was followed by Sherman, who presided over the Indian Wars until his retirement in 1883. Sherman was followed by Sheridan, who served until his death in 1888. Schofield was next, serving until 1895. General Nelson A. Miles, a self-made man who commanded a brigade in the Army of the Potomac, followed Schofield. Highly ambitious, he later served as the prison warden of Jefferson Davis for the two years of the latter's imprisonment. He was also the captor of the Indian chief Geronimo. He served until 1903 and was the last Civil War major general to die (May 15, 1925).

General Warren was not able until 1879 to obtain a formal hearing to clear his name after his abrupt removal by Sheridan on the field of Five Forks. The tribunal deliberated for more than two years before finally exonerating him. The exoneration came too late. Warren died three months before its results were published. Today, one condemns the army, not Warren (or the similarly maligned Gen. Fitz-John Porter), for the unconscionable delay in permitting justice to be done.

CHAPTER XIV
No Such Army Since the Days of Julius Caesar

I beg to present you as a Christmas gift the City of Savannah with 150 heavy guns, plenty of ammunition and also about 25,000 bales of cotton." So Sherman telegraphed to President Lincoln on December 16, 1864. The march to the sea was over. The army that had disappeared from the view of an anxious North in November had emerged victorious at Fort Pulaski near the mouth of the Savannah River in December and had restored communications with the North. The incredible campaign that had begun that spring in Chattanooga now ended both in Nashville and in Savannah. The Confederacy that had remained following Vicksburg and Chattanooga was now neatly split in half. For practical purposes, only the Carolinas and southern Virginia carried on the Southern cause.

The campaign had started on May 7 at Tunnel Hill, that fateful elevation that Sherman had been unable to wrest from Gen. Pat Cleburne during the battle of Chattanooga. Now Sherman had 98,000 men confronting 53,000 Confederates under Joe Johnston across the valley. Grant had given Sherman a three-fold mission: invade the interior of the South Atlantic states, damage their war resources, and break up Johnston's army. Sherman accordingly drove straight down the Western and Atlanta Railroad to Atlanta, the Southeast's main industrial and communications center.

Sherman's first tactical maneuver exemplified his conduct of the entire campaign. Using the armies of Thomas and Schofield to hold Johnston in place, he sent General McPherson's army to the south to emerge on the railroad in the rear of General Johnston. Johnston escaped the pincers but at the cost of yielding miles of territory. So the pattern persisted in battle after battle, until Johnston finally dug in upon the largest natural barrier on his path of retreat, Kennesaw Mountain. Sherman, for once, substituted a frontal assault for a flanking maneuver. He was made to regret it. In short order, he lost 2,000 men to Johnston's 500 and thereafter resumed flanking operations.

When Johnston was maneuvered into abandoning the last natural obstacle before Atlanta, the Chattahoochee River barrier, President Davis gave up on him and his tactics. On July 17 he replaced Johnston with Gen. J. B. Hood, who immediately went over to the offensive and attacked General Thomas's army at Peachtree Creek. Hood incurred 4,800 casualties and fell back into the city.

Sherman did not pursue but skirted Atlanta to the north in order to strike eastward against Decatur, a station located on the Georgia Railroad between Atlanta and Savannah. On July 22, Hood caught McPherson's army in an isolated position to the east of the city, but faulty coordination caused his attack to misfire. McPherson's army escaped, causing more casualties than they received, but General McPherson was killed. He was replaced as commander of the Army of the Tennessee by Gen. O. O. Howard, formerly the head of the Army of the Potomac's "infernal Dutchmen."

Sherman now turned his attention to the two railroads that ran north to Atlanta from Montgomery, Alabama, and Macon, Georgia. The Union moved to cut the railway from Montgomery. On July 27, as Howard's army was moving from north to south, Hood hit Howard on the flank at Ezra Church. Howard's flank, however, was protected by the corps of Gen. John Logan, which threw back Hood, again inflicting heavy casualties upon him.

Hood's offensive capacity was now diminished, but he still held the city and the railway to Macon. Sherman then sent the Federal army south of the city on a broad sweep to his right. On August 28, Federal forces captured a section of the Macon near Jonesboro. Hardee's corps was forced to retreat. His last railroad gone, Hood had no option but to abandon the city. On September 2, Sherman occupied it.

Superficially, it appeared that Sherman and Hood had now shifted roles. Sherman was defending the city, while Hood's army was threatening Sherman's railway connections with Chattanooga. Such a comparison would, however, be illusory. Sherman knew precisely what he wanted and how he would accomplish it in spite of Hood. Moreover, he had the power to back up his intentions. Hood was reduced to employing ever more unlikely tactics to attempt to bring about Sherman's withdrawal.

As expressed in letters to Generals Halleck and Rawlins, both dated September 1863 (a year before Sherman's capture of Atlanta), Sherman's philosophy was straightforward and unyielding. His letter to Halleck stated:

> War . . . should be "pure and simple" as applied to the belligerents. I would keep it so, till all traces of the war are effaced; till those who appealed to it are sick and tired of it, and come to the emblem of our nation and sue for peace. I would not coax them, or even meet them halfway, but make them so sick of war that generations would pass away before they would again appeal to it.

Sherman's letter to Rawlins stated:

> I would make this war as severe as possible, and show no symptoms of tiring till the South begs for mercy; indeed, I know, and you know, that the end would be reached quicker than by any seeming yielding on our part.

As Sherman had a philosophy, so he had a plan to accomplish it. He would evacuate the civilian population of the city of Atlanta and destroy its industrial, military, and transportation capabilities, leaving the hapless civilians to fend for themselves as best they could. Atlanta's citizens begged him to relent, and General Hood protested on their behalf. These remonstrances Sherman brushed aside, as follows:

> I give full credit to your statements of the distress that will be occasioned by [the order], and yet shall not revoke my orders, simply because my orders are not designed to meet the humanities of the case. . . .

You cannot qualify war in harsher terms than I will. War is cruelty and you cannot refine it, and those who brought war into our country deserve all the curses and maledictions a people can pour out. You might as well appeal against the thunderstorm as against these terrible hardships of war.

But Sherman reminded them in a letter to Atlanta officials:

Now that war comes home to you, you feel very different. You deprecate its horrors, but you did not feel them when you sent carloads of soldiers and ammunition and molded shells and shot to carry war into Kentucky and Tennessee, and desolate the homes of hundreds and thousands of good people who only asked to live in peace at their old homes and under the Government of their inheritance.

In a letter to Hood, Sherman said:

If we must be enemies, let us be men, and fight it out as we propose to do, and not deal in hypocritical appeals to God and humanity.

These comments hit a nerve throughout the entire South. This was the "dirty underbelly" of all that fine talk about "the states' right to secede" and "our sacred duty to preserve the Southern way of life" that had swept the South since Lincoln's election. Nobody had counted on this. In the beginning, some Southerners had really believed that peaceful separation was possible and were content to let it happen even though it was not their preferred choice. When war came, they believed it would be short, remote, and chivalrous. Now they found themselves caught in a revolution as violent and unpredictable as that experienced by the citizens of Paris in the days of the Reign of Terror. Southerners, even those with stout hearts, began to wonder for the first time how the conflict might be ended before everything worth preserving was swept away.

They would have been horrified if they could have predicted the next move. Sherman intended nothing less than to cut his supply lines and to march down what would become a fifty-mile-wide corridor of destruction from Atlanta to the sea. He recognized that this was perfectly possible, telling Halleck, "Where a million people find subsistence, my army won't starve."

In part, Sherman's intended action was a recognition of military necessity. The army, having captured Atlanta, could not stay there. The long, tenuous rail supply line stretching all the way to Louisville, Kentucky, could neither be defended nor sustained. Similarly, Sherman's army could not "occupy" Georgia without effectively taking itself out of any further active participation in the war. Sherman, however, recognized that occupation was not necessary as long as the Southern civilian population was made to feel the sting of war. He reasoned that if war became painful enough, then Southerners would force their leaders to give up the illusion of Southern nationhood and sue for peace. His point of view was forcibly expressed by the following quotations from a letter to Roswell Sawyer, dated January 31, 1864:

War is simply power unrestrained by constitution or compact. The people of the South having appealed to war are barred from appealing to our Constitution, which they have practically and publicly defied.

I believe that some of the rich and slave-holding are prejudiced to an extent that nothing but death or ruin will extinguish, but hope, as the poorer and industrial classes of the South realize their relative weakness and their dependence upon the fruits of the earth and the good will of their fellow men, they will discover the error of their ways. To those who submit to the rightful law and authority, all gentleness and forbearance; but to the petulant and persistent secessionists, why, death is mercy and the quicker he or she is disposed of, the better.

All of this strikes even the modern ear as being somewhat blood-curdling. Sherman nonetheless never had the intention of emulating Attila the Hun. The "rules of the game," as laid down in his Special Order 120 (November 1864), spell out his terms of engagement:

The army will forage liberally on the country during the march [but] soldiers must not enter the dwelling of the inhabitants or commit any trespass. In districts and neighborhoods where the army is unmolested, no destruction of such property should be permitted; but should guerrillas or bushwhackers molest our march, or should the inhabitants burn bridges, obstruct roads or otherwise manifest local hostility, then army commanders should order and enforce a devastation more or less relentless, according to the measure of such hostility.

In other words, barring guerrilla warfare, the real estate and personal property of unoffending residents should be left alone, although crops and livestock could be seized freely. Sherman was well aware that he could not completely enforce these orders, although he would later boast that:

No city was ever occupied with less disorder or more system than that of Savannah, and it is a subject of universal comment that, though an army of 60,000 men lay camped around it, women and children of a hostile people walk its streets with as much security as they do in Philadelphia.

Sherman's words and actions must be seen within the context of the times. Southern leaders in the spring of 1864 were giving no indication whatever of a desire to end the war. In fact, if anything, their dedication to their cause grew increasingly intense as the likelihood of its success diminished. In July 1864, President Jefferson Davis advised self-appointed Northern peace emissaries:

. . . now [the war] must go on . . . unless you acknowledge our right to self-government. We are not fighting for slavery. We are fighting for independence and that, or extermination, we will have.

Similarly, in May 1864 as the Overland Campaign started, Lee predicted: "If victorious, we have everything to live for. If defeated, there will be nothing left to live for." As late as February 1865, he added: "[the South] cannot barter manhood for peace nor the right of self-government for lives or property."

Given such sentiments on the part of their enemy, attitudes in the North were changing. No longer was this a "brother's war." It had become relentless and remorseless. The North had evolved from a war aim of capturing territory ("On to Richmond") to that of beating Southern armies and finally to one of terrorizing and impoverishing the civilian population as being the only means of appealing to it over the heads of their political leaders. Sherman was the first of the North's leaders to make this ultimate transition.

Over one brief month Sherman carried out his plan of "making Georgia howl." Behind him the state of Georgia was demoralized. He had also planted seeds of despair among Georgia's soldiers serving away from home in the various armies. Now, as for their brothers in Tennessee and Virginia, their personal property was destroyed and their families were left destitute. They had little left for which to fight.

Occupying Savannah in December 1864, the western commander rested his men and contemplated their next move. The population of Georgia and the Carolinas cowered. Their previously well-ordered world had been shattered in less than a year. Now they could only contemplate in horror what might next occur and pray that they be given a brief respite. Their hope was that General Grant would order Sherman to Virginia to merge his western army with the Army of the Potomac. Failing this, they might at least assume that the weather would be their ally and that the combination of winter rains and large, full, eastward-flowing rivers would preclude the Federals' turning north before spring.

Such hopes might have been realized. General Grant, in fact, proposed to Sherman that his army be transported to Virginia, but Sherman demurred. He presumed (correctly) that the Army of the Potomac alone would be sufficient to subdue Lee. If not, Grant might obtain reinforcements from General Thomas's Army of the Cumberland, which had now decimated Hood's army, thus largely ending Confederate resistance in the west.

Sherman therefore counterproposed that his force should continue immediately on the march, moving northward through the

Carolinas until it reached Virginia's southern border. There, it could assist Grant in closing the trap on both Lee and the small Confederate force that was then assembling in the Carolinas. In this manner the war should be ended by spring. In the interim, retribution could be delivered to the "cradle of rebellion," South Carolina. Sherman planned to commence his march on February 1. South Carolina watched in horror as it became apparent not only that an invasion would occur but also that its onset was imminent.

Sherman in later years would boast that his campaign through the Carolinas was his proudest accomplishment, the march to the sea in Georgia being a "lark" by comparison. The earlier march had been conducted over dry land in pleasant weather. Now the army would be marching in midwinter during a year of unusually heavy rains. Moreover, before reaching their objective, the men would be required to cross nine large rivers and a sodden countryside. Conventional wisdom deemed this to be impossible.

To perform the "impossible," Sherman organized a "pioneer corps" of 6,600 men, mostly lumberjacks from Michigan and Minnesota and rail-splitters from Illinois and Indiana. The main function of this unit would be to "corduroy" roads so as to permit 2,500 wagons and 600 ambulances to accompany the army. Corduroying was necessary because all roads were then unpaved. The best roads were either gravel-topped and graded for drainage or those designated "plank" roads. These consisted of highways that had been "paved" by nailing wooden boards side by side to longitudinal supports placed on either side of the highway.

Even these improved roads were virtually nonexistent in North and South Carolina. The typical "highway" was a compressed dirt path perhaps fifteen to twenty feet wide. Paving materials such as asphalt did not exist and, in any event, could not have been carried in bulk. The only practical way of "paving" a road was to lay log timbers, derived from cutting trees, over the surface of the road. The ridged surface so created gave rise to the term "corduroy road."

Corduroying roads was neither complicated nor difficult. It was merely tedious and laborious. It involved cutting innumerable trees, topping them, removing their lower branches, and then splitting the resulting bare trunks longitudinally to produce two semi-circular timbers. These would be laid, flat side down, perpendicularly across a muddy patch in a road to keep heavy wagons from bogging down at that location.This was adequate, provided there were only occasional bad patches on the road surface to be bridged. It did have its drawbacks, however. If the traffic was heavy or the mud was deep, then the logs would soon be pushed below the surface, and it would be necessary to repeat the process.

Another hazard of corduroying sometimes occurred when a wagon traversed the corduroy off center. In such event, the weight of the wagon wheel hitting the end of a log could elevate the opposite end of that log so as to penetrate the bottom of the wagon. The log, now hanging vertically below the wagon, would firmly implant itself in the muddy roadbed. This would immediately anchor the wagon, bring it to a sudden stop, and block all further progress of the wagon train. Because teamsters were notably profane, the reaction up and down the line of march to such an event can be readily imagined. The only remedy was to saw the offending timber in two, thus enabling the stuck wagon to be pulled off the road for repairs.

There was a second, better method of corduroying roads that avoided this problem and resisted road destruction caused by heavy use, but it required more preparation by the pioneers. This consisted of laying longitudinal support timbers on either side of the road and notching such timbers so that transverse logs could be fitted into the supports. To be really secure, the logs would then be lashed into place, and a second longitudinal support would be laid and lashed on either side across the top of the transverse logs. Thus, a log "mat" would be created and used to make a facsimile of a plank road.

This method was essential when the army was crossing a flooded countryside where the road surface was under water. In such cases not only were log mats required, but the mats themselves would need to be anchored. The log mat was Sherman's "secret weapon." It alone enabled him to traverse regions that others deemed impassable.

Among other functions, corduroy roads were used to transport wounded or injured men. The standard army ambulance was designed to carry up to five litter patients or eight sitting wounded. Like the supply wagon, it had no springs to cushion road shocks, although sometimes straw or branches would be laid in the wagon bed to soften the impact. Nonetheless, the agony that the wounded (who were unsedated) must have suffered riding over such roads for miles in these wagons defies description.

Sherman's army continued to number about 60,000, the same level that was reached the preceding fall when Thomas and Schofield were detached to complete Hood's destruction. The army remained divided into two "wings" of equal size. As in Georgia, these would march in two parallel columns, approximately thirty miles apart, and be mutually supporting, given twenty-four-hour notice. Either wing, however, was deemed capable of withstanding any force that the Confederates should be able to bring against it.

On the right would be the former Army of the Tennessee, now commanded by Gen. O. O. Howard. Under Howard were two army corps commanded by two former congressmen, John Logan and Francis Blair of Illinois and Missouri, respectively. Howard was something of an oddity among generals in that he was not profane, neither smoked nor drank, and was a fervent Christian and abolitionist. In spite of these "shortcomings," he was well regarded by his fellow officers and men as a skillful and humane general who conserved soldiers' lives. Logan and Blair were exceptions to the rule that politicians make bad generals. Both were political generals who had become proficient at war and could hold their own against any West Pointer.

On the left was the other wing, composed of the old Army of the Cumberland, renamed the Army of Georgia. (Thomas's force at Nashville now carried the former title.) The Army of Georgia was commanded by Gen. Henry Slocum, who was, according to Sherman, "one of the best soldiers and best men that ever lived." One of its corps was commanded by a Union general with the unlikely name of Jefferson Davis; the other, by Gen. A. S. Williams. Davis and Williams were competent West Pointers, although Williams was later relieved for not being "sufficiently aggressive."

During the latter part of January, the two wings reached their jumping-off points, and on February 1, 1865, the campaign began. Conventional wisdom was right in one respect. Neither General Sherman nor his "pioneers" were miracle workers who could literally walk on water. They thus could not follow a coastal route that would require them to cross major river estuaries. That, however, was never their intention.

There existed in South Carolina parallel "ridges" of higher ground that separated the various eastward-flowing rivers from one another. The army intended to march along the ridges into the interior and to cross the rivers upstream at points where they were narrower. The army's ultimate goal was Goldsboro, North Carolina, selected because it was at the junction of two railways that connected the city to the North Carolina shore. Arrival at Goldsboro would ensure the resumption of Sherman's supplies and communications.

As Sherman had discovered in Georgia, a Y-shaped advance had the particular advantage of enabling the army to feint to either the right or the left. It thus forced the opposing commander to divide his army to defend cities on either side of its path. This advantage was heightened by the speed of the Union advance, because the Confederate commander was thereby denied the luxury of a last-minute consolidation when the actual direction of the Northern advance became clear. By that time, Sherman would have already outflanked his forces. The Southern general would therefore be forced to continually retreat without contest before Sherman's advance.

On February 1, Sherman's left wing crossed the Savannah River (the boundary between Georgia and South Carolina) at Sister's Ferry, twenty miles upstream from the city. The right wing had previously been transported up the coast to Hilton Head. From there it moved north to Pocotaligo on the Charleston and Savannah Railroad, which it immediately incapacitated. The onslaught of South Carolina had begun.

To Sherman's men, South Carolina was not just another state but the symbol of where treason began. As soon as they crossed its borders, they embarked upon a campaign of destruction that was born of their frustration at having had the course of their own lives interrupted and threatened. Sherman deliberately used the fear that this sentiment provoked among the populace to tactical advantage. "My aim," he said, "was to whip the rebels, to humble their pride, to follow them to their inmost recesses, and make them fear and dread us. 'Fear of the Lord is the beginning of wisdom.'"

The soldiers carried out their instructions, direct and implied, to the letter. A major in Slocum's wing observed, "The army burned everything it came near in the state of South Carolina. Our track through the state is a desert waste." Another infantryman commented, "South Carolina has commenced to pay an installment, long overdue, on her debt to justice and humanity." Among the first towns to be struck was Barnwell, which suffered because of its association with Robert Barnwell Rhett, the "Father of Secession." All that the army left behind were ashes and the suggestion that the town be renamed "Burnwell." Howard's and Slocum's wings would then rendezvous near the town of Branchville on the Charleston and Augusta Railroad, where they would spend two days in track destruction.

Railroad demolition had become a professional specialty of Sherman's soldiers. Demolition gangs would start by raising one rail, still attached to its ties, to a vertical position over the other rail. The still-assembled track would next be rolled forward until a full section had been unearthed. The ties would then be knocked off with a sledge and stacked in a pile over which the separated track would be laid. Bonfires would be made of the piles of ties and tracks, and the tracks became heated to a red-hot state. The heated track would finally be wrapped around a tree or pole to form a "Sherman bowtie" or "hairpin."

The foregoing was considered sufficient, until the soldiers discovered that the process of simply bending track was reversible. To prevent future reclamation, the Federals added the refinement of twisting the hot track laterally as it was being wrapped around its tree. This made such track permanently unusable (short of rerolling it). Because the South's only track-producing rolling mill then in existence, the Tredegar Iron Works in Richmond, was otherwise engaged, a railroad so destroyed could be restored only by cannibalizing other less vital trackage. When Sherman finished, the South could no longer be said to have a railway "system."

To reach the Charleston and Augusta Railroad, Howard had only the Salkehatchie River to cross, but Slocum needed also to cross both the Savannah River and the three-mile-wide Cousawhatchie swamp. Crossing the swamp entailed building a 300-foot bridge and corduroying approaches that were as much as three feet underwater. Amazingly, Slocum arrived only two days after Howard. During the next 2 days the two wings combined to turn thirty miles of railroad into scrap metal.

It was now clear that Columbia, the state capital, was Sherman's next target, but this Confederate deduction was made too late to be of use. The defending commander, General Beauregard, had a force of about 22,000, but as Sherman had foreseen, it was divided. General Hardee had three divisions of infantry at Charleston, and Gen. D. H. Hill had two divisions of cavalry at Augusta. Hill also awaited the imminent arrival of 3,000 survivors of Hood's army under General Stevenson.

Hardee and Hill had hoped to merge forces south of Columbia, but Sherman's advance precluded this. Beauregard reluctantly abandoned Columbia and combined his forces at Chester, fifty miles north of the capital. General Joe Johnston, observing events from western North Carolina, remarked with amazement, "When I learned that Sherman's army was marching through the Salk swamps, making its own corduroy roads at the rate of a dozen miles a day and more, I made up my mind that there had been no such army in existence since the days of Julius Caesar."

Columbia lay at the conqueror's "mercy," a highly qualified virtue. Its situation was worsened by two fateful events. Cotton bales had been removed from warehouses and left in the streets to await transport (which never arrived) to the countryside for burning before the city was captured, and Union troops entering the city were greeted by former slaves offering drinks from their former masters' "liberated" wine cellars. A great fire became inescapable. It laid waste eighty-four of the city's 124 blocks.

Thus ended General Beauregard's tenure as army commander. Lee (now commander in chief of all Confederate armies) sought to reinstate Gen. Joe Johnston, but President Davis bristled. Davis disliked Johnston even more than he did Beauregard. Lee curtly informed him that no other choice was possible, and Davis grudgingly assented.

Forty miles north of Columbia, Sherman made a sharp right turn, after having feinted north in the direction of Charlotte, North Carolina. Incessant rains, however, were finally having an effect. Sherman's army became bogged down for several days in crossing the Wateree River. One member of Slocum's wing, after toiling for three days through mud and chest-high icy water, commented, "It looks like Uncle Billy struck this river end-wise." Within a week, however, the sun returned. Both wings of the army then crossed the Wateree and headed for Fayetteville, North Carolina.

It was now apparent that Sherman was heading for a rendezvous with Schofield (who had just captured Wilmington, the Confederacy's last port). Having left South Carolina, the army changed its mood. No longer were they an avenging army. Sherman ordered his men to "deal as moderately and fairly by North Carolinians as possible." In short order, both wings crossed the Cheraw, Lumber, and Cape Fear Rivers and entered Fayetteville.

General Johnston (now commanding 30,000 men) knew that he must fight before Sherman's 60,000-man force combined with Schofield's approaching army of 30,000 if there were to be any chance of success. He thought he saw an opportunity at Bentonville, a town near the Neuse River (where Goldsboro was also located). Slocum's wing had become strung out along its line of march. Carlin's division of Davis's corps was now alone at the head of the formation. Behind him was Davis's other division, that of James Morgan. Following at a distance were the two available divisions of Williams's corps. Johnston's plan was to entrap Carlin (and possibly Morgan) by having cavalry retreat before him. Carlin would thus be induced to press forward until he was in a position to be attacked on three sides by pre-positioned Confederate infantry. Unfortunately for Johnston, Bragg's division, then retreating from Wilmington, was not as close as Johnston believed and could not reach the battle on time. Thus, when the trap was sprung, the Confederates were inadequate to the task. Carlin's division, with Morgan's support, was able to fight its way out.

Following the battle of Bentonville, Johnston retired to Raleigh. Sherman occupied Goldsboro and joined Schofield, thus completing the mission of his campaign. Neither side knew it as yet, but the last battle of the western army had just been fought.

AFTERMATH

Sherman then departed to attend the River Queen conference at City Point, leaving Schofield in command. Sherman took this opportunity to press upon Grant his desire to have the marching army participate in cornering Lee. Grant was opposed because of the effect this would have on the morale of the Army of the Potomac. Sherman accordingly turned his army toward Raleigh, North Carolina. While on the march, he learned from Grant of Lee's surrender at Appomattox.

General Joe Johnston, recognizing that the plight of his army had become hopeless, sought first to use Governor Zebulon Vance of North Carolina as an intermediary but later agreed upon a direct meeting with Sherman at the Bennett farmhouse (near Durham). Sherman initially proposed terms identical to those given Lee, but Johnston suggested a more comprehensive approach. He pointed out that, unlike Lee, he was not surrounded. Thus, he could escape and lead Sherman on a prolonged chase. Similarly, other Confederate forces were still at large in Alabama and Louisiana and could hold out for extended periods. To avoid this, Johnston offered to surrender all the remaining forces of the Confederacy if Sherman would agree to a general armistice.

This made sense to Sherman. He was not a politician (he was, in fact, an antipolitician) and was anxious to fulfill his repeated promise to the South to change from avenger to friend as soon as hostilities ended. He also recalled Lincoln's River Queen dictum that a peace of reconciliation be established. He therefore eagerly seized the opportunity that Johnston presented. Together, the two generals entered an agreement under which all Confederate forces would be disbanded, their arms would be deposited in state arsenals, soldiers would abide by Federal and state authority, and existing state governments would be preserved but would be "reorganized" by the president. They also agreed to guarantee all citizens "their political rights and franchises, as well as their rights of person and property, as defined by the Constitution."

This was, to put it mildly, politically naive, but it also reflected Sherman's lack of awareness of Lincoln's admonition to Grant not to discuss political questions in any surrender negotiation. When the text of Sherman's agreement was received in Washington, Secretary of War Stanton (the emerging "strongman" of the post-assassination cabinet of the new President Johnson) and the Congress exploded.

Even Grant on initial perusal realized that it "wouldn't do at all." Stanton accused Sherman of planning a coup d'état.

The agreement was "wrong" in virtually every particular. In effect, it ended the war on a status-quo-antebellum basis. Not a single mention was made of the black population. Moreover, because the Thirteenth Amendment had by then passed the Congress but had not yet been ratified by the states, the agreed-upon protection of property, "as defined by the Constitution," left even emancipation in a state of uncertainty.

The plan to stack arms in state capitals seemed to many like a device for having them available in case of a future attempt at rebellion, and the restoration of state government and political rights appeared to absolve all Confederates from war guilt. Sherman went overnight from conquering hero to political goat in the popular estimation.

The administration sent Grant to deliver its official disapproval to Sherman, Grant being considered the appropriate emissary to preclude Sherman's turning ugly. Grant had no such concern, but he welcomed the task as a means of helping his friend suffer only minimal embarrassment. Grant used the assassination of the president rather than substantive arguments as the basis for persuading Sherman to disavow his work. He also for the first time showed Sherman the text of Lincoln's telegram reserving political questions to himself. This pacified Sherman, who commented that "it would have saved a world of trouble" if someone had thought to send him a copy when it was originally written.

Sherman then recontacted Johnston. The latter was cowed by the thought of Sherman's soldiers seeking revenge for Lincoln's death if hostilities continued and so readily agreed to a duplication of the Appomattox terms. Within weeks, the remaining Confederate forces in the west, upon being granted the same terms, also individually surrendered. The war was finally over.

President Jefferson Davis and his cabinet became fugitives following the fall of Richmond. Davis was finally captured in Georgia on May 10, 1865, and was sent to prison in Fortress Monroe. After two years pending trial, he was released on bail and was never prosecuted. He lived abroad until 1877, when he returned to Mississippi. There, in 1881, he wrote *The Rise and Fall of the Confederate Government.* He died in 1889. Never well liked, he was nonetheless respected for remaining proud and unrepentant to the end.

The abortive peace pact had only one aftereffect. It confirmed for General Sherman two of his most cherished beliefs, notably that Secretary Stanton was the vilest reptile on the face of the earth, and that politics, politicians, and all their works were to be despised above all else. When, years later, Sherman was approached to become a Republican candidate for president, he responded with what has become the classic disclaimer in American politics: "If nominated, I will not run! If elected, I will not serve!" To the end of his days, he never understood what was wrong with the Bennett Farm agreement and believed that Lincoln would have approved it.

General Johnston was elected to the U.S. House of Representatives in 1878 (from Virginia) and in 1885 was appointed commissioner of railroads by President Grover Cleveland. Johnston died in 1891 of complications following a head cold that he suffered from having stood bareheaded in February weather as a pallbearer at Sherman's funeral. At the time a friend suggested that he put on his hat, but the eighty-four-year-old Johnston responded, "If I were in his place and he in mine, he would not put on his hat."

In 1865, General Howard became the head of the Freedmen's Bureau for the education and advancement of black citizens; he was also a founder of Howard University. Slocum later served three terms in the House of Representatives and was on the board of the Gettysburg Monument Commission.

Both Generals Logan and Blair resumed their political careers after the war. Logan became a radical Republican congressman and senator and ran unsuccessfully for vice president in 1884. Blair was the Democratic nominee for vice president in 1868 and was appointed to the Senate in 1871 to fill an unexpired term. Blair died in 1875; Logan, in 1886.

General Jefferson Davis remained a professional army officer and fought in the Indian wars.

General Beauregard returned to New Orleans after the war and became a railroad president and supervisor of the Louisiana lottery. He refused offers to command several foreign armies. He died in 1893.

Haunting questions remain. Was the war necessary, and, once having started, could it have been settled short of the South's unconditional surrender? In my estimation, conditions for war were not present before the John Brown raid of 1859. That event made war inevitable by so frightening the moderate majority of Southern politicians as to drive them into the arms of the fire-eaters, theretofore a vocal but ineffective minority.

The war's inevitability was also profoundly increased by two grave misconceptions. The first arose from the very different ways in which Northerners and Southerners experienced patriotism and allegiance. The South, a more settled society, based its allegiance on an almost European sense of blood and soil. One was faithful to the state of one's ancestors and to the soil of his inheritance. One's state thus was all important, and the union of which it was a part was mostly a matter of convenience and self-interest rather than one of fundamental concern. To the North, a society of immigrants and pioneers, a sense of place was secondary. Its all-pervasive ideal was that of the Constitution and the political freedoms and economic opportunities that it guaranteed. To sever the bond between the states was to attack the core of the Northerner's concept of his nation and its destiny.

Neither side truly understood the other beforehand. Lincoln's First Inaugural appeal to a mystic sense of union thus fell on uncomprehending ears, and the South had to be disabused of its presumption that a peaceful separation would occur when the North realized that an unwilling coalition of states was both futile and pointless. By the time that mutual comprehension occurred, it was too late.

The second misconception was that the South believed that cotton was king and that its monopoly of it would coerce both the North and Great Britain into yielding to Confederate demands. The South even embargoed cotton exports during 1861 to demonstrate its control of the market. By the time it realized its error, its ports were blockaded. The South then discovered what all monopolists inevitably learn. No monopoly lasts forever. In time, markets adjust as either new sources of supply are created, substitute products are found, or commodity demand shifts. What was once invaluable becomes commonplace. To its chagrin, the South again realized its error too late.

The second part of the question—could the war have been settled short of unconditional surrender—is more conjectural. It is safe to say that no realistic possibility of a negotiated peace existed prior to the spring of 1864. At that time, however, many factors conspired to create a window of opportunity that could have been used.

Both sides were exhausted, but the North's exhaustion was psychological, whereas the South's was all too physical. The North was traumatized by the war's cost in lives either ended or ruined. Materially, however, it was enjoying unequaled prosperity. Its industries were expanding in diversity, size, and productivity. Its financial system not only coped with wartime needs but also provided the capital necessary to build factories and railroads. Finally, the government, now freed from Southern obstruction, was efficiently handling such civil matters as homesteading, a transcontinental railway, and the establishment of a land grant college system.

The South's situation was diametrically opposite. Plantation slavery had been destroyed. Southern currency was debased by hyperinflation. The transportation system was ruined, the population had been reduced to subsistence levels, and the government was on the verge of collapse.

Consider also demographics. The North still had a large reservoir of able-bodied, white, native males that a more equitable military draft system could have mobilized, if necessary. It never became necessary, however, because of two other major population "pools" from which an increasing number of recruits were being drawn—liberated slaves and working-class immigrants. Southern manpower, however, was already stretched beyond its limits. There were insufficient white males to fill the Southern armies while simultaneously maintaining the country's industrial, agricultural, and transportation systems. Even a remarkable effort by Southern womanhood (in spite of gender barriers) could not redress the balance. Moreover, the existence of large numbers of semiliberated slaves diverted white men and women to overseer roles rather than adding manpower.

In addition, the appointment of U. S. Grant as commander of the armies, together with the emergence of a new breed of Union general as Grant's principal lieutenants, further added to the growing imbalance between the sections. These generals were both able and tough. Now war-tested and adapted to the command of volunteer troops, they also had great depth of numbers. At the top were Grant, Sherman, Thomas, Meade, and Sheridan. A second echelon, consisting of McPherson, Schofield, Hancock, Ord, Wilson, Slocum, Howard, Logan, and Blair, was available as replacements if needed. A third rung of leadership, at the division level, by men such as Birney, Gibbon, Griffin, Canby, A. J. Smith, Getty, Geary, and Chamberlain (and many others) provided added support. Although the South could not have foreseen the emergence of the "total war" doctrine, it might have sensed that this new leadership class was apt to be much more unyielding and unforgiving than their predecessors. Southern armies were concurrently beginning to suffer critical losses among general officers, a trend that would accelerate in 1864.

Finally, the South had suffered three decisive defeats in the last half of 1863. As a result it had lost the initiative in Virginia, had lost the last vestige of control over the Mississippi and the Trans-Mississippi Confederacy at Vicksburg, and had lost the gateway to the inner South at Chattanooga. All possibility of gaining either military supremacy or the intervention of foreign powers was gone. The South's only hope was that war weariness would induce the North to accept peace without union. In the spring of 1864, that hope seemed faint indeed.

The South, therefore, had every rational reason to attempt to negotiate the best terms possible before the 1864 campaign began. Why didn't they? The simple answer is that the principal war aims of the two sides remained diametrically opposed and therefore nonnegotiable: the South demanded independence and slavery; the North would settle for nothing less than union and emancipation.

We must, however, examine these premises more closely. Southern independence was always an artificial entity, born more of hatred and fear of the North than genuine desire. Even Jefferson Davis was a latecomer to this cause. There is good reason to suppose that the South could conceivably have accepted a restored union if the relationship of the individual states to the central government were defined to its liking.

As for slavery, Lincoln's quotation is apt: "Broken eggs can never be mended, and the longer the breaking proceeds the more will be broken." By 1864, slavery's demise, even in the Deep South, was inevitable. The open question was how it would be replaced. What the South really wanted was racial segregation, and it could have employed its bargaining power to that end. Lincoln was not nonnegotiable on this point, given the racial biases of his age. Something probably could have been worked out if there were agreement among all parties that "justice" had been served.

If not only the opportunity but also the basis for negotiations existed, why didn't they occur? Ultimately the answer is simply that humans are fallible. They act from mixed motives, and rational judgments, wisely or unwisely, are usually influenced by emotions.

The first such emotion was undoubtedly fear. Southern political and military leaders were well aware that the North deemed them to have committed treason, compounded by armed rebellion. The penalty for such acts normally was death. The leaders were thus justifiably worried about a campaign of retribution, with or without Lincoln's consent or color of law. The second emotion was pride. Southern leaders, like their Revolutionary forebearers, had staked their "lives, fortunes, and sacred honor" on the cause. To sacrifice it simply because they were undergoing privations was unthinkable, particularly since they had drawn their fellow citizens into the struggle. Only true hopelessness could justify reneging, and that concept was elusive.

It was also impossible in March 1864 to find a Southern political leader willing to stake his ultimate historical reputation on compromise. Although a late convert to the cause of Southern independence, Jefferson Davis by then had become a bitter-ender who opposed surrender even if the South were overrun and who espoused guerrilla warfare and passive resistance in such contingency. His previous comment about independence or extermination was not hyperbole. The Confederate cabinet and Congress were unwilling to take a public stand against him.

There was no opposition party and little sense of a popular mandate behind any particular faction. Unfortunately, the strongest faction held "right-wing" views, not those of the "left." This group had coalesced around Vice President Stephens and Governors Vance (North Carolina) and Brown (Georgia). Their view was that the Richmond regime had become as tyrannical as the Washington government because it too usurped wartime emergency powers in violation of states' rights. They were thus not ideal candidates to discredit Davis and sue for peace. Nonetheless, they were the group selected when the attempt was finally made.

It did not occur in March 1864 (when some bargaining along the above lines might have succeeded) but in January 1865 (when the South's residual bargaining power was practically nil). At Davis's instruction (provoked by congressional clamor), Vice President Stephens led a delegation to explore terms with Lincoln. Davis stipulated, however, that the delegation was not authorized even to discuss terms short of independence. That, of course, guaranteed failure, which Davis then described as evidencing a Northern desire for tyrannical domination of a prostrate South. He thus used the failure in order to discredit the peace faction to his own short-term political advantage but to his region's detriment. So ended abortively the only attempt at a negotiated peace.

The final unknown element in this analysis concerns the Southern generals. By 1864 a handy definition of the extent of the Confederacy was that it consisted of the land lying between the Confederate armies. Only the armies still gave life to the country. Similarly, the national leader whom the Southern people recognized was not Jefferson Davis but Robert E. Lee. In the spring of 1864, could not Lee have disavowed the demands of Jefferson Davis? Moreover, with the endorsement of such subordinates as Longstreet, Stuart, Johnston, and Beauregard, could not Lee have peremptorily taken peace negotiations into his own hands? Certainly, he could have. It also seems likely that his lieutenants would have supported him. He did not do so, however, and there is no evidence that he ever even considered it.

Lee was a very private person. Therefore, to analyze his feelings is highly conjectural. This much, however, is sure. Lee was not a careerist politician. His sole ambition was to do his duty as he construed it, to wit: follow the dictates of his state, right or wrong, and, in the best American tradition, subordinate the military hierarchy to civil authority. He seems to have been simply incapable of carrying out a coup d'état, no matter how necessary he might have considered it. One particular incident is revealing.

By March 1865, the proverbial handwriting on the wall was, figuratively, in letters that were ten feet tall and totally legible to all, certainly including Lee. As he was planning his "last gasp" attempt to break out at Fort Stedman, he confided to General Gordon that the odds against the Confederacy were overwhelming and that their current offensive was probably a forlorn hope. Gordon responded that if things were that bad, the best thing to do would be for Lee to immediately impress the political authorities with the need to request a cease-fire to seek the best terms possible. Lee nodded sadly but said that he could find no one in Richmond who would either take responsibility to do this or authorize him to do so. Without the color of that authority, Lee, himself, would not move.

The union was now restored, but it would be a very different union than what had prevailed since Jefferson's presidency. No longer would the federal government be Southern, Democratic, decentralized, and agriculturally oriented. Thenceforth, it would be Northern, Republican, capitalist, and increasingly centralized. It remained to be seen how Lincoln's "new birth of freedom" would be realized. It still remains to be seen.

Last Steamboat North, Last Train to Springfield

One of the conceits of the nineteenth century was that technology invariably brought progress. The world, according to then contemporary opinion, had been in an upward spiral since the inception of the Industrial Revolution. As the fruits of invention became increasingly available to the peoples of the world, an unending era of unrivaled prosperity would occur, and little by little, the evils associated with want and inequality would recede.

The experience of the twentieth century, however, has effectively dispelled this pleasant illusion. During this century we have watched as technology has been employed not only amorally and dispassionately but also in active support of terrorism and tyrannization. It therefore comes as no surprise to the modern reader when the same instrument that theretofore was used beneficially suddenly turns oppressive or painful when used to a contrary purpose.

Central to the nineteenth-century conception of technology as progress was the use of the steam engine, the driving force for all the century's machinery. Steam ran the machine tools and factory lines, it turned the spindles and ran the looms of the textile industry, it pumped the nation's mines free of water and polluted air, and it ran the steamboats and railway locomotives that provided the transportation system. It was the main icon of the new secular religion of progress.

This paean to progress could even be stretched to cover the use of steamboats and railways as instruments of war. General Sherman was the leading proponent of that point of view. War, he noted, was cruelty, a pure, unrelieved hell resulting from the disavowal of law and governance and a resort to the law of the jungle. It was misery undiluted that could not be mitigated in any way. Therefore, the only way to deal with it was to end it quickly. Then the erstwhile conquerors could revert to civilization and the benefits thereof. If sophisticated instruments of war hastened that day, then this too was progress.

This was a point of view cherished during the last year of the war by many Northerners. It seems, therefore, somehow a fitting coda on the war that when it did finally end, the first two peacetime uses of steam transportation were tragic rather than triumphant.

In his Second Inaugural address, Lincoln had queried whether the conflict was fated to continue until "every drop of blood drawn with the lash shall be paid with another drawn with the sword." These following two steam-related events seemed to wring out those last drops.

THE SS *SULTANA*

On April 27, 1865, about three weeks after the surrender at Appomattox, thousands of Union soldiers were billeted at Camp Fisk (near Vicksburg on the Mississippi River) awaiting transportation to the North. Most of these men had been prisoners of war (POWs), some for as long as two years or more. While at Camp Fisk, their paperwork was being processed. Specifically, they would first be "exchanged" against lists of captured Confederates, and upon exchange they would be mustered out. This exchange was necessary because the Trans-Mississippi Confederacy still had not surrendered. On the surface that seemed absurd; an exchanged Confederate was now legally free to proceed to Texas and reenlist in the remaining Confederate army. It was presumed, however, that the beneficial example of seeing his Union counterpart discharged upon exchange would dissuade the Confederate from such a rash act. Union expectations in this regard were undoubtedly correct.

So it was that, on April 27, more than 1,800 discharged Union soldiers had been fully processed and were now awaiting transportation. Such transportation existed in the form of the steamboat *Sultana,* one of many commercial vessels that carried freight and cabin passengers up and down the Mississippi River. These vessels constituted the easiest way to transport home those soldiers who had been discharged from the army while serving in Louisiana, Mississippi, or western Tennessee.

The government's standard contract called for a fixed-fee payment to the steamboat owner of five dollars for each enlisted man and ten dollars for each officer. For this the soldier received only a space on deck without any creature comforts such as a cabin or meals being provided. However, because soldiers in the field were used to deprivation (particularly these soldiers, who had been POWs), the men were happy to put up with any discomfort necessary to gain a fast passage home. A soldier on coming aboard sought out a place on the deck or cabin tops to put down his blanket and ensured that he had access to a bucket for his bodily needs. He made his meals from his own provisions and cooked these in a communal pot with his neighbors, using water drawn from the ship's boilers.

The steamship lines sought this business avidly. After all, the entire fee could be retained as profit, because the vessel was providing the soldiers with nothing except boiler water. It thus behooved the steamship company to load as many soldiers as it could. This frequently meant paying kickbacks to a mustering-out officer to induce him to direct each batch of new civilians to a particular ship. So it was that the *Sultana*, which could safely handle 300 surplus passengers, actually left Vicksburg with 1,866 discharged troops, 75 cabin passengers, 85 crew, 60 horses, and 100 hogs. No deck area was left unutilized. Movement about the ship was impossible.

The *Sultana* proceeded on a northbound course until it reached a point approximately 90 miles below Memphis. There, at 3:00 A.M., its boiler blew. Of the total number on board, more than 1,500 were lost due to the blast, exposure to live steam, or drowning. Helping to raise the total was the fact that the river was at high water with a swift current, making the Arkansas shore difficult to reach.

The cause of the explosion was never definitively ascertained. The ship had experienced boiler trouble on its passage downriver, and repairs had been made. It may be that these were faulty, but that fault was not immediately apparent. It could also have been that the metal plate used to make the repair was not sufficiently tough to withstand boiler pressure. Metallurgy was not then an exact science, and the quality of metal castings could vary tremendously between one order and another.

Another theory is that the explosion was caused by superheated steam arising from there being too little feed water in the boilers. The fact that large amounts of water were drawn off for cooking purposes gives credence to this theory, although the time of the occurrence, 3:00 A.M., does not. Finally, there is the obvious fact that the engines were being strained to drive the weight of almost 1,900 extra men and more than 150 animals upstream against a faster current than normal. The boat's engineer may well have tied down the boiler's safety valve to gain greater steam pressure, or the valve might have become stuck due to dirt or corrosion. Possibly many of these factors contributed to the disaster.

The event could not be allowed to pass without blame being assessed. The officer singled out was Capt. Frederick Speed, the mustering-out officer at Camp Fisk in charge of arranging transportation. He was court-martialed and, after a trial of five months, was dismissed from the service.

What could not be remedied, however, was the pain of the veterans' family members. Their grief can only be imagined and must have been worse than that of the family whose son had died in battle. The families of the *Sultana* victims had already been in despair for months or years about their relatives' well-being in a Southern prison camp, where conditions were rumored to be horrendous. Suddenly, by a stroke of Providence, they received word that their relative had, against all odds, survived and would be returning within weeks. Several weeks later, they then received the appalling news that their hopes had been dashed and the men had perished. This must have seemed almost too cruel to bear, as if God himself were mocking them.

Last drops of blood indeed.

PRESIDENT LINCOLN'S FUNERAL TRAIN

With the start of the military campaigning season in late March 1865, General Grant telegraphed President Lincoln to advise him that major developments were imminent in Virginia and showed great promise of finally leading to the war's end. Grant suggested that the president might well wish to visit him at his headquarters at City Point, Virginia, to await events. Lincoln needed no urging. This was the climax that he had awaited during four years of carnage. President and Mrs. Lincoln boarded the *River Queen*, a steamer outfitted for their use, and proceeded to City Point.

The first order of business was to convene a conference aboard the *River Queen* to discuss the anticipated impending collapse of the Southern armies and government. Besides Lincoln and Grant, the meeting was attended by General Sherman, who had come up from North Carolina for this purpose, and by Admiral Porter.

This was only Lincoln's second meeting with Sherman, the first having occurred back in 1861 before Sherman held any official position. Sherman had not then been impressed and had concluded that Lincoln was a lightweight. Lincoln now expressed his pleasure at the general's presence but queried whether it was wise for him to leave his army. Sherman responded that Howard, Slocum, and Schofield were able lieutenants and capable of handling anything that might ensue. Lincoln then turned to the subject at hand, indicating that he wished for a peace of reconciliation without reprisals. His intent was to get at least 10 percent of the prewar electorate in each seceding state to swear to the oath of allegiance. Upon that occurrence each such state would be considered reunited and capable of resumed voting for federal office. Everything else was negotiable, except that the Thirteenth Amendment (emancipation) must be accepted and the Confederate war debt repudiated.

Lincoln's pronouncements had a profound effect on both Grant and Sherman and, through them, on the country as well. Lee's and Johnston's surrenders were both accepted in this conciliatory spirit. Thereafter, whatever generals could do to heal the country's wounds, the generals on both sides did.

After the meeting, Lincoln walked Sherman to his horse, as the general was leaving to return to his own headquarters. After urging Sherman to continue to press hard, Lincoln confided, "You know, Sherman, the thing I always liked about you and Grant is that, unlike my other generals, you never found fault with me." This must have come as something of a surprise to Sherman, because all his life he had been constantly cussing out all politicians (including his own brother, Senator John Sherman) individually, as a class, and as a profession. In fact, there were times when it was not even clear that he favored a democratic system of government. Whatever Sherman may have previously believed, however, his admiration for Lincoln had been growing ever since his arrival at the conference. He was increasingly impressed by the breadth of Lincoln's vision and knowledge and was moved by his compassion. Now he was awestruck. Sherman was never to meet Lincoln again, but from then until the day he died, some thirty years later, he considered Lincoln the greatest man he ever met. In fact, he would shortly get himself into considerable political difficulty by trying to carry out his understanding of Lincoln's instructions to the letter.

The predicted events now occurred. On April 1, 1865, the decisive battle of Five Forks took place. Lee's line broke, exposing his last road and railroad to Grant's capture. Petersburg, and hence Richmond, were no longer tenable. Lee managed to withdraw from Petersburg, but within a matter of days Grant's army, with Sheridan in the lead, cornered him. Lee had no option but to surrender.

On April 4, Lincoln decided to visit Richmond, now evacuated by all but its black population and devastated by fire. Walking its streets with only twenty escorts, the president eventually wound up at the Confederate White House and sat at his opposite number's desk. During his visit he was tremendously moved by the expression of gratitude from the black population, who greeted him as their liberator. Lincoln finally cried out, "Don't kneel to me. You must kneel to God only and thank Him for your freedom."

The president was clearly exhilarated the next day as the *River Queen* returned to Washington. During the trip home, the Lincolns attended a band concert at which the "Marseillaise" was played in honor of the Lincolns' guest, Lafayette's grandson. Following that, Lincoln requested "Dixie," noting that the song was now "federal property."

After the concert, the president was asked to read some passages from Shakespeare, one of his favorite pastimes. Lincoln had a highly sensitive appreciation of the bard and had committed an astounding portion of his work to memory. One of his favorite plays was *Macbeth,* from which, this day, he selected the following passage:

> Duncan is in his grave.
> After life's fitful fever he sleeps well.
> Treason had done his worst; nor steel, nor poison,
> malice domestic, foreign levy, nothing
> can touch him further.

The passage seemed to engross him, and he read it a second time.

On the night of April 10, news of Lee's surrender arrived in Washington. Spontaneously, a crowd gathered and marched on the White House with the intent of "serenading" the president. Lincoln greeted them but suggested that they return the following night, when he would have a few words to say. The crowd left somewhat subdued. They really hadn't wanted to listen to a speech. What they wanted was for Lincoln to lead them in a few cheers for Grant, Sherman, Thomas, and the rest, and then perhaps to sing with them the "Battle Cry of Freedom" or "Marching Through Georgia" before leaving.

Instead, when they returned on the eleventh, they were greeted by Lincoln, candle in hand, reading a prepared speech on the subject of presidential reconstruction. Their disappointment was palpable.

On Good Friday (April 14) the first item on the presidential agenda was a cabinet meeting to which General Grant had been invited. The president arrived looking more rested and under less strain than had been observed for some time. When the group assembled, the president asked Grant whether he had received any news from Sherman. When Grant responded in the negative, Lincoln mentioned that he was sure that something would soon be received. When asked by Secretary Wells on what he based this assurance, he responded, "Actually, this is in your domain, Neptune." (Neither the somewhat pompous Secretary of the Navy Gideon Wells nor the very pompous Secretary of War Edwin Stanton particularly enjoyed the president's playful affectation of referring to them, respectively, as "Neptune" and "Mars"; still, he was the president, and so the two cabinet officers had little choice but to stand on their dignity when others snickered.)

Lincoln went on to describe how the previous night he again had a recurring dream. In the dream he was standing on the deck of "a singular, indescribable vessel" that was proceeding rapidly through the water toward a distant and ill-defined shore. He continued by saying that the dream always foretold the occurrence of a major event, usually a battle. He had had the dream before Antietam, Murfreesboro, Vicksburg, and Wilmington, all of which, he observed, were Union victories. He stated, therefore, that he was sure that the dream must presage Johnston's surrender to Sherman. General Grant (who was never willing to concede anything to General Rosecrans) grumped that a few "victories" such as Murfreesboro would have destroyed the army. Nonetheless, Lincoln remained steadfast in his impression. The cabinet then turned to the business of reconstruction.

That night the president was assassinated by the actor John Wilkes Booth, at Ford's Theater. Abraham Lincoln had foretold his own death.

There are other stories about Lincoln's having a presentiment of his own death. In one, he had a dream that he had awakened one morning to hear the sound of many people weeping. He arose and walked through the public rooms of the White House. The rooms were all empty, but everywhere he heard the sound of weeping. Finally, he entered the East Room, where he saw the weeping people around a catafalque in the middle of the room. He turned to one woman and asked what happened, and she responded, "The president has been killed by an assassin."

Perhaps the most eerie such tale concerned an occurrence on the night of his election in November 1860. Lincoln returned late that night to his home in Springfield, Illinois, after spending many hours at the telegraph office awaiting election returns. He was exhausted, and before climbing the stairs to go to bed, he collapsed into a chair in the parlor. Across the parlor was a large mirror, and when Lincoln looked up, he saw in the mirror two images of his face, one largely superimposed on the other. One image was vibrant, but the other exhibited a sickly pallor. Lincoln stood and approached the mirror to get a better look. As he did, the second image disappeared. When he went back to the chair, however, the second image reemerged, only to disappear again when he approached the mirror a second time. The following morning he described the incident to his wife. She looked aghast as she told him that she interpreted it to mean that he would be elected twice to office but would die during the second term.

There was really no precedent in 1865 for a presidential state funeral. Only two presidents had previously died in office. The first, William Henry Harrison, survived his inauguration by only a month or so and was not well known. The second, Zachary Taylor, was popular because of his generalship in the Mexican War. However, the divisions between North and South had already become sufficiently severe that no national ceremonial event could be contemplated.

Lincoln's closed coffin lay in state, surrounded by an honor guard, for three days—first in the East Room of the White House, then in the Capitol rotunda. It was then put aboard a crepe-draped train for the journey back to Springfield. The train's itinerary was designed to duplicate in reverse Lincoln's preinaugural trip in February 1861.

The funeral car in which Lincoln lay was built by USMRR as the president's special car in 1863 in Alexandria, Virginia. Its first use, however, was for the funeral trip. It was a heavy car, mounted on four sets of four-wheel trucks, and was painted chocolate brown. On its side were the words "United States." Under this was the national coat of arms. The car had a drawing room, bedroom, and parlor, all connected by an aisle running the full length of the coach.

The body was placed aboard on April 21, 1865, and the funeral train departed at 8:00 A.M. It consisted of nine cars, with the remaining eight carrying family, honor guard, and many mourners. The train, pulled by a Baltimore and Ohio Railroad engine, arrived in Baltimore at 10:00 A.M. There, Lincoln's coffin was placed in the rotunda of the Merchants Exchange.

The funeral train departed Baltimore at 3:00 P.M., now drawn by a Pennsylvania Railroad locomotive, with Harrisburg as its destination. It arrived at the Pennsylvania capital at 10:00 P.M. During the following day the casket lay in the state capitol. The funeral train departed Harrisburg at noon on April 23 for Philadelphia, pulled by Pennsylvania Railroad engine 331. The casket was there displayed in Independence Hall.

At 4:00 A.M. on April 24 the train left Philadelphia for Jersey City, then the casket was taken by ferry to New York's City Hall. The funeral car itself was ferried across the Hudson River, then it later departed for Albany as part of the newly formed funeral train. On April 26, the New York Central Railroad took charge and brought the train to Buffalo, where the casket was displayed in St. James Hall during the day of April 27.

Various railroads then took the train through Erie, Cleveland, and Columbus. Then it went to Chicago, where the casket was displayed at the Clark Street Court House.

The last leg of the trip, to Springfield, Illinois, was handled by the Chicago, Alton, and St. Louis Railroad. The train arrived in the Illinois capital on May 3, whereupon the coffin was taken to the hall of the House of Representatives, where Lincoln had served in the 1830s and 1840s. On May 4 the body was temporarily interred pending transfer at a later time to an elaborate monument then being erected by the state of Illinois.

The grief of the nation was expressed throughout the long trip. In every town bonfires were ignited, cannons boomed, and bells tolled dirges as the funeral train went through. Eulogies were offered at every stop, and crowds jammed the streets in all of the cities where the casket was displayed.

Duncan was indeed in his grave, no longer to be touched by any domestic or foreign foe. Did he and the brave members of his generation leave to us, their distant descendants, any lasting legacy of their titanic struggle?

It is easy to be cynical and respond in the negative. The Civil War at its heart was about race relations. At first, some progress seemed to have been made. The Thirteenth, Fourteenth, and Fifteenth Amendments were enacted, some important civil rights legislation was passed, and, in the South, Reconstruction regimes ensured that blacks received certain political and economic rights and access to education. However, in less than a dozen years, these hopes were dashed. The black night of Southern restoration and Northern indifference obscured the promise of justice.

The cause was not dead. One hundred years later it again sprang to life in Montgomery, Alabama, and Atlanta, Georgia. Great progress was again made, but a counterrevolution was also provoked. Can anyone, even today, say that he or she can visualize the day when America will be a truly color-blind society?

Yet, that is not all there is to the legacy. The Civil War also remains an evocative experience because it reminds us that there is a second aspect to the American dream. Part of that dream is, and always was, that people should be free to pursue their individual (and selfish) aspirations wherever these may lead, while Adam Smith's "invisible hand" ensures that the common good will be thereby benefited. Lincoln, however, more frequently articulated a traditional corollary to the dream: that having received freedom, citizens have an obligation to give back duty and service. From these would be derived the genuine American commonwealth. It is a tradition we honor when we become volunteers, for example, as firemen, local officials, or members of a philanthrophic organization. By this dictum America, to be itself, must be not only free, but just. That lamp for the moment is somewhat dim, but in the fullness of time it will be restored.

It follows, therefore, that whenever any American leader embarks upon a cause with the intent of unifying and utilizing our best instincts rather than capitalizing on our worst, he or she almost instinctively chooses the steps of the Lincoln Memorial as the site from which to declare such intent. The republic will always prosper if it can be truly said of us and of succeeding generations that our contribution was as freely given as that of Abraham Lincoln and the men and women who fought the Civil War.

BIBLIOGRAPHY

Abdill, G. B. *Civil War Railroads*. Seattle, Washington: Superior Publishing Company, 1961.

Barrett, John. *Sherman's March through the Carolinas*. Chapel Hill: University of North Carolina Press, 1956.

Billings, John D. *Hardtack and Coffee*. 1887; reprint, Lincoln: University of Nebraska Press, 1993.

Catton, Bruce. *Mr. Lincoln's Army*. Garden City, New York: Doubleday and Company, Inc., 1951.

——*Glory Road*. Garden City, New York: Doubleday and Company, Inc., 1951.

——*A Stillness at Appomattox*. Garden City, New York: Doubleday and Company, Inc., 1951.

——*This Hallowed Ground*. Garden City, New York: Doubleday and Company, Inc., 1956.

——*Grant Moves South*. Boston: Little Brown and Company, 1960.

——*Grant Takes Command*. Boston: Little Brown and Company, 1960.

——*Centennial History of the Civil War*. 3 vols. Garden City, New York: Doubleday and Company, Inc., 1961.

——*Reflections on the Civil War*. Garden City, New York: Doubleday and Company, Inc., 1981.

Ellis, Hamilton. *The Lore of the Train*. Gothenburg, Sweden: AB Nordbok, 1971.

Faust, Patricia. *Encyclopedia of the Civil War*. New York: Harper and Row, 1986.

Foote, Shelby. *The Civil War: A Narrative*. 3 vols. New York: Random House, Inc., 1963.

Hunter, Louis C. *Steamboats on the Western Rivers*. New York: Dover Publications, Inc., 1993. Reprint, Cambridge, Massachusetts: Harvard University Press, 1949.

Lymon, Daryl. *Civil War Quotations*. Conshohocken, Pennsylvania: Combined Books, Inc., 1995.

Nevins, Allan. *The Ordeal of the Union*. 8 vols. New York: Charles Scribners Sons, 1947–71.

O'Connor, Richard. *Thomas: Rock of Chickamauga*. New York: Prentice Hall, Inc., 1948.

Sears, Stephen. *To the Gates of Richmond*. New York: Ticknor and Fields, 1992.

Smith, George, and Judah, Charles. *Life in the North*. University of New Mexico Press, 1966.

Steiner, Paul. *Disease in the Civil War*. Springfield, Illinois: Charles C. Thomas Publications, 1968.

Stover, John. *American Railroads*. Chicago: University of Chicago Press, 1961.

Trudeau, Noah. *The Last Citadel*. Boston: Little Brown and Company, 1991.

Vandiver, Frank E. *Jubal's Raid*. New York: McGraw Hill Book Company, Inc., 1960.

Index

Alabama, 81-82, 116, 123, 138, 143
Alexander, General, 109
Alexandria, La., 116–18
Alexandria, Va., 54–55, 65, 161
"Anaconda" (Union plan, 1861–62), 35, 49, 187
Anderson, Col. Adna, 131
Anderson, Robert, 23
Andrew, Gov. John, 2, 16
Annapolis, 6–7, 11
Antietam, battle of, 58, 66–68, 141, 162
Appomattox Court House, 184, 199–200, 218–19, 228
Appomattox River, 145–47, 151, 153, 171, 190, 198–99
Arkansas, 115
Army of the Cumberland (renamed Army of Georgia), 17, 81, 91–92, 95–100, 104–105, 107, 110, 126, 130, 133, 138, 210, 213
Army of the James, 151, 153, 163
Army of Northern Virginia, 60, 66, 73, 111, 124, 150, 154, 193, 195
Army of the Ohio, 126
Army of the Potomac, 20, 22, 32–35, 50–51, 53–54, 57, 60–62, 64–66, 68, 74, 91, 93, 99–100, 104–105, 107, 114, 124, 126, 130, 141, 143, 145, 150–52, 162–63, 168–69, 177, 184, 186, 189, 197, 202, 205, 210, 218
Army of the Tennessee, 75–76, 93, 105, 107, 110–11, 116, 125–27, 133, 145, 205, 213
Army of West Virginia, 166
Atlanta, 93, 109–110, 114, 116, 125, 129, 133–34, 136–38, 169, 189, 204–208

Bailey, Lt. Col. Joseph, 119–20, 122–23
Bailey, Capt. Theodorus, 45–47
Baltimore, 14, 164–65
Baltimore Riots, 3–7, 50, 156

Banks, Gen. Nathaniel, 81, 86, 88, 100, 114–23, 183
Barnard, Maj. John Gross, 33, 160
Barry, Col. William F., 20
Beauregard, Gen. P. G. T., 140, 151–55, 158–59, 216, 220, 225
Belle Plain, Va., 70–72
Bentonvile, 217
Berlin, Md., 68–70
Bermuda Hundred, 145–46, 153–54
Black troops, 111, 135, 152, 174–80
Blair, Gen. Francis, 213, 220, 223
Blockade, naval (southern ports), 35, 37–38, 221
Booth, John Wilkes, 234
Boston, 7
Bragg, Gen. Braxton, 13, 59, 66, 75, 89, 92–94, 96–98, 101–102, 104–108, 110, 114, 125, 127, 129, 133–35, 140, 145, 155, 189, 217
Brown's Ferry, 101–102
Buckingham, Governor, 16
Buckner, General, 14, 94
Bull Run, battles of, 20, 24, 31–32, 34–35, 50–53, 59, 63, 65, 156, 158–59, 161, 167, 199
Burnside, Gen. Ambrose, 51, 67–74, 94, 105, 133–34, 141, 171–77, 179–80, 183–84, 195
Butler, Gen. Ben, 1–2, 6–8, 14, 16, 41–48, 114, 151, 153, 163, 168, 184

Canby, Gen. E .R. S., 122
Carlin, General, 217
Carolinas, 90, 111, 131, 204, 210–11, 214–17
Casualties, Confederate, 22, 58, 62, 136, 138, 142–44, 195, 198–99, 205
Casualties, Union, 22, 40, 46, 58, 136–37, 142–44, 169, 180, 187–88, 205
Cavalry, 34, 76, 81, 105, 110, 124, 129, 135–36, 138–40, 146, 165–67,189,193, 196–97, 216–17
Centerville, 51–53, 57, 65, 158–59

Chamberlain, Gen. Joshua, 183, 200–201
Champion Hill, battle of, 87
Chancellorsville, battle of, 93,104, 110, 142, 162
Chantilly, battle of, 66, 161
Chattanooga, 93–95, 97–103, 109, 113–14 116,126– 27, 129–30, 133–35, 138, 151, 189, 204, 206, 223
Chickahominy River, 58–61, 146–47
Chickamauga Creek, 93–94, 99, 101, 109, 129–30, 133, 140
Citizen militia, 157–59
City Point, Va., 145, 182, 190–92, 196, 217, 231
Cleburne, Gen. Pat, 106, 109–11, 155, 204
Cold Harbor, battle of, 143–44, 151, 169
Columbia, S. C., 216
Commissary (War Department), 24
Confederate Department of Alabama, Mississippi and eastern Louisiana, 129, 136
Constitution, USS (Old Ironsides), 8
Corduroying roads, 211–12, 216
"Cracker Line " (supply route), 101–102, 104, 134, 150–51
Crittenden, General, 95, 97
Crook, General, 166–67
Custer, Gen. George Armstrong, 167, 196

Davis, Capt. Charles, 48
Davis, Jefferson (Confederate President), 13, 59, 87, 89–96, 98, 105, 110–11, 127, 133, 135–36, 152, 154–55, 169, 189, 202, 205, 209, 216, 219–20, 223–25
Davis, Gen. Jefferson (Union general), 213, 220
Delaware, 13
Democratic Party, 1
Dennison, Governor, 50
Devin, General, 196
"Dimmock Line" fortifications (Petersburg), 151–52, 170

Disease, infectious, 21–22, 15, 30, 33, 48, 73, 187
Dodge, Gen. Grenville, 131

Early, Gen. Jubel, 144–67. 189–90, 193, 196
Elliot's Salient, 170–71, 175
Emory, General, 166–67

Fair Oaks (Seven Pines), battle of, 58–59
Farragut, Adm. David Glascow, 39–49, 51, 75, 140, 188–90
Ferrero, Gen. Edward, 174–75, 177, 179–80, 184
Five Forks, battle of , 196–98, 203
Foote, Admiral, 140
Forrest, Gen. Nathan Bedford, 76, 97–98, 105, 110–11, 125–26, 129–30, 133, 135–39, 155
Fort DeRussy, 165
Fortifications (Washington), 160–63, 177
Fort Fisher, 110
Fort Jackson, 40, 42–47, 51, 75
Fort Monroe, 54–56
Fort Morgan, 188
Fort Pemburton, 78
Fort Pickens, 38
Fort Pulaski, 204
Fort St. Philip, 40, 42–47, 51, 75
Fort Slocum, 165
Fort Stedman, 193, 195, 226
Fort Stevens, 165–66
Fort Sumter, 2, 16, 23
Fox, Gustavus, 38
Franklin, battle of, 111, 138
Franklin, Gen. William, 116, 166
Fredericksburg, 18, 52, 64, 67, 69–70, 72, 74, 116, 134, 142, 162, 179
Funkhouser, Capt. R. D., 195–96

Georgia, 81, 90, 93, 111, 115–16, 125–27, 130, 136, 138, 208, 210
Gerdes, Lt. F. H., 44
Gettysburg, 91–93, 104, 142–43, 153–54, 162, 196, 198, 201

Gilbert, Gen. Charles, 17–18
Gillmore, Gen. Q. A., 151
Gordon, Gen. John B., 155, 193–94,
    201, 226
Granger, General, 94, 97, 107–10
Grant, Gen. Ulysses, 13, 35, 42,
    48–49,51, 75–82, 86 –92, 99–101,
    104–109, 112–17, 126, 129–30,
    134, 138–40, 143–46, 150–51,
    153–55, 162–69, 172–73, 175, 177,
    180–82, 184, 187, 189–93, 196,
    199–200, 202, 204, 210–11,
    217–19, 222–23, 233–34
Gregg, General, 87
Grierson, Brig. Gen. Benjamin, 82,
    86, 135, 183
Griffin, General, 198
Gunboats, 40, 44–45

Halleck, General, 48, 69–70, 74–75,
    92, 115, 206, 208
Hancock, Gen. Winfield Scott,
    152–54, 170, 175, 187, 223
Hardee, General, 98, 127, 205, 216
Hardie, Lt. Col. James, 33
Harpers Ferry, 66, 68–69, 165
Hartford, USS (Flagship),44, 46, 188
Hartranft, General, 195
"Heavies" force, 161, 163, 165, 167,
    177
Hicks, Gov. Thomas, 7–8
Hill, Gen. A. P., 98, 187
Hill, Gen. D. H., 216
Hoke, General, 153
Holmes, Capt. Oliver Wendell,
    166–67
Hood, Gen. John Bell, 111, 125,
    127, 137–40, 189, 205–207, 210,
    213
Hooker, Gen. Joe, 100–101,
    104–107, 109–110, 141–42
Howard, Gen. O. O., 110, 205, 213,
    215, 220, 223, 231
Howlett Line, 153–54
Hunter, Gen. David, 164–66, 168

Illinois, 22
Indiana, 19, 125

Iowa, 19

Jackson, 86–88
Jackson, Gen. John K. ("Mudwell"),
    105
Jackson, Gen. Stonewall, 53–54,
    60–61, 65, 72, 86, 104, 116, 142,
    157, 159, 164
James River, 52, 58, 62–64, 144–47,
    149, 152–53, 163–64, 182, 190–91
Jamestown, 52
Johnson, Andrew, 110, 218
Johnston, Gen. A. S., 140
Johnston, Gen. Joe, 52–53, 58–60,
    87–90, 111, 114, 127, 129, 138–40,
    143, 155, 158–59, 189, 194, 201,
    204–205, 216–18, 220, 225, 231,
    234

Kearney, Gen. Philip, 20–21, 66
Kentucky, 13, 35, 48, 59, 66, 76, 125
Keyes, General, 59
Knoxville, 94, 105, 110, 129, 133–34

Ledlie, Gen. James, 177, 179, 184,
    195
Lee, Gen. Robert E., 50, 53, 59–63,
    65–67, 71–73, 75, 80, 93, 98, 111,
    114, 124, 139, 142–46, 149–55,
    162–64, 167–69, 171, 175, 177,
    180–84, 187–190, 192–202,
    209–11, 216, 218, 225–26, 231–33
Lee, "Rooney", 197–98
Lee, Gen. Stephen, 136
Lincoln, Abraham, 63–64, 66–67,
    69, 70, 74, 77, 88, 92,
    99–100,113–15, 122, 130, 133,
    141–43, 156, 158, 162, 169, 188,
    192, 196, 204, 207, 218–19,
    220–21, 224–26, 228,230–35, 237
Logan, Gen. John, 183, 205, 213,
    220, 223
Log mats, 212
Longstreet, Gen. James, 58, 60, 65,
    72, 94–98, 101, 105, 133–34, 137,
    140, 225
Lookout Mountain, 98, 100–102,
    104–106, 126, 134

Loring, Brig. Gen. W. W., 87
Louisiana,115, 122–23
Louisville, 102–103, 208
Lyon, General, 35
Lytle, Gen. William, 95

McArthur, Arthur, 109
McArthur, Douglas, 109
McCallum, Gen. Dan C., 130–31, 192
McClellan, Gen. George B., 30–36,
  50–54, 56–58, 60–67, 73, 124, 144,
  190, 192
McClernand, Gen. John, 77, 80,
  87–89
McCook, General, 95, 97
McDowell, Gen. Irwin, 33, 53, 61,
  65, 158–59
Mclean, Wilmer, 199–200
McPherson, Gen. James, 87–89,
  126, 204–205, 223
Magruder, General, 57–58
Mahone, Gen. William, 184
Malvern Hill, battle of, 62–63, 93
March to the Sea (Sherman), 125,
  130, 138–39, 204, 207–208,
  210–11, 213–16
Maryland, 3–5, 8, 12–14, 59, 66
Marcy, Col. Randolf, 31
Meade, Gen. George, 92, 126, 139,
  142–43, 146 , 154, 162, 168–69,
  171–73, 175–76, 179–80, 184, 198,
  223
Mechanisville, 60, 62
Meigs, Montgomery, 24, 26, 32, 102,
  131
Memphis, 76, 126, 129, 135–36
Merritt, General, 167
Mexico, 115
Michigan, 18
Miles, Gen. Nelson A., 202
Minutemen tradition, 2, 156–57,
  159, 185
Missionary Ridge, 105–110, 134
Mississippi, 73, 76, 82, 86, 91, 94,
  114, 122–23, 126, 133, 138
Mississippi River, 35, 38–42, 44–45,
  48, 51, 75, 77–82, 85–86, 91,
  115–16, 121,123, 223, 229
Missouri, 13, 35, 110

Mobile, 49, 110, 114, 123, 188
Monroe Doctrine, 115
Morale, Union, 64, 66, 125, 142
Morgan, James, 217
Morgan, John Hunt, 96, 125, 130
Mortar schooners, 41–42,44–45
"Mud March", 73, 141

Nashville, 102–103, 109, 123, 126,
  130–31, 138–39, 204, 213
Naval forces, Confederate, 40, 42,
  44–45, 47–48, 188
Naval forces, Union, 41–46, 54,
  68–70, 79, 82, 84–85, 116–18, 188,
  191
Newcomen, Thomas, 9
New Orleans, 37–40, 42–49, 51, 75,
  122, 157
Norfolk, 35, 38, 127, 182
North Carolina, 51, 134

Ohio, 22, 125
Olmsted, Frederick Law, 33
Ord, General, 170, 223
Ordnance, War Department, 24
"Overland Campaign", 143, 162,
  167, 169, 174, 184, 197, 209

Patronage, 16–17
Patterson, Gen. Robert, 158–59
Pemberton, Gen. John, 76, 78,
  81–82, 86–89, 94, 113–14, 140, 155
Peninsular Campaign, 36, 52–58,
  61, 63–64, 116, 124, 141, 144, 161
Pennsylvania, 66, 91
Petersburg, 145–46, 150–51,
  153–54, 161, 164, 167–71, 175,
  178, 180–83, 190–93, 196–98,
  232
Philadelphia, 3, 6–7, 164
Pickett, General, 196–98
Pickets, 186–87, 194
Pinkerton, Allen, 51
Pioneer Corps, 211–13
Pleasants, Lt. Col. Henry, 169–174,
  177–78
Polk, General, 97–98, 127, 155
Pontoons, 55–56, 58–59, 61, 64,
  67–74, 100–102, 106, 122, 147–50

Pope, Gen. John, 13, 35, 42, 63, 65–66
Porter, Col. Andrew, 31
Porter, Adm. David Dixon, 41, 44, 49, 79, 82, 84, 86, 116, 118–23, 140, 231
Porter, Fitz-John, 60–63, 203
Port Hudson, 75
Ports blockaded, 38–39
Potomac River, 3, 33, 54–55, 66–70, 72, 143, 159–61, 165
Potter, Gen. Robert, 171–72, 177, 179
Price, Gen. Sterling, 110, 155
Prisoners of War (POW), 228

"Quaker cannons", 52
Quartermasters, War Department, 24–28, 32, 101–103

Railroads, 3, 6–8, 10–12, 22–23, 26, 51, 76, 98, 127–38, 145, 182–83, 187, 189, 191–93, 199, 205–206, 214–15, 235–36
Ramsay, George, 30
Rapidan River, 43, 187
Rappahannock River, 52, 64–65, 67–68, 70, 73, 74, 93, 148
Rawlins, Brig. Gen. John, 113, 206
Red River, 75, 79, 81, 85, 115, 118–23, 136, 140, 166
Reese, Sgt. Harry, 178
Rhett, Robert Barnwell, 215
Richmond, 2, 36, 46, 52–53, 58–62, 65, 114, 124, 142–45, 151, 158, 164, 171, 175, 180, 187, 193, 199, 219, 225–26, 232
Ricketts, Gen. James, 165–66
Ripley, James, 24, 29–30
Roanoke Island, 51
Rosecrans, Gen. William, 91–100, 109–110, 134, 234

Savannah, 204–205, 209–210
Sawyer, Roswell, 208
Schofield, Gen. John, 126, 138–40, 202, 204, 213, 217, 223, 231
Scott, Gen. Winfield, 27, 35, 49, 187
Secession, 2–5, 12, 14, 39, 47, 49,

143, 169, 207–208, 215
Self-government, Southern view, 209
Selma, 114, 139
Shenandoah Valley, 3, 53, 60, 65–66,86,114,116, 146, 158, 163–67, 189–90, 193
Sheridan, Gen. Philip, 109, 124, 126, 139–40, 166–67, 184, 189–90, 193, 196–99, 202, 223
Sherman, Gen. William T., 23–24, 81, 86–90, 104– 107, 109–12, 114–16, 120, 123, 125–27, 129–30, 133–40, 168–69, 189–90, 202, 204–11, 213–20, 223, 227, 231–34
Shiloh, battle of ,48, 64, 75, 159, 168
Shreveport, 115, 117–18
Sickles, Gen. Dan,32
Siegal, Gen. Franz, 114
"Silk Stocking" regiment, 19
Slavery, 4, 12–13, 109, 222–24
Slocum, Gen. Henry, 213, 215–17, 220, 223, 231
Smith, Gen. A. J., 116–17, 136
Smith, Gen. E. Kirby, 117–18, 123, 201
Smith, Gen. W. F "Baldy", 100–101, 106, 150–54, 170
Smith, William Sooy, 135
Spaulding, Maj. Ira, 68–72, 74, 148
Spotsylvania, 18
Stanton, Edwin, 92, 130, 218–20, 233
Steamboats, 23, 82–85
Steam engine, 8–11
Steam locomotive, 10–11, 227
Steele, Gen. Frederick, 117–18
Stevens, Gen. Isaac, 66
Stoneman, George, 34
Stone's River, battle of, 91–92
Stuart, J. E. B., 34, 60, 124, 225
Sturgis, Brig. Gen., Samuel, 135
Sultana (steamboat), 228–30
Sumner, Gen. Edwin, 59, 69–70, 72–73
Supply, need for and importance of, 24–27, 30, 32–33, 39–40, 65, 67, 75–76, 81, 86, 90, 92, 99, 101–104,

115, 126–30, 134–35, 138, 145–47,
164, 182–83, 187–89, 191–92, 196,
199, 207–208, 214
Surrender, 199–201, 218–19, 228,
231, 233
Susquahanna River, 7

Taylor, General, 24
Taylor, Gen. Richard, 117–18,
121–23, 136, 140, 201
Taylor, Zachary, 117
Tennessee, 35, 42, 48, 51, 76, 81–82,
91, 93, 99 125–27, 131, 135
Tennessee, CSS, 188
Tennessee River, 48, 98, 100–102,
106, 137–38, 168
Terry, General, 123, 154
Texas, 115
Thomas, Gen. George H., 13, 35,
49, 92, 94–95, 97, 100–101,
104–109, 123, 126, 134, 138–40,
204–205, 210, 213, 223, 233
Transportation system, 22–27, 39,
182–83, 189, 211–13, 222, 227
Trans-Mississippi Confederacy, 75,
115, 117, 223, 228
Tripler, S., medical director, 33

Uniforms, 19–21
U.S. Military Railroad System (USM-
RR), 128, 130–32, 182, 192, 235
U.S. Naval Academy, 7–8, 123

Van Dorn, Gen. Earl, 76, 125,
129–30
Vicksburg, 48–49, 75–82, 84, 86–92,
99–100, 104, 113, 115, 117, 129,
135, 138, 140, 144, 204, 223, 229
Virginia, 13, 31, 35, 39, 47–48, 50,
53, 65, 67, 69, 114–15, 126,
143–45, 204, 210–11
Virginia (*Merrimac*), 38
Vliet, Brig. Gen. S., 32
Volunteer enlistment, 16, 18–19

Wallace, Gen. Lew, 165–66
War aims, 223
War, assessment of, 221–26, 236–37

War Democrat, 88
War Department, 30–31, 33, 54,
68–70, 73, 92, 96, 159
"War Governors", 15–16, 29
War philosophy (Sherman),
206–10, 228
Warren, General, 179, 187, 196–98,
202–203
Washington, 2–3, 5–7, 12, 16, 24,
31, 51–54, 61, 65, 68–70, 76, 80,
114, 131, 156, 158–66, 189–90,
218, 225, 233
Watt, James, 9
Weapons, 8, 28–30, 33–34, 57,
78–79, 96, 161, 181–82
Wells, Gideon, 38, 233
West Point, 60, 62, 91, 100, 113,
164, 167, 185, 213
West Virginia, 50–51, 53–54
Wheeler, Gen. Joe, 105, 125, 130,
133–35, 137, 139
Whig Party, 1
Wilcox Landing, 146–47, 149
Wilder, Gen. John T., 96
Williamsburg, 52, 57
Willcox, Gen. Orlando, 177, 179,
195
Williams, Gen. A. S., 213, 217
Williams, Gen. Seth, 33
Wilson, General, 139, 223
Wing dams, 119–21
Wood, General, 94–95, 97, 109
Woodbury, Brig. Gen. Daniel,
69–70, 74
Wright, Maj. W. W., 131

Yazoo River, 77–79, 81, 87
York River, 52, 58, 62, 146, 181
Yorktown, 52, 57–58, 161, 181